Recent Developments in Intelligent Nature–Inspired Computing

Srikanta Patnaik
SOA University, India

A volume in the Advances in
Computational Intelligence
and Robotics (ACIR) Book
Series

www.igi-global.com

Published in the United States of America by
   IGI Global
   Information Science Reference (an imprint of IGI Global)
   701 E. Chocolate Avenue
   Hershey PA 17033
   Tel: 717-533-8845
   Fax: 717-533-8661
   E-mail: cust@igi-global.com
   Web site: http://www.igi-global.com

                     Library of Congress Cataloging-in-Publication Data

Names: Patnaik, Srikanta, editor.
Title: Recent developments in intelligent nature inspired computing /
   Srikanta Patnaik, editor.
Description: Hershey, PA : Information Science Reference, [2017] | Includes
   bibliographical references.
Identifiers: LCCN 2016058437| ISBN 9781522523222 (hardcover) | ISBN
   9781522523239 (ebook)
Subjects: LCSH: Natural computation.
Classification: LCC QA76.9.N37 R43 2017 | DDC 006.3/8--dc23 LC record available at https://
lccn.loc.gov/2016058437

This book is published in the IGI Global book series Advances in Computational Intelligence and
Robotics (ACIR) (ISSN: 2327-0411; eISSN: 2327-042X)

British Cataloguing in Publication Data
A Cataloguing in Publication record for this book is available from the British Library.

Advances in Computational Intelligence and Robotics (ACIR) Book Series

ISSN:2327-0411
EISSN:2327-042X

MISSION

While intelligence is traditionally a term applied to humans and human cognition, technology has progressed in such a way to allow for the development of intelligent systems able to simulate many human traits. With this new era of simulated and artificial intelligence, much research is needed in order to continue to advance the field and also to evaluate the ethical and societal concerns of the existence of artificial life and machine learning.

The **Advances in Computational Intelligence and Robotics (ACIR) Book Series** encourages scholarly discourse on all topics pertaining to evolutionary computing, artificial life, computational intelligence, machine learning, and robotics. ACIR presents the latest research being conducted on diverse topics in intelligence technologies with the goal of advancing knowledge and applications in this rapidly evolving field.

COVERAGE

- Neural Networks
- Evolutionary Computing
- Robotics
- Synthetic Emotions
- Fuzzy Systems
- Computational Logic
- Automated Reasoning
- Computational Intelligence
- Algorithmic Learning
- Intelligent control

IGI Global is currently accepting manuscripts for publication within this series. To submit a proposal for a volume in this series, please contact our Acquisition Editors at Acquisitions@igi-global.com or visit: http://www.igi-global.com/publish/.

Titles in this Series

For a list of additional titles in this series, please visit: www.igi-global.com

www.igi-global.com

701 E. Chocolate Ave., Hershey, PA 17033
Order online at www.igi-global.com or call 717-533-8845 x100
To place a standing order for titles released in this series,
contact: cust@igi-global.com
Mon-Fri 8:00 am - 5:00 pm (est) or fax 24 hours a day 717-533-8661

Table of Contents

Section 1
Physics-Inspired Computational Techniques

*Alireza Askarzadeh, Kerman Graduate University of Advanced
Technology, Iran*
*Esmat Rashedi, Kerman Graduate University of Advanced Technology,
Iran*

Jose M. Lanza-Gutierrez, Universidad Politecnica de Madrid, Spain
Ricardo Soto, Pontificia Universidad Católica de Valparaíso, Chile
*Broderick Crawford, Pontificia Universidad Católica de Valparaíso,
Chile*
Juan A. Gomez-Pulido, University of Extremadura, Spain
*Nicolas Fernandez, Pontificia Universidad Católica de Valparaíso,
Chile*
Carlos Castillo, Pontificia Universidad Católica de Valparaíso, Chile

Section 2
Bio-Inspired Computational Techniques

Section 3
Collective Intelligence-Based Computational Techniques

Detailed Table of Contents

Section 1
Physics-Inspired Computational Techniques

This section consists of chapters using physics-based approaches i.e., the nature-inspired computational techniques are based upon the basic principles of physics such as the principle of how harmony is achieved while composing music or the underlying principle of electro-magnetism or even the physics behind black hole concept. All these principles of physics along with other principles form the basis of the Physics-Inspired computational techniques.

Harmony search (HS) is a meta-heuristic search algorithm which tries to mimic the improvisation process of musicians in finding a pleasing harmony. In recent years, due to some advantages, HS has received a significant attention. HS is easy to implement, converges quickly to the optimal solution and finds a good enough solution in a reasonable amount of computational time. The merits of HS algorithm have led to its application to optimization problems of different engineering areas. In this chapter, the concepts and performance of HS algorithm are shown and some engineering applications are reviewed. It is observed that HS has shown promising performance in solving difficult optimization problems and different versions of this algorithm have been developed. In the next years, it is expected that HS is applied to more real optimization problems.

    Jose M. Lanza-Gutierrez, Universidad Politecnica de Madrid, Spain
    Ricardo Soto, Pontificia Universidad Católica de Valparaíso, Chile
    Broderick Crawford, Pontificia Universidad Católica de Valparaíso,
        Chile
    Juan A. Gomez-Pulido, University of Extremadura, Spain
    Nicolas Fernandez, Pontificia Universidad Católica de Valparaíso,
        Chile
    Carlos Castillo, Pontificia Universidad Católica de Valparaíso, Chile

Group technology has acquired a great consideration in the last years. This technique allows including the advantages of serial production to any manufacturing industry by dividing a manufacturing plant into a set of machine-part cells. The identification and formation of the cells are known as the Manufacturing Cell Design Problem (MCDP), which is an NP-hard problem. In this paper, the authors propose to solve the problem through a swarm intelligence metaheuristic called ElectroMagnetism-like (EM-like) algorithm, which is inspired by the attraction-repulsion mechanism of particles in the context of the electromagnetic theory. The original EM-like algorithm was designed for solving continuous optimization problems, while the MCDP is usually formulated by assuming a binary approach. Hence, the authors propose an adaptation of this algorithm for addressing the problem. Such adaptation is applied for solving a freely available dataset of the MCDP, obtaining competitive results compared to recent approaches.

    Premalatha Kandhasamy, Bannari Amman Institute of Technology,
        India
    Balamurugan R, Bannari Amman Institute of Technology, India
    Kannimuthu S, Karpagam College of Engineering, India

In recent years, nature-inspired algorithms have been popular due to the fact that many real-world optimization problems are increasingly large, complex and dynamic. By reasons of the size and complexity of the problems, it is necessary to develop an optimization method whose efficiency is measured by finding the near optimal solution within a reasonable amount of time. A black hole is an object that has enough masses in a small enough volume that its gravitational force is strong enough to prevent light or anything else from escaping. Stellar mass Black hole Optimization (SBO) is a novel optimization algorithm inspired from the property of the gravity's relentless pull of black holes which are presented in the Universe. In this paper SBO algorithm is tested on benchmark optimization test functions and compared with the Cuckoo Search, Particle Swarm Optimization and Artificial Bee Colony systems. The experiment results show that the SBO outperforms the existing methods.

Section 2
Bio-Inspired Computational Techniques

Bio-Inspired computational techniques usually take motivation from various biological systems or processes existing in nature. The motivating features of biological systems or processes include adaptability and robustness that attracts to mimic them to develop computational techniques based upon them. Artificial Immune Systems, Viral Systems, foraging behaviour of mammals, hunting strategy adopted by predators etc. form the basis of some interesting biology-inspired computational techniques.

The designers of Artificial Immune Systems (AIS) had been inspired from the properties of natural immune systems: self-organization, adaptation and diversity, learning by continual exposure, knowledge extraction and generalization, clonal selection, networking and meta-dynamics, knowledge of self and non-self, etc. The aim of this chapter, along its sections, is to describe the principles of artificial immune systems, the most representational data structures (for the representation of antibodies and antigens), suitable metrics (which quantifies the interactions between components of the AIS) and their properties, AIS specific algorithms and their characteristics, some hybrid computational schemes (based on various soft computing methods and techniques like artificial neural networks, fuzzy and intuitionistic-fuzzy systems, evolutionary computation, and genetic algorithms), both standard and extended AIS models/architectures, and AIS applications, in the end.

In this paper optimal design of time modulated linear antenna arrays (TMLAA) with optimal placement of nulls in the desired direction of elevation plane has been dealt with the approach based on evolutionary algorithm like collective animal behaviour (CAB). Analysis has been done in theoretical and practical environment. Firstly the current excitation weights of the linear array of isotropic elements have been optimized by CAB is applied to improve null performance of TMLAA by Radio Frequency (RF) switch in MATLAB environment. The nulls positions of a TMLAA can be reduced significantly by optimizing the static excitation amplitudes and proper design of switch-on time intervals of each element. The CAB adjusts the current excitation amplitude of each element to place deeper nulls in the desired directions. Secondly the obtained optimal current excitation weight of the array factor is practically implemented in computer simulation technology- microwave studio (CST- MWS) environment. The array of microstrip patch antenna has been designed to operate at 5.85 GHz.

Chapter 6

    Yoshinori Suzuki, Iowa State University, USA
    Juan David Cortes, Iowa State University, USA

Based on recent viral transmission events in the swine species, we present a new framework to implement and execute tabu search (TS). The framework mimics the gradual evolutionary process observed when certain flu viruses move from one host population to another. It consists of three steps: (1) executing TS on a smaller subset of the original problem, (2) using one of its promising solutions as an initial solution for a marginally larger problem, and (3) repeating this process until the original problem is reached and solved. Numerical experiments conducted with randomly-generated vehicle routing instances demonstrate interesting results.

Section 3
Collective Intelligence-Based Computational Techniques

Sometimes a group of insects or animals or birds move together in search of food source or shelter. Collective Intelligence deals with the intelligence of a group emerging as the result of actions and reactions among the individual elements of the swarming group. The individual elements of a group follow simple rules and interact with each other for sharing information among them to achieve the overall goal such as finding food source or shelter. Most of the insect colonies such as ants, bees, termites, wasps, lion pride, fish schools and flock of birds etc., form the basis of this category-based nature-inspired computational technique since self-organization and decentralization are the identifying as well motivating features of these colonies.

Each hydropower system incorporates with appropriate hydro turbine, and hydro governor unit. In the current work, an Automatic Generation Control (AGC) of two equal hydropower systems with Proportional-Integral-Derivative (PID) controller was investigated. The gain values of the PID controllers were tuned using Ant Colony Optimization (ACO) technique with one percent Step Load Perturbation (1% SLP) in area 1. The Integral Square Error (ISE), Integral Time Square Error (ITSE), Integral Absolute Error (IAE) and Integral Time Absolute Error (ITAE) were chosen as the objective function in order to optimize the controller's gain values. The experimental results reported that the IAE based PID controller improved the system performance compared to other objective functions during sudden load disturbance.

Location management is a very critical and intricate problem in wireless mobile communication which involves tracking the movement of the mobile users in the cellular network. Particle Swarm Optimization (PSO) is proposed for the optimal design of the cellular network using reporting cell planning (RCP) strategy. In this state-of-the-art approach, the proposed algorithm reduces the involved total cost such as location update and paging cost for the location management issue. The same technique is proved to be a competitive approach to different existing test network problems showing the efficacy of the proposed method through simulation results. The result obtained is also validated for real network data obtained from BSNL, Odisha. Particle Swarm Optimization is used to find the optimal set of reporting cells in a given cellular network by minimizing the location management cost. This RCP technique applied to this cost minimization problem has given improved result as compared to the results obtained in the previous literature.

Chapter 9
Intelligent Demand Forecasting and Replenishment System by Using Nature-
Inspired Computing 190

Pragyan Nanda, SOA University, India
Sritam Patnaik, National University of Singapore, Singapore
Srikanta Patnaik, SOA University, India

The fashion apparel industry is too diverse, volatile and uncertain due to the fast changing market scenario. Forecasting demands of consumers has become survival necessity for organizations dealing with this field. Many traditional approaches have been proposed for improving the computational time and accuracy of the forecasting system. However, most of the approaches have over-looked the uncertainty existing in the fashion apparel market due to certain unpredictable events such as new trends, new promotions and advertisements, sudden rise and fall in economic conditions and so on. In this chapter, an intelligent multi-agent based demand forecasting and replenishment system has been proposed that adopts features from nature-inspired computing for handling uncertainty of the fashion apparel industry. The proposed system is inspired from the group hunting behaviour of crocodiles such as they form temporary alliances with other crocodiles for their own benefit even after being territorial creatures.

Chapter 10
Role Allocation in a Group of Control Objects: General Purpose Approach.... 206

Viacheslav Abrosimov, Smart Solutions, Russia

The efficiency of control objects that fulfill economic and military tasks in groups depends on the correct role allocation among them. This paper develops a role allocation algorithm for control objects jointly fulfilling a collective task. Control objects are represented as intelligent agents with some capabilities and needs. The problem is solved by ranking the agents based on their closeness to given roles in terms of their functionality and characteristics. The efficiency of the suggested approach is illustrated by allocating the role of reconnaissance aircraft in the group attack problem with a protected target.

Preface

Nature has always been a never-ending source for inspiration as it has its own amazing ways of solving complex problems efficiently. Over the last few decades, nature-inspired computing has emerged as a new computing paradigm and attracted the attention of researchers as well academia for solving conventional complex problems. As it is observed, nature solves the complex real-time problems in its own natural and sophisticated ways such as evolution of species, foraging food in scarce environment, survival of species in adverse conditions, using intelligent strategies for setting traps and capturing prey, maintaining a hierarchy in a group according to certain criteria, attracting mates for mating and building shelter etc. Behind all these seemingly complex phenomena of nature, simple rules are hidden as the species in nature do not understand complex things. They follow simple rules at individual level which gradually emerges as a complete phenomena or collective intelligence of the species or group. For example in case of an ant colony, the individual ants follow the pheromone trail (a chemical trail released by ants when they find food source) of their preceding ants while releasing pheromone trail for ants starting from nest after them. Although the chemical pheromone has a tendency to evaporate with time but the laying of pheromone by ants at regular interval prevents the evaporation and keeps the pheromone smell strong for guiding other ants. Similarly, in a flock of birds, each individual bird maintains its velocity and position while flying with respect to its neighbouring birds and hence do not collide with them while flying in as flock for foraging food. Thus, these simple rules followed at individual level leads to the collective achievement of the ultimate goal of the group. Scientists and researchers have been studying these phenomena of nature over decades to understand the working principle behind them. As a whole the complexity underlying these natural phenomena is beyond our understanding capability but when the complex system is broken into single components, their working principles can be observed and understood. Once understood, they further try to replicate the same into artificial systems for solving real-time complex problems by breaking them into modules and following similar simple rules. Now, these artificial systems being inspired from natural phenomena have high adaptability as a significant feature to survive uncertain environments of real world problems. Other significant features of these artificial systems that have been inherited from nature include its self-organizing nature, sharing of information among individuals in an optimal and decentralized manner.

The natural phenomena forming the basis for the nature-inspired computational techniques gets inspiration from various fields existing in nature and can be categorized into physics-inspired, chemistry-inspired, bio-inspired and collective intelligence based ones. Nature-inspired computing follows the bottom up approach while the top down approach of the traditional A.I. makes it complicated for decision making. Nature-inspired computing approaches are usually based upon the distributed arrangement of relatively simple and low-level elements known as agents that interact with each other as well with the environment.

Some of the most widely nature-inspired computing techniques that have been widely used to solve complex optimization problems are ant colony optimization (ACO), particle swarm optimization (PSO), artificial bee colony (ABC), bat algorithm (BA), firefly algorithm (FFA), and harmony search (HS) etc. The major reason behind the wide acceptance of these nature-inspired computing techniques is their adaptable, self-organizing and decentralized behaviour. All these features make nature-inspired computing techniques best suited for solving problems related to dynamic and uncertain environments. Manufacturing, supply chain and logistics, demand forecasting, stock market prediction are some of the areas that involves dynamic and uncertain environment with large number of constraints, thus leading to complicacy in decision making. Nature-inspired computing thus presents its ability in solving complex problems that are beyond traditional problem solving technique's capabilities. Although nature inspired algorithm presents diversity in their applications but still many open problems and research gaps do exist in this emerging research area.

The book on "Intelligent Nature-Inspired Computing" provides a wide coverage while balancing emphasis between theoretical as well as practical illustration of the existing as well as new techniques. The book discusses the latest progress in some of the existing nature-inspired computing techniques such as Harmony Search (HS) and Artificial Immune System (AIS) along with laying base for newly proposed approaches such has Stellar mass Black Hole (SBO) approach and group hunting strategy of crocodiles. This book can provide a base for beginners, scholars, researchers as well as experts working on nature-inspired computing. Also engineers working on similar real world problems can find it useful. Further the book provides an extensive index listed at the end of the book that can be used by the readers for ease of access of significant concepts.

ORGANIZATION OF THE BOOK

The book is logically organized into 10 chapters broadly categorized into three major sections. A brief description of each of the chapters follows:

Chapter 1 gives a brief study about the Harmony Search Algorithm. The chapter discusses the basic concept of harmony search and its application to various engineering areas. It further identifies the challenges faced by various application fields while applying Harmony Search Algorithm.

Chapter 2 first discusses the manufacturing cell design problem in detail which is the division of manufacturing plant into a set of machine-part cells. The chapter then further applies a physics based Electro-Magnetism-like (EM-like) algorithm to solve the manufacturing cell design problem using a binary approach while the original EM-like algorithm was developed for continuous optimization problems.

Chapter 3 presents a novel physics based Stellar mass Black Hole Optimization algorithm that takes inspiration from the physical properties of black hole that maintains a gravitational pull on the matters surrounding it. The authors further present analysis of experimental and comparative results obtained by testing on benchmark functions.

Chapter 4 describes the principle lying under the working of antibodies and antigens forming the Artificial Immune System (AIS). The authors present a detailed review of the representation of components of AIS algorithm, metrics and their properties. Further they discuss the architecture of some AIS-based hybrid models along with the applications.

Chapter 5 deals with the optimal design of linear antenna arrays using the evolutionary-based collective animal behaviour (CAB) approach. The author provides both theoretical and practical analysis of the evolutionary approach for solving the design problem.

Chapter 6 presents a framework for the implementation and execution of Tabu Search (TS) on the basis of viral transmission strategy. The authors present a detailed discussion on how certain viruses change their hosts gradually along with numerical results.

Chapter 7 investigates an Automatic Generation Control (AGC) of hydro power system with Proportional-Integral-Derivative (PID). The authors adopt Ant Colony Optimization (ACO) technique for tuning the PID controller and argue that ACO improves the system performance.

Chapter 8 presents a Particle Swarm Optimization (PSO) based approach for optimizing the cellular network design as a cost minimization problem. The authors contend that the PSO-based approach reduces the total cost due to location management problem.

Chapter 9 investigates the factors responsible for the volatility and uncertainty in consumer demands of fashion apparel industry. The authors further integrate the group hunting strategy adopted by crocodiles with multi-agent based system for demand forecasting and replenishment. The authors argue that the proposed system can handle uncertainty and volatility of the fashion apparel industry.

Chapter 10 investigates a correct role allocation problem that occurs during the execution of military tasks to accomplish the collective task. They next develop a role allocation based algorithm for solving the optimal role allocation of aircrafts in a group attack problem.

Srikanta Patnaik
SOA University, India

Acknowledgment

First and foremost, the editor would like to thank and acknowledge the contributors of this handbook for their support and patience. The editor would also like to thank the reviewers for their valuable and suggestions for improving the material of the handbook as without their support, this handbook would not have been successful. The editors would also like to acknowledge the help of all the people involved in this project.

Also the editor would like to convey his sincere thanks to Mariah Gilbert and Colleen Moore for their endless support. Finally, the editor would like to express his gratitude to the IGI-Global publication team for their extensive efforts during various phases of the Handbook development.

Srikanta Patnaik
SOA University, India

Introduction

Nature-inspired computing has been considered as a successful practice over the past few decades. This relatively new computing paradigm consists of some of the most powerful and widely accepted optimizing tools for handling real world problems. Although a significant number of literatures have been emerged over last few years, still this field of research succeeds in attracting the attention of peer researchers. Design and derivation of new emerging techniques with improved tuning of significant parameters, thus leading to the enhanced performance of complex systems is quite challenging.

Recent Developments in Intelligent Nature-Inspired Computing delivers many interesting contributions received from the researchers belonging to diverse fields and working in the area of nature-inspired computing. The book presents selected computing techniques widely covering the base categories of nature-inspired computing as well as diverse applications ranging from manufacturing cell design problem to optimal antenna array design, from automatic generation control of power system to intelligent demand forecasting and replenishment system. It also provides a strong foundation for some of the nature-inspired techniques such as Harmony Search (HS) and Artificial Immune System (AIS) and welcomes new algorithmic techniques for solving some of the complex problems of real world with interesting results. The book gives equal emphasis to both the theoretical background as well as practical implementation of the nature-inspired computing techniques.

The book highlights emerging nature-inspired computing techniques that might become strong foundation for many upcoming approaches for solving complex problems in future along with the cutting-edge progress in existing approaches. The book has been organized into three major sections on the basis of the categories; the computing techniques belong to, for the ease of the targeted audience. The book provides a complete understanding of the existing as well as newly proposed nature-inspired techniques along with addressing various issues making the deployment of the techniques challenging. The intended audience for the book may range from naïve researchers and practitioners of nature-inspired computing to experts with deep knowledge in this respective area.

Srikanta Patnaik
SOA University, India

Section 1
Physics–Inspired Computational Techniques

This section consists of chapters using physics-based approaches i.e., the nature-inspired computational techniques are based upon the basic principles of physics such as the principle of how harmony is achieved while composing music or the underlying principle of electro-magnetism or even the physics behind black hole concept. All these principles of physics along with other principles form the basis of the Physics-Inspired computational techniques.

Chapter 1
Harmony Search Algorithm:
Basic Concepts and Engineering Applications

Alireza Askarzadeh
Kerman Graduate University of Advanced Technology, Iran

Esmat Rashedi
Kerman Graduate University of Advanced Technology, Iran

ABSTRACT

Harmony search (HS) is a meta-heuristic search algorithm which tries to mimic the improvisation process of musicians in finding a pleasing harmony. In recent years, due to some advantages, HS has received a significant attention. HS is easy to implement, converges quickly to the optimal solution and finds a good enough solution in a reasonable amount of computational time. The merits of HS algorithm have led to its application to optimization problems of different engineering areas. In this chapter, the concepts and performance of HS algorithm are shown and some engineering applications are reviewed. It is observed that HS has shown promising performance in solving difficult optimization problems and different versions of this algorithm have been developed. In the next years, it is expected that HS is applied to more real optimization problems.

DOI: 10.4018/978-1-5225-2322-2.ch001

INTRODUCTION

Most often, engineering optimization problems have non-linear and non-convex objective functions with intense equality and inequality constraints along with various types of decision variables. As a result, solving such optimization problems using traditional methods faces with increasing difficulties. Meta-heuristic optimization algorithms can be efficient alternatives to conquer the difficulty of complex optimization problems. Originally invented in (Geem et al. 2001), HS is a meta-heuristic optimizer inspired by the music improvisation process. In music improvisation process, a predefined number of musicians attempt to tune the pitch of their instruments to achieve a pleasing harmony (best state). In nature, a harmony is defined by a special relation between several sound waves that have different frequencies. The quality of the improvised harmony is determined by aesthetic estimation. In order to improve the aesthetic estimation and find the best harmony, the musicians make practice after practice.

There are similarities between musicians improvisation and optimization processes. In an optimization problem, the ultimate aim is to find the global optimum of the objective function under consideration by tuning a predefined number of decision variables. Indeed, in an optimization problem the decision variables make a solution vector. Then, the values of the decision variables are put into the objective function and the quality of the solution vector is calculated. The solution vector is updated during the iterations until the global optimum is obtained.

Comparison of musical and optimization processes reveals the following similarities:

- In musical process, the quality of a harmony is determined by aesthetic estimation. In an optimization process, the quality of a solution vector is determined by the objective function value.
- In musical process, the ultimate goal is to obtain the best (fantastic) harmony. In an optimization process, the ultimate goal is to obtain the global optimum.
- In musical process, musicians change the pitch of their instruments. An optimization algorithm changes the values of the decision variables.
- In musical process, any attempt to play a harmony is called practice. In an optimization, each attempt to update a solution vector is called iteration.

In general, when a musician wants to tune the pitch of his/her instrument (for example fiddle, saxophone, etc) and sound a note, he/she utilizes one of the three possible ways. Theses rules are the main body of HS algorithm.

1. He/she can sound a note from the possible range randomly.
2. He/she can sound a note from his/her memory.
3. He/she can sound a note near-by one note from his/her memory.

In the following next sections, HS implementation for optimization, HS variants and HS applications have been explained in detail.

HS IMPLEMENTATION FOR OPTIMIZATION

In HS algorithm, a feasible solution is called harmony and each decision variable of the solution is corresponding to a note. HS includes a harmony memory (HM) in which a predetermined number of harmonies (*N*) have been stored. Suppose the goal is to minimize/maximize a fitness function (*f*) subject to *d* decision variables. This optimization problem is defined as follows:

$$Min.\left(or\ Max. \right) \quad f\left(x_1, x_2, ..., x_d\right) \tag{1}$$

where *f* is the fitness function, x_i (*i* = 1,2,...,*d*) is decision variable *i* and *d* denotes the problem dimension.

In order to implement HS algorithm for optimization, the following steps should be used:

Step 1. A harmony memory is initialized.
Step 2. A new harmony is improvised.
Step 3. The new harmony is included in the HM or excluded.
Step 4. Steps 2 and 3 are repeated until the stopping criterion is met. When the stopping criterion is met, go to
Step 5. The best harmony stored in HM is returned as the found optimum solution.

The details of each step are as follows:

Step 1. Initialization of HM

In HS, at first, *N* harmonies are produced in the search space and stored in HM. Table 1 shows the structure of the HM.

As Table 1 shows, harmony *i* can be specified by a vector, harmony $i = [x_{i,1} x_{i,2} ... x_{i,d}]$. In order to initialize the HM, Eq. (2) can be used. The last column of HM is the fitness function values corresponding to each harmony. For example, f_i means

Table 1. The structure of harmony memory

	x_1	x_2	...	x_d	f
Harmony 1	$x_{1,1}$	$x_{1,2}$	...	$x_{1,d}$	f_1
Harmony 2	$x_{2,1}$	$x_{2,2}$	...	$x_{2,d}$	f_2
⋮	⋮	⋮		⋮	⋮
Harmony N	$x_{N,1}$	$x_{N,2}$	...	$x_{N,d}$	f_N

the value of the fitness function for harmony 1. This value is calculated by putting the decision variables of harmony 1 into the fitness function.

$$x_{i,j} = l_j + rand \times \left(u_i - l_j\right) \qquad i = 1,2,...,N; \quad j = 1,2,...,d \tag{2}$$

where l_j and u_j are the lower and upper bounds of decision variable j, respectively, and *rand* is a random number with uniform distribution from [0 1]. Mathematically, the HM is shown by the following expression:

$$HM = \begin{bmatrix} Harmony\ 1 \\ Harmony\ 2 \\ \vdots \\ Harmony\ N \end{bmatrix} = \begin{bmatrix} x_{1,1} & x_{1,2} & \cdots & x_{1,d} & f_1 \\ x_{2,1} & x_{2,2} & \cdots & x_{2,d} & f_2 \\ \vdots & \vdots & & \vdots & \vdots \\ x_{N,1} & x_{N,2} & \cdots & x_{N,d} & f_N \end{bmatrix} \tag{3}$$

Step 2. Improvisation of a New Harmony

The next step is to improvise a new harmony, $x_{new} = [x_{new,1} x_{new,2} ... x_{new,d}]$. The main feature of HS algorithm in comparison with other metaheuristics such as genetic algorithm (GA) is that in HS, a new harmony is generated by use of all the existing harmonies. For generation of decision variable j, the following procedure is conducted. This procedure in done for all the decision variables until a new harmony is obtained.

Stage 1

A random number with uniform distribution from [0 1] is generated (*rand*). If *rand* > *HMCR*, the decision variable of the new harmony ($x_{new,j}$) is randomly generated by Eq. (4). *HMCR* which is the abbreviation of harmony memory considering rate varies between 0 and 1.

$$x_{new,j} = l_j + rand \times \left(u_i - l_j\right)$$ (4)

Otherwise, if $rand \leq HMCR$, one of the harmonies stored in HM is randomly selected, for example k where $1 \leq k \leq N$. Then, $x_{new,j}$ is selected by the corresponding value of harmony k from HM as Equation 5.

$$x_{new,j} = x_{k,j}$$ (5)

Stage 2

In order to escape from local optima, HS makes use of pitch adjustment mechanism by which the improvised note may be shifted to a neighbour value with respect to the possible range. In HS, there is a parameter named pitch adjusting rate (*PAR*) which varies between 0 and 1. Small values of *PAR* leads to having a weak pitch adjustment mechanism and large values of *PAR* result in having a rich pitch adjustment mechanism. In order to perform pitch adjustment mechanism, after stage 1, a random number from [0 1] with uniform distribution is generated (*rand*). If $rand \leq PAR$, the improvised note should be shifted to a neighbour value by using Equation 6. Otherwise, if $rand > PAR$, the improvised note does not change.

$$x_{new,j} = x_{new,j} + bw \times \left(rand - 0.5\right) \times \left|u_j - l_j\right|$$ (6)

where *bw* is called the bandwidth of generation and *rand* is a random number between 0 and 1 with uniform distribution. The term of $\left(rand - 0.5\right)$ generates a random number from [-0.5 0.5]. Since the users donot know that it is better to increase the value of the decision variable or decrease its value, the term of $\left(rand - 0.5\right)$ is used to randomly select the direction of movement. In Eq. (6), the term of $\left|u_j - l_j\right|$ is used to control the scale of the decision variables since in an optimization problem, the scale of the decision variables may vary significantly such as -10^4 to 10^4 in one dimension and -10^{-5} to 10^{-5} in another one.

Step 3. Replacement

After Step 2, we have a new feasible harmony. The fitness function of the new harmony (f_{new}) is calculated. In this Step, we compare the new harmony and the worst harmony stored in HM. Suppose harmony h ($1 \leq h \leq N$) is the worst harmony stored in HM in terms of the fitness function value. In this case, if f_{new} is better than fit_h, harmony h is removed from the HM and the new harmony is replaced. Otherwise, if f_{new} is worse than fit_h, the new harmony is abandoned.

Step 4. Stopping Criterion

Most often, the stopping criterion of optimization algorithms is to reach to a pre-defined number of iterations (t_{max}). When this criterion is met, the algorithm is terminated and we go to Step 5. Otherwise, Steps 2 and 3 are repeated until the stopping criterion is satisfied.

Step 5. Final result

In this Step, the best harmony stored in HM is returned as the optimum solution of the problem under consideration. Figure 1 shows the flow chart of HS implementation for optimization.

HS has three parameters, namely, *HMCR*, *PAR* and *bw*. The role of these parameters on HS performance is as follows:

- **HMCR:** The value of *HMCR* which belongs to [0 1], denotes the probability of using historical values stored in HM for playing a note. Small values of *HMCR* result in random search (with the probability of 1-*HMCR*) and vice versa. For example, *HMCR* of 0.9 means that the note will be sound from the HM by the probability of 0.9 and will be sound randomly by the probability of 0.1 from the possible range.

- **PAR:** By this value which belongs to [0 1], each value improvised from the HM, has a change to be replaced by a value located at the vicinity of the selected value from HM. In HS, this chance is provided and controlled by the probability of *PAR*. As a result, large values of *PAR* increase the probability of pitch adjustment and vice versa.

- **bw:** If the pitch adjustment mechanism is selected, the value of *bw* controls the step size of movement. By using large values of *bw*, the distance between the new value and the HM value increases. Indeed, we can tune the global and local search by *bw* value.

As the first investigation, the Rosenbrock's banana test function, defined by Equation 7, is used to illustrate the performance of HS algorithm. Figure 3 indicates the schematic of the test function. The global minimum of this function is 0 which is located at $x_1 = 1$ and $x_2 = 1$. HS algorithm is used to find the solution of the Rosenbrock's banana test function. The parameter setting of HS is as follows: $N = 20$, $HMCR = 0.95$, $PAR = 0.8$, $bw = 0.2$ and $t_{max} = 10000$.

$$Min. \quad f\left(x_1, x_2\right) = Ln\left(1 + (1 - x_1)^2 + 100(x_2 - x_1^2)^2\right) \tag{7}$$
$$-10 \leq x_1, x_2 \leq 10$$

HS algorithm can successfully find the global solution of the Rosenbrock's banana test function. Figure 4 shows the position of the initial solutions stored in HM. Figures 5 to 8 shows the position of the produced solutions after 100, 1000, 5000 and 10000 iterations, respectively. As can be seen, HS algorithm can provide a good balance between diversification and intensification during its search process.

In order to evaluate the search power of the classical HS algorithm, Griewank test function in 30 dimensions is used as a multimodal high-dimensional test function where there are many local optima over the search range. The expression of this function is shown by Equation 8. The global minimum of this function is 0 which is located at $(0,0,....,0)$.

$$Min. \; f(x) = \frac{1}{4000} \sum\nolimits_{i=1}^{n} (x_i)^2 - \prod\nolimits_{i=1}^{n} \cos(\frac{x_i}{\sqrt{i}}) + 1 \tag{8}$$
$$-600 \leq x_i \leq 600 \qquad i = 1, 2, ..., 30$$

In order to solve the Griewank test function, the parameter setting of HS is as follows: $N = 50$, $HMCR = 0.9$, $bw = 0.1$ and $t_{max} = 50000$. Table 1 shows the impact of different PAR values on the performance of HS over the Griewank test function. The statistical results reported in this table have been obtained over 30 independent runs. As can be seen, the best performance is achieved when the value of PAR is set to 0.1. In Table 1, $PAR = rand$ means that the value of PAR is adjusted by a random number between 0 and 1 drawn from a uniform distribution.

Figure 8 and Figure 9 show the convergence rate of HS algorithm during the first 5000 iterations. These figures show the fitness function value of the best harmony stored in HM at each iteration. It is clear that HS finds a good region of the search space at the first iterations and tries to converge to the solution.

Table 2 represents the impact of different bw values on the performance of HS over the Griewank test function. In this case, the parameter setting of HS is as follows: $N = 50$, $HMCR = 0.9$, $PAR = 0.1$ and $t_{max} = 50000$. It is observed that by use of $bw = 0.01$, HS can find better results than the other values for the studied test function.

Figure 1. Flow chart of harmony search algorithm for optimization

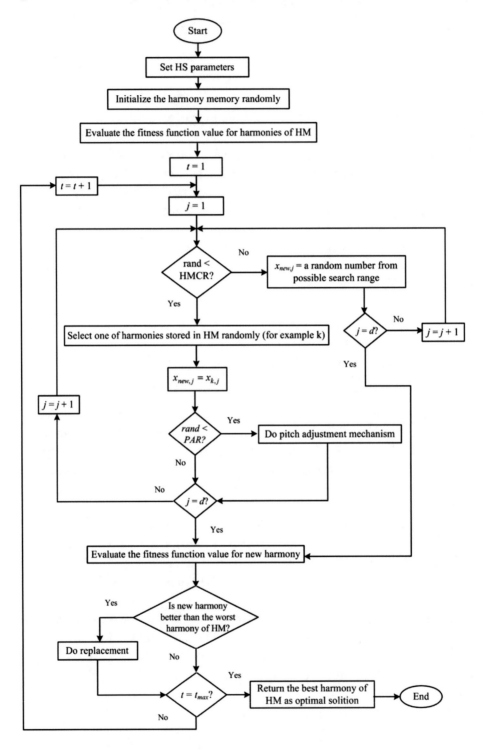

Figure 2. The graph of the Rosenbrock's banana test function

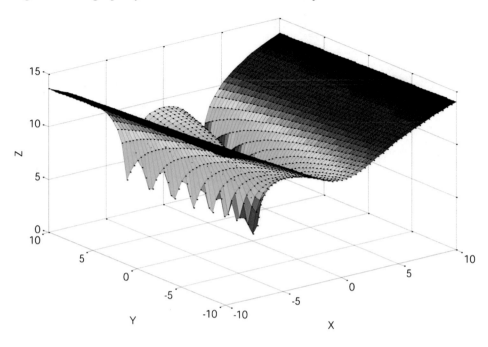

Figure 3. The initial positions memorized in HM

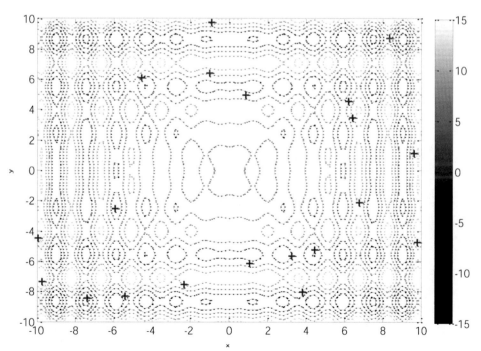

Figure 4. The positions generated by HS algorithm during the first 100 iterations

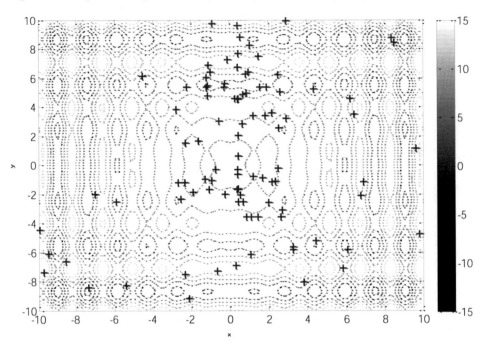

Figure 5. The positions generated by HS algorithm during the first 1000 iterations

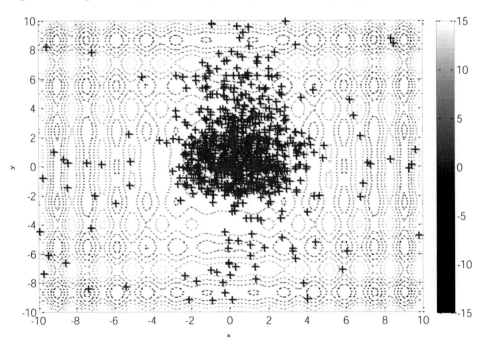

Figure 6. The positions generated by HS algorithm during the first 5000 iterations

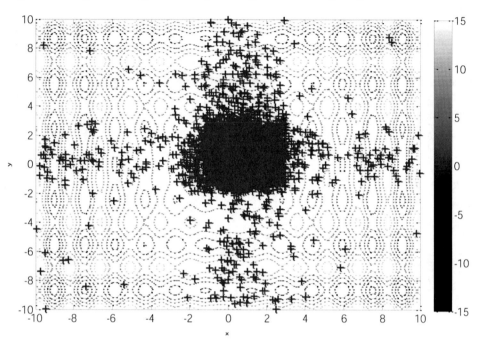

Figure 7. The positions generated by HS algorithm during the first 10000 iterations

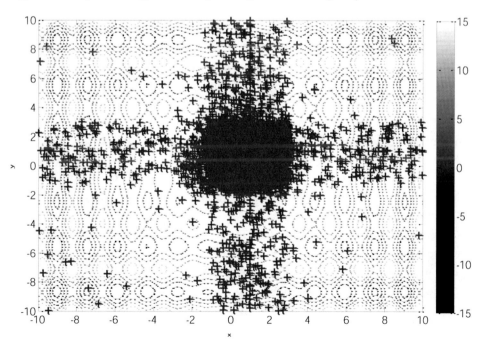

Table 2. Performance of HS algorithm on Griewank function considering different PAR values

Index	PAR = 0.1	PAR = 0.3	PAR = 0.5	PAR = 0.7	PAR = 0.9	PAR = rand
Average	1.39	2.86	4.59	6.38	7.89	4.70
Standard Deviation	0.07	0.20	0.47	0.44	0.97	0.32
Minimum	1.26	2.39	3.28	5.53	4.93	4.07
Maximum	1.54	3.35	5.32	7.12	9.90	5.45

Table 3. Performance of HS algorithm on Griewank function considering different bw values

Index	bw = 0.001	bw = 0.01	bw = 0.1	bw = 1	bw = rand
Average	1.20	1.03	1.39	9.33	3.74
Standard Deviation	0.06	0.03	0.07	2.02	0.46
Minimum	1.09	0.87	1.26	6.06	2.53
Maximum	1.31	1.07	1.54	13.47	4.39

COMPARATIVE STUDY OF VARIOUS VARIANTS

Investigations on HS performance show that this algorithm has a good ability in exploration and can discover the potential solution rapidly. However, the local search ability of HS is weak so that no better solution is expected at the latter iterations of HS algorithm. In the literature, various variants have been devised to improve the searching ability of HS.

Like other optimization algorithms, parameter setting of HS algorithm is a challenging task. Since *PAR* and *bw* have a great influence on the quality of the final solution, proper parameter setting of HS increases the probability of finding the global solution more and more. The absence of general rules for doing parameter setting of HS algorithm has guided the research towards developing new variants of HS which focus on parameter setting.

In this context, one of the most famous and popular variants of HS algorithms is the investigation made by (Mahdavi et al. 2007). They have proposed time-varying values for *PAR* and *bw*. Based on their suggestion, the value of *PAR* increases linearly during the iterations as follows:

Figure 8. Convergence rate of HS algorithm for solving the Griewank function considering different PAR values during the first 5000 iterations
For a more accurate representation of this figure, please see the electronic version.

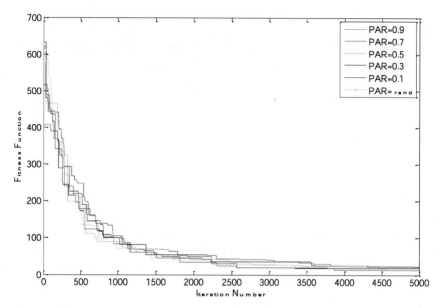

Figure 9. Convergence rate of HS algorithm for solving the Griewank function considering different bw values during the first 5000 iterations
For a more accurate representation of this figure, please see the electronic version.

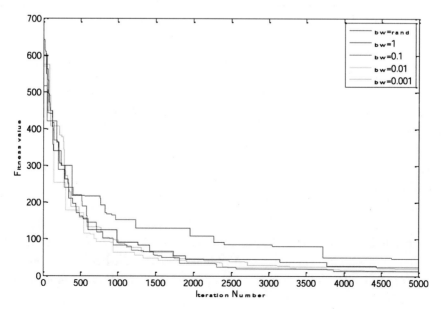

13

$$PAR^t = PAR_{\min} + \frac{PAR_{\max} - PAR_{\min}}{t_{\max}} \times t \tag{9}$$

where PAR^t is the PAR value at iteration t, t_{max} is the maximum number of iterations, PAR_{min} is the minimum PAR value and PAR_{max} is the maximum PAR value.

The value of bw decreases nonlinearly during the iterations by the following exponential function:

$$bw^t = bw_{\max} \times \exp\left(Ln(\frac{bw_{\min}}{bw_{\max}}) \times \frac{t}{t_{\max}}\right) \tag{10}$$

where bw_{max} and bw_{min} are the maximum bandwidth and minimum bandwidth, respectively.

Based on this idea that a successful search should be proceeded progressively at the beginning of the algorithm and then gradually settled down, (Wang and Huang 2010) have developed a self-adaptive HS algorithm which utilizes a decreasing linear PAR during the iterations to prevent overshooting and oscillation. Indeed, this idea is the opposite of the idea used by (Mahdavi et al. 2007). Also, they have used the maximal and minimal values in the HM to conduct pitch adjustment mechanism instead of using the parameter of bw. For this aim, one of the following equations is used for doing the pitch adjustment:

$$x_{new,j} = x_{new,j} + \left[\max(HM^j) - x_{new,j}\right] \times rand \tag{11}$$

$$x_{new,j} = x_{new,j} - \left[x_{new,j} - \min(HM^j)\right] \times rand \tag{12}$$

where $\max(HM^j)$ and $\min(HM^j)$ are the highest and the lowest values of variable j in HM. By use of this pitch adjustment mechanism, the decision variables will not violate the boundary constraint.

There are other investigations which have developed HS variants with the aim of finding the best parameter setting. In (Geem 2006; Mukhopadhyay et al. 2008), optimum setting of bw has been discussed. In (Geem et al. 2005; Chakraborty et al. 2009), the parameter of PAR has been modified. In the first, it is proposed to replace the PAR parameter by a mutation operator borrowed from differential evolution (DE) algorithm and in the latter, a multi-pitch adjusting rate has been proposed. In (Hasancebi et al. 2009), the dynamic variation of $HMCR$ and PAR values has been proposed.

There are investigations which have tried to eliminate the burden of manually finding the best parameter setting of HS algorithm. In (Geem, Sim 2010), an additional matrix is used for memorizing operation types (random selection, memory consideration, or pitch adjustment) in each variable. At each iteration, the parameters of *HMCR* and *PAR* are recalculated based on the matrix information. In (Askarzadeh, Zebarjadi 2014), the following equations have been proposed for tuning the HS parameters based on random numbers drawn from a uniform distribution between 0 and 1:

$$HMCR = 0.9 + 0.1 \times rand \tag{13}$$

$$PAR = \frac{1 - rand}{2} \tag{14}$$

$$bw = rand \tag{15}$$

In the pitch adjustment mechanism of original HS algorithm, the direction is selected randomly and the step size is determined by *bw*. Some researchers have tried to introduce new pitch adjustment mechanisms. In (Omran, Mahdavi 2008), a global-best HS (GHS) has been developed in which the pitch adjustment is only based on the best harmony of HM and there is no need to *bw*. In (Wang, Huang 2010), a variant, named self-adaptive HS (SAHS), has been proposed in which a new harmony is improvised based on the maximal and minimal values of HM. In some investigations, the hybridization of HS algorithm with concepts borrowed from the other meta-heuristic algorithms such as differential mutation (Wang, Li 2013) and particle swarm optimization (Pandi, Panigrahi 2011) has been investigated and satisfactory results have been reported.

APPLICATIONS

To date, HS is utilized to solve various engineering optimization problems. Some of the works have been reviewed below.

Electrical Engineering

The hybridization of HS and DE was developed in (De et al. 2015) for designing a CMOS inverter. The heuristic algorithm found the best design variables to optimize the system performance. The design variables were the ratio of the channel width to the channel length of the CMOS transistors and the output load capacitance.

Telecommunication

In telecommunication, HS was used for optimal designing of wireless sensor networks (WSN), antenna and radar. The pattern synthesis of linear antenna arrays was investigated in (Guney,Onay 2011). Pattern synthesis is the process of determining the parameters of an antenna array to achieve the target antenna radiation pattern. HS with a local search procedure utilized to solve the Spread-Spectrum Radar Polyphase (SSRP) codes design in (Gil-López et al. 2012). The variables are the magnitudes of the phase differences for the SSRP and the goal was the minimization of the module of the largest among the samples of the autocorrelation function. HS with a local search procedure was used for node localization in the wireless sensor networks with noisy distance-related measurements in (Manjarres et al. 2013). There were two objective functions of CF and CV. CF is the squared error between the estimated and the measured inter-node distances of the nodes that are in the connectivity range of each others and CV is the number of connectivity neighborhood constraints which are not satisfied by the candidate topology. The design of low complexity sharp Modified Discrete Fourier Transform (MDFT) filter bank using hybrid HS and Gravitational search algorithm were reported in (Sakthivel,Elias 2015). Filter coefficients are optimized to design a low complexity sharp MDFT filter bank with low power consumption, low chip area and high speed of operation.

Pattern Recognition and Image/Speech Processing

In the field of pattern recognition, there are two famous topics of classification and clustering. HS could be adopted to design a classifier or a clustering algorithm. The application of HS in recognizing patterns in image or speech data are reported in some researches.

Classification

Classification is the process of assigning category labels to any type of data. Two important parts of classification systems are classifiers and features. HS could help to improve the accuracy of the system by improving the classifier or selecting the best set of features. In (Kulluk et al. 2012), six benchmark classification problems were solved by an artificial neural network (ANN) which trained using self-adaptive global best version of HS. The process of training feed-forward NNs using HS was performed by optimizing the weights of links between the neurons to minimize the error. A hybrid harmony-based classifier was developed in (Karimi et al. 2012). HS produced if-then rules that determine the label of the data according to its attributes. Authors in (Wang et al. 2015b) used HS as a feature selection method for email classification. HS found the best discriminative features in regard to the document frequency and term frequency. Email classification could help for filtering spam. A self-adaptive HS utilized in (Huang et al. 2014) for local feature selection in the classification of music genre. Music features were five acoustic characteristics and the number of music genres was ten. The goal was the maximization of classification precision. In (Inbarani et al. 2015), the hybridization of HS and rough set theory was developed to select the best set of features to maximize the cassification accuracy. A hybrid HS combined with stochastic local search was produced in (Nekkaa,Boughaci 2015) to find the beneficial features for the classification outcome optimization. The support vector machine (SVM) was used as the classifier and its parameters (penalty parameter C and the gamma parameter for the RBF kernel) were tuned by an iterative search. A self-adjusting HS was produced in (Zheng et al. 2015a) to maximize the classification accuracy of C4.5 classifier by feature selection.

Clustering

Clustering is about discriminating data into some groups (called clusters), in such a way that data in a group are similar to each other and different from the other groups. Harmony K-means algorithm was produced in (Mahdavi,Abolhassani 2009) for document clustering. Documents were represented using term weights. HS found the center of the clusters and then the results were refined by K-means.

Image Processing

In the image processing algorithms, heuristic optimization algorithms like HS are useful for optimizing, tuning and enhancing the processing results. There are various works in this regard. In (Cuevas 2013), block matching for motion estimation was handeled by HS. The fitness function was the matching quality of each motion vector candidate. A window arround the current block was searched for the best matched block. The motion vector is the position difference between the current block and the best match block. In images, the saliency map is calculated by combining various information like color, intensity, orientation, and other feature maps. Saliency map is useful for target detection. To have more target conspicuity in the saliency map, a modified Gaussian HS was used in (Li,Duan 2014). Tuning the parameters of Deep Belief Networks was performed using HS in (Papa et al. 2015). Binary mage reconstruction was solved by this network to minimize the mean square error beween reconsrtucted and original image. Image restoration by projections onto convex sets was tackled in (Pires et al. 2015) where its parameters were optimized by HS. HS found the best parameters to maximize the improvement signal to noise ratio (ISNR).

Speech Processing

HS was used to solve part-of-speech (PoS) tagging problem in (Forsati,Shamsfard 2015) and find the best tagging quality. PoS is about syntactic tagging to every word in a sentence according to the context.

Water Management

To design and manage water distribution and water supply networks, there are some optimization problems that could be handled by HS. Water distribution network design problem was solved in (Geem 2012) by a diversity improved version of HS to minimize the construction cost. The problems have design constraints of nodal pressure and quantity and the decision variables are the diameter of the pipes. In (Baek et al. 2010), HS was employed to optimize the simulation of hydraulic under abnormal operating conditions in water distribution systems. HS built the model to minimize the error between the assumed and the calculated heads at the demand nodes. Pump scheduling problem in water distribution systems was tackled in (Kougias,Theodossiou 2013) using the polyphonic HS. The objectives were the minimization of quantity of pumped water and electricity and maintenance cost. The design of groundwater remediation systems was tackled by a probabilistic multi-objective fast HS in (Luo et al. 2014; Luo et al. 2012) to minimize the remediation cost and contaminant mass remaining in aquifer. Authors in (Atrabi et al. 2015) used HS for reservoir operation optimization to minimize the water supply deficit and flood damages of a reservoir. The subjected constraint was mass balance limitation.

Mechanical Engineering

In mechanical engineering, HS was utilized for optimizing mechanical process and mechanical design problems. Authors in (Abhishek et al. 2016) used a fuzzy embedded HS for tuning the machining process parameters of the carbon fiber reinforced polymer (CFRP) composites. These composites are used for manufacturing engineering components especially in aerospace and automobile industries. A fuzzy inference system was used to model the multiple performance characteristics into a single objective function. Some well-known constraint mechanical design optimization problems namely the pressure vessel design problem, the tension/compression spring design problem, and the welded beam design problem were solved in (Mun,Cho 2012) by a modified HS. Authors in (Razfar et al. 2011) found optimal cutting parameters in face milling process by HS to minimize the surface roughness. The surface roughness was modeled by feed forward artificial neural networks. Surface roughness formation and cutting force mechanisms modeling were also developed in (Zinati,Razfar 2012) by HS and artificial neural networks.

Chemical Engineering

Thermodynamic models in chemical engineering are useful for synthesis, design, optimization, and control of process systems (Merzougui et al. 2012). The parameter estimation of these models could be solved by heuristic optimization. HS was applied in (Merzougui et al. 2012) for estimation of binary interaction parameters in the liquid–liquid phase equilibrium model. The objective function was the data fitting between observed and calculated data. The support vector regression (SVR) estimated the relationship function between amount of asphaltene precipitation and titration data in (Fattahi et al. 2015). HS was tuned the SVR learning parameters and the data fit accuracy was defined as the objective function. This method is useful in petroleum industry.

Power Engineering

In the field of power engineering, there are many optimization problems like economic dispatch (ED), optimal power flow (OPF), unit commitment (UC), modeling problems, designing, and power system planning problems. HS was examined to solve these problems in various reported works.

Economic Dispatch

ED is defined by optimal determination of the generator power outputs while supporting the load demand. It has two types of static or dynamic dispatch and it has some equality and inequality constraints. Authors in (Arul et al. 2013a) utilized HS with chaotic self-adaptive differential mutation operator for optimal solving of dynamic ED with some constraints. The constraints were about real power balance, real power generation limits, and generating unit ramp-rate limits. The objective function was the total fuel cost. Combined heat and power economic dispatch optimized by HS in (Javadi et al. 2012). Three types of thermal units including co-generation, electrical only, and heat-only units were considered and the energy production cost was minimized. Authors in (Jeddi,Vahidinasab 2014) employed modified HS for economic load dispatch to minimize the generation cost while satisfying unit operating limits, power balance constraints, ramp-rate limits, and spinning reserve constraints. The modified HS was produced using wavelet mutation and a memory consideration scheme based on the roulette wheel. Authors in (Khazali,Kalantar 2011) used HS to find the settings of control variables to optimize the power transmission loss, voltage stability, and voltage profile in economic power dispatch problem. Control variables were generator voltages, tap positions of tap changing transformers and the amount of reactive compensation devices. Authors in (Niu et al. 2014) proposed HS with arithmetic crossover operation for solving five different types of ED problems, including static dispatch with valve point effects, ED with prohibited operating zones, ED with multiple fuel cells, combined heat and power ED, and dynamic ED. A differential HS was employed in (Wang,Li 2013) for solving the non-convex ED to minimize the total fuel cost. Constraints of generating capacity, power balance, ramp rate limit, and prohibited operating zones were handled by a repair procedure and three simple selection rules. Authors in (Arul et al. 2013a) solved non-convex ED using HS for generation cost minimization. The constraints of real power balance, generation limit, prohibited operating zones, ramp-rate, and system spinning reserve, were tackled by penalization. Non-convex ED was also solved in (Arul et al. 2014) by an improved version of HS.

Optimal Power Flow

OPF is defined by the minimization of generation costs and loss in power system variables under some equality and inequality constraints. OPF problem was solved using improved HS in (Sinsuphan et al. 2013) to minimize the total production cost under constraints for real and reactive power flow and variable limits. OPF was also solved by HS in (Sivasubramani,Swarup 2011) with the objectives of the total fuel cost, real power loss, and voltage stability index minimization. The authors in (Arul et al., 2013b) proposed a chaotic self-adaptive differential HS to solve OPF problems with non-smooth and non-convex cost functions.

Unit Commitment

UC is the problem of determining schedules of generating units including on/off states of the units and how much they generate hourly. The objective of UC is to minimize the total operating cost. UC is a large-scale, non-convex, and constraint problem. Security constrained unit commitment problem was handled in (Samiee et al. 2013) to minimize the fuel cost and startup and shut down costs of thermal units while satisfying constraints for: AC power flow constraints, up/down time duration, ramp rate, operating zones, system spinning, AC security, and reactive power generation. To handle these constraints, a hybrid method composed of tri-state algorithm and infeasible solution rejection technique was produced. The unit commitment problem was solved by an improved version of HS in (Morsali et al. 2014) to minimize the operation, start-up and shut-down costs. This objective function was subjected to the load demand constraints and ramp rate limits. To solve this problem, HS control parameters of memory size, *HMCR*, *PAR* and *bw* was adapted. In (Paqaleh et al. 2010), to solve UC by HS, the considered objectives were the fuel costs of generating units, the start-up costs of the committed units and shut-down costs of the decommitted units and the constraints were the power balance, spinning reserve capacity of generating units, unit ramp-up and ramp-down rates, minimum up/down time limit, and spinning reserve requirement.

Modeling

Grouping-based global HS was proposed in (Askarzadeh,Rezazadeh 2011) for modeling the voltage as a function of the current in proton exchange membrane fuel cell (PEMFC). HS found the parameters of the modele to fit the simulated data and minimize the error. Authors in (Askarzadeh,Zebarjadi 2014) used HS for wind power modeling by finding the optimum parameters of the model. Optimum parameters minimize the error between the model and actual wind powers. Authors in (Askarzadeh,Rezazadeh 2012) utilized HS for modeling the current as a function of the voltage in solar cells. HS identified the model parameters to minimize the difference between experimental data and the model results.

Designing and Planning

Optimum design of a PV/wind hybrid system was experimented in (Askarzadeh 2013b). A hybridization of HS with chaotic search and simulated annealing was used to find the number of PV panels, wind turbines and batteries which minimize the total annual cost of the system in the presence of some constraints. A discrete HS was proposed in (Askarzadeh 2013a) for determining the optimum size of wind–photovoltaic hybrid energy systems which minimize the total annual cost. Power network partitioning was solved by HS in (Ezhilarasi,Swarup 2012b) to minimize the number of nodes in a cluster and the interconnections between the clusters. Optimally partitioning the network into clusters enhances the computational complexity by parallel processing. This problem was also solved in (Ezhilarasi,Swarup 2012a) by HS and a graph bi-partitioning method called Kernighan–Lin strategy. Authors in (Javaheri,Goldoost-Soloot 2012) employed HS for optimal locating and sizing of FACTS devices in power systems to minimize the total generation cost. The optimal placement and sizing of capacitors in power distribution networks was handled in (Sirjani,Bade 2015) by an improved global HS, to minimize the power loss and total cost. The problem constraints were load unbalancing, mutual coupling and harmonics. Power transmission expansion planning was solved in (Rastgou,Moshtagh 2014) by improved HS to minimize the construction costs, congestion cost, and security cost. A hybrid self- adaptive global HA was utilized in (Shivaie et al. 2015) for reliability-based Distribution Expansion Planning (DEP). There were four objectives of the investment, maintenance, operation, and expected customer interruption costs with the problem constraints of operational restrictions, Kirchhoff's laws, radial structure limitation, voltage limits, and capital expenditure budget restriction.

Civil Engineering

In civil engineering, there are many complicated optimization problems that was solved by HS such as optimizing building structures, road construction, and solving structural design problems.

Optimizing Structural Designs

Special seismic moment reinforced concrete frames are used in buildings to resist earthquakes. Ref (Akin,Saka 2015) utilized HS for optimal design of these frames under earthquake loads to minimize the frame cost. The frame design variables are consisted of two groups of column design variables and beam design variables. Authors in (Amini,Ghaderi 2013) used the hybridization of HS with ant colony search algorithm for optimal locating of dampers in structural systems. The objective function was defined by the dynamic response of the system and the configuration and forces of the dampers which was minimized. Two improved HS algorithms were proposed in (Degertekin 2012) for optimally designing of truss structures. Size and shape of truss structures was also optimized in (Kaveh,Javadi 2014) with a hybrid method of PSO and HS to minimize the truss weight. A social HS model was employed for design of the composite floor with minimum cost in (Kaveh,Ahangaran 2012). Design variables were related to the concrete slab, steel beams, and the shear studs. Four classical weight minimization problems of steel frames were designed using an enhanced HS in (Maheri,Narimani 2014). Damage under ambient vibration in structural systems was detected by HS in (Miguel et al. 2012). HS produced numerical model for structural damage and minimized its difference with the experimental model. The structural damage was estimated from a model update process using damage-induced changes in the modal features. Steel frame optimization was solved in (Murren,Khandelwal 2014) to obtain least-weight designs subjected to design and drift constraints. A hybrid HS was proposed in (Segura et al. 2015) for optimizing the sustainability of post-tensioned concrete box-girder pedestrian bridges. HS found the structural design variables and the geometry for minimizing the costs while satisfying the constraints for structural safety and durability. Authors in (Bekdas 2015) designed post-tensioned axially symmetric cylindrical reinforced concrete walls and minimized the total material cost using

HS. These walls are used in storage tanks for liquids and solids. In (Carbas,Saka 2012), topological design of domes was performed by improved HS to minimize the weight of each dome. Optimal design of steel frames was developed in (Degertekin 2008) by HS to determine the design variables of steel and minimize the weight of the frame. Optimal sensor placement on gantry crane structures was solved by HS in (Jin et al. 2015). These sensors are used to evaluate the safety and reliability of structures. The number and the location of the sensors were determined by HS to improve the performance. Optimal design of geosynthetic-reinforced retaining walls was performed in (Manahiloh et al. 2015) by HS to minimize the construction cost in the presence of design constraints.

Road Transportation

The optimum signal settings in a road transportation with a hybridization of HS and hill climbing was performed in (Ceylan,Ceylan 2012) for minimizing the travel time and the fuel consumption. In (Salcedo-Sanz et al. 2013), the reconfiguration of one-way roads in a city by providing alternative routes was solved by a two-objective HS. The proposed method guaranteed the mobility of citizens. The value of this function was estimated by a Monte Carlo simulation. A modified HS was produced in (Lee,Mun 2014) to establish a dynamic model for describing the resistance for rutting and fatigue cracking of asphalt concrete mixture. HS found the parameters of the model to fit to the laboratory tests.

Financial Tasks

A self adaptive differential HS was used in (Dash et al. 2014) for designing a single hidden layer feed forward neural network. The optimized neural network was used for prediction of a financial time series data that was the closing price and volatility of five different stock indices. Forecasting of financial data was performed in (Dash et al. 2015) by an integrating model of a interval type2 fuzzy logic system and an artificial neural network. A proposed differential HS was used for optimizing the parameters of the fuzzy time series models for stock market volatility prediction. A stochastic replenishment intervals multiproduct inventory model with dynamic demand was solved by HS in (Taleizadeh et al. 2012) to minimize costs of holding, purchasing and shortage. Multi-site order planning problem was handled by HS in (Guo et al. 2015). This problem was defined in a make-to-order manufacturing environment considering multiple production uncertainties. The goal is to attain production objectives by effectively determining the allocation of customer orders to several self-owned or collaborative production plants placed in different regions.

Product Transportation

Multi-server location–allocation problem was tackled by multi-objective HS in (Hajipour et al. 2014). This problem is about placing a number of facilities in between a number of customers located at fixed points to minimize the transportation cost. Shipping cost in a transportation problem was minimized by hybridization of HS and simulated annealing in (Hosseini et al. 2014). In this problem, some vehicles transport goods from suppliers to the customers via three transportation systems. The problem of emergency air transportation was solved in (Zheng et al. 2015b) by a hybridization of biogeography-based optimization and HS, to maximize delivery efficiency. This problem is about the transportation of amounts of n different types of relief supplies from a set of m air freight hubs to the closest airport to the target disaster area.

Job Scheduling

Multi-objective flexible job shop scheduling problem solved by a Pareto version of HS with multiple harmony generation strategies in (Gao et al. 2014). HS with one-point crossover and iterative local search was employed in (Li et al. 2015) to solve the flow line manufacturing cell scheduling problem and minimize the total tardiness and mean total flow time. Cellular manufacturing system is a production system which needs cell scheduling before starting the production process. Two-sided assembly lines are kind of assembly lines in which tasks operations can be performed in them. Non dominated HS was proposed in (Purnomo,Wee 2014) to solve the task assignment problem in a two-sided assembly line with zone constraints. The objective was the maximization of the production rate and the distribution of the workload in the assembly line. Flexible job-shop scheduling problem was solved in (Gao et al. 2015) by discrete HS. The objectives were the weighted combination of the maximum of the completion time and the mean of earliness and tardiness.

Function Optimization

There are some enhanced versions of HS for numerical optimization examined by some standard function optimization: improved HS (Ashrafi,Dariane 2013), HS with a novel selection schemes (Al-Betar et al. 2012; Al-Betar et al. 2013), island-based HS (Al-Betar et al. 2015), Geometric Selective HS (Castelli et al. 2014), HS with dynamic control parameters (Chen et al. 2012), a learning automata-based HS (Enayatifar et al. 2013), HS with mutation operators (Hasan et al. 2014), global dynamic HS (Khalili et al. 2014), improved HS (Contreras et al. 2014), parameter adaptive HS (Kumar et al. 2014), intelligent global HS (Valian et al. 2014), HS with Gaussian mutation (Dai et al. 2015), HS with the population based incremental learning (Gao et al. 2012), hybridization of HS and cuckoo search (Wang et al. 2015a). High-dimensional multimodal optimization problems was solved by HS in (Tuo et al. 2015). 0–1 knapsack problems was solved in (Kong et al. 2015a, b) by new versions of binary HS. Furthermore, it was solved in (Layeb 2013) by a hybrid quantum HS.

CONCLUSION

As one of the powerful optimization algorithms, HS has attracted significant attention for solving different types of optimization problems during the recent years. The advantages of HS algorithm are easy implementation, simple concept, fast convergence speed and few parameters to adjust. Owing to these merits, HS has been considerably used to solve various problems in different fields like power system, communication, software, civil, water engineering, and pattern recognition. Study of the literature indicates that HS can effectively and efficiently solve different types of engineering optimization problems. In the literature, various variants of HS algorithm can be found which focus on improving improvisation process, harmony memory consideration and parameter setting. There are other variants which try to enhance the performance of HS by borrowing some ideas from the other metaheuristic such as GA, PSO, DE and chaotic search. By comparing the results obtained by HS and other algorithms it can be drawn that HS could be a good candidate to solve complex optimization problems.

ACKNOWLEDGMENT

The authors would like to thank Editor and Reviewers for their helpful comments.

REFERENCES

Abhishek, K., Datta, S., & Mahapatra, S. S. (2015). Multi-objective optimization in drilling of CFRP (polyester) composites: Application of a fuzzy embedded harmony search (HS) algorithm. *Measurement*, *77*, 222–239. doi:10.1016/j.measurement.2015.09.015

Akin, A., & Saka, M. P. (2015). Harmony search algorithm based optimum detailed design of reinforced concrete plane frames subject to ACI 31805 provisions. *Computers & Structures*, *147*, 79–95. doi:10.1016/j.compstruc.2014.10.003

Al-Betar, M. A., Awadallah, M. A., Khader, A. T., & Abdalkareem, Z. A. (2015). Island-based harmony search for optimization problems. *Expert Systems with Applications*, *42*(4), 2026–2035. doi:10.1016/j.eswa.2014.10.008

Al-Betar, M. A., Doush, I. A., Khader, A. T., & Awadallah, M. A. (2012). Novel selection schemes for harmony search. *Applied Mathematics and Computation*, *218*(10), 6095–6117. doi:10.1016/j.amc.2011.11.095

Al-Betar, M. A., Khader, A. T., Geem, Z. W., Doush, I. A., & Awadallah, M. A. (2013). An analysis of selection methods in memory consideration for harmony search. *Applied Mathematics and Computation*, *219*(22), 10753–10767. doi:10.1016/j. amc.2013.04.053

Amini, F., & Ghaderi, P. (2013). Hybridization of Harmony Search and Ant Colony Optimization for optimal locating of structural dampers. *Applied Soft Computing*, *13*(5), 2272–2280. doi:10.1016/j.asoc.2013.02.001

Arul, R., Ravi, G., & Velusami, S. (2013). Solving optimal power flow problems using chaotic self adaptive differential harmony search algorithm. *Electric Power Components and Systems*, *41*(8), 782–805. doi:10.1080/15325008.2013.769033

Arul, R., Ravi, G., & Velusami, S. (2013a). Chaotic self-adaptive differential harmony search algorithm based dynamic economic dispatch. *International Journal of Electrical Power & Energy Systems*, *50*, 85–96. doi:10.1016/j.ijepes.2013.02.017

Arul, R., Ravi, G., & Velusami, S. (2013b). Non-convex economic dispatch with heuristic load patterns, valve point loading effect, prohibited operating zones, ramp-rate limits and spinning reserve constraints using harmony search algorithm. *Electrical Engineering*, *95*(1), 53–61. doi:10.1007/s00202-012-0241-y

Arul, R., Ravi, G., & Velusami, S. (2014). An improved harmony search algorithm to solve economic load dispatch problems with generator constraints. *Electrical Engineering*, *96*(1), 55–63. doi:10.1007/s00202-012-0276-0

Ashrafi, S. M., & Dariane, A. B. (2013). Performance evaluation of an improved harmony search algorithm for numerical optimization: Melody Search (MS). *Engineering Applications of Artificial Intelligence*, *26*(4), 1301–1321. doi:10.1016/j. engappai.2012.08.005

Askarzadeh, A. (2013a). Developing a discrete harmony search algorithm for size optimization of wind–photovoltaic hybrid energy system. *Solar Energy, 98*(Part C), 190–195. doi:10.1016/j.solener.2013.10.008

Askarzadeh, A. (2013b). A discrete chaotic harmony search-based simulated annealing algorithm for optimum design of PV/wind hybrid system. *Solar Energy, 97*, 93–101. doi:10.1016/j.solener.2013.08.014

Askarzadeh, A., & Rezazadeh, A. (2011). A grouping-based global harmony search algorithm for modeling of proton exchange membrane fuel cell. *International Journal of Hydrogen Energy, 36*(8), 5047–5053. doi:10.1016/j.ijhydene.2011.01.070

Askarzadeh, A., & Rezazadeh, A. (2012). Parameter identification for solar cell models using harmony search-based algorithms. *Solar Energy, 86*(11), 3241–3249. doi:10.1016/j.solener.2012.08.018

Askarzadeh, A., & Zebarjadi, M. (2014). Wind power modeling using harmony search with a novel parameter setting approach. *Journal of Wind Engineering and Industrial Aerodynamics, 135*, 70–75. doi:10.1016/j.jweia.2014.10.012

Atrabi, H. B., Kourosh, Q., Rheinheimer, D. E., & Sharifi, E. (2015). Application of harmony search algorithm to reservoir operation optimization. *Water Resources Management, 29*(15), 5729–5748. doi:10.1007/s11269-015-1143-3

Baek, C. W., Jun, H. D., & Kim, J. H. (2010). Development of a PDA model for water distribution systems using harmony search algorithm. *KSCE Journal of Civil Engineering, 14*(4), 613–625. doi:10.1007/s12205-010-0613-7

Bekdas, G. (2015). Harmony search algorithm approach for optimum design of post-tensioned axially symmetric cylindrical reinforced concrete walls. *Journal of Optim Theory Application, 164*(1), 342–358. doi:10.1007/s10957-014-0562-2

Carbas, S., & Saka, M. P. (2012). Optimum topology design of various geometrically nonlinear latticed domes using improved harmony search method. *Struct Multidisc Optim, 45*(3), 377–399. doi:10.1007/s00158-011-0675-2

Castelli, M., Silva, S., Manzoni, L., & Vanneschi, L. (2014). Geometric Selective Harmony Search. *Information Sciences, 279*, 468–482. doi:10.1016/j.ins.2014.04.001

Ceylan, H., & Ceylan, H. (2012). A Hybrid Harmony Search and TRANSYT hill climbing algorithm for signalized stochastic equilibrium transportation networks. *Transportation Research Part C, Emerging Technologies, 25*, 152–167. doi:10.1016/j.trc.2012.05.007

Chakraborty, P., Roy, G. G., Das, S., Jain, D., & Abraham, A. (2009). An improved harmony search algorithm with differential mutation operator. *Fundamenta Informaticae*, *95*, 1–26.

Chen, J., Pan, Q., & Li, J. (2012). Harmony search algorithm with dynamic control parameters. *Applied Mathematics and Computation*, *219*(2), 592–604. doi:10.1016/j.amc.2012.06.048

Contreras, J., Amaya, I., & Correa, R. (2014). An improved variant of the conventional Harmony Search algorithm. *Applied Mathematics and Computation*, *227*, 821–830. doi:10.1016/j.amc.2013.11.050

Cuevas, E. (2013). Block-matching algorithm based on harmony search optimization for motion estimation. *Applied Intelligence*, *39*(1), 165–183. doi:10.1007/s10489-012-0403-7

Dai, X., Yuan, X., Wu, L. (in press). A novel harmony search algorithm with gaussian mutation for multi-objective optimization. *Soft Comput.*

Dash, R., Dash, P. K., & Bisoi, R. (2014). A self adaptive differential harmony search based optimized extreme learning machine for financial time series prediction. *Swarm and Evolutionary Computation*, *19*, 25–42. doi:10.1016/j.swevo.2014.07.003

Dash, R., Dash, P. K., & Bisoi, R. (2015). A differential harmony search based hybrid interval type2 fuzzy EGARCH model for stock market volatility prediction. *International Journal of Approximate Reasoning*, *59*, 81–104. doi:10.1016/j.ijar.2015.02.001

De, B. P., Kar, R., Mandal, D., & Ghoshal, S. P. (2016). Optimal design of high speed symmetric switching CMOS inverter using hybrid harmony search with differential evolution. *Soft Computing*, *20*(9), 3699–3717. doi:10.1007/s00500-015-1731-4

Degertekin, S. O. (2012). Improved harmony search algorithms for sizing optimization of truss structures. *Computers & Structures*, *92–93*, 229–241. doi:10.1016/j.compstruc.2011.10.022

Degertekin, S. O., & Hayalioglu, M. S. (2010). Harmony search algorithm for minimum cost design of steel frames with semi-rigid connections and column bases. *Struct Multidisc Optim*, *42*(5), 755–768. doi:10.1007/s00158-010-0533-7

Enayatifar, R., Yousefi, M., Abdullah, A. H., & Darus, A. N. (2013). A novel harmony search algorithm based on learning automata. *Communications in Nonlinear Science and Numerical Simulation*, *18*(12), 3481–3497. doi:10.1016/j.cnsns.2013.04.028

Ezhilarasi, G. A., & Swarup, K. S. (2012a). Network decomposition using Kernighan–Lin strategy aided harmony search algorithm. *Swarm and Evolutionary Computation*, *7*, 1–6. doi:10.1016/j.swevo.2012.07.002

Ezhilarasi, G. A., & Swarup, K. S. (2012b). Network partitioning using harmony search and equivalencing for distributed computing. *Journal of Parallel and Distributed Computing*, *72*(8), 936–943. doi:10.1016/j.jpdc.2012.04.006

Fattahi, H., Gholami, A., Amiribakhtiar, M. S., & Moradi, S. (2015). Estimation of asphaltene precipitation from titration data: A hybrid support vector regression with harmony search. *Neural Computing & Applications*, *26*(4), 789–798. doi:10.1007/s00521-014-1766-y

Forsati, R., & Shamsfard, M. (2015). Novel harmony search-based algorithms for part-of-speech tagging. *Knowledge and Information Systems*, *42*(3), 709–736. doi:10.1007/s10115-013-0719-6

Gao, K. Z., Suganthan, P. N., Pan, Q. K., Chua, T. J., Cai, T. X., & Chong, C. S. (2014). Pareto-based grouping discrete harmony search algorithm for multi-objective flexible job shop scheduling. *Information Sciences*, *289*, 76–90. doi:10.1016/j.ins.2014.07.039

Gao, K. Z., Suganthan, P. N., Pan, Q. K., Chua, T. J., Cai, T. X., & Chong, C. S. (2015). Discrete harmony search algorithm for flexible job shop scheduling problem with multiple objectives. *Journal of Intelligent Manufacturing*, *27*(2), 363–374. doi:10.1007/s10845-014-0869-8

Gao, X. Z., Wang, X., Jokinen, T., Ovaska, S. J., Arkkio, A., & Zenger, K. (2012). A hybrid PBIL-based harmony search method. *Neural Computing & Applications*, *21*(5), 1071–1083. doi:10.1007/s00521-011-0675-6

Geem, Z. (2006). *Improved harmony search from ensemble of music players. In Knowledge-based intelligent information and engineering systems* (pp. 86–93). Heidelberg: Springer. doi:10.1007/11892960_11

Geem, Z. W. (2012). Effects of initial memory and identical harmony in global optimization using harmony search algorithm. *Applied Mathematics and Computation*, *218*(22), 11337–11343. doi:10.1016/j.amc.2012.04.070

Geem, Z. W., & Sim, K. B. (2010). Parameter-setting-free harmony search algorithm. *Applied Mathematics and Computation*, *217*(8), 3881–3889. doi:10.1016/j.amc.2010.09.049

Geem, Z. W., Tseng, C. L., & Park, Y. (2005). *Harmony search for generalized orienteering problem: best touring in China. In Advances in natural computation* (pp. 741–750). Berlin: Springer.

Gil-López, S., Ser, J. D., Salcedo-Sanz, S., Pérez-Bellido, Á. M., Cabero, J. M., & Portilla-Figueras, J. A. (2012). A hybrid harmony search algorithm for the spread spectrum radar polyphase codes design problem. *Expert Systems with Applications, 39*(12), 11089–11093. doi:10.1016/j.eswa.2012.03.063

Guney, K., & Onay, M. (2011). Optimal synthesis of linear antenna arrays using a harmony search algorithm. *Expert Systems with Applications, 38*(12), 15455–15462. doi:10.1016/j.eswa.2011.06.015

Guo, Z. X., Yang, C., Wang, W., & Yang, J. (2015). Harmony search-based multi-objective optimization model for multi-site order planning with multiple uncertainties and learning effects. *Computers & Industrial Engineering, 83,* 74–90. doi:10.1016/j.cie.2015.01.023

Hajipour, V., Rahmati, S. H. A., Pasandideh, S. H. R., & Niaki, S. T. A. (2014). A multi-objective harmony search algorithm to optimize multi-server location–allocation problem in congested systems. *Computers & Industrial Engineering, 72,* 187–197. doi:10.1016/j.cie.2014.03.018

Hasan, B. H. F., Abu Doush, I., Al Maghayreh, E., Alkhateeb, F., & Hamdan, M. (2014). Hybridizing Harmony Search algorithm with different mutation operators for continuous problems. *Applied Mathematics and Computation, 232,* 1166–1182. doi:10.1016/j.amc.2013.12.139

Hasancebi, O., Erdal, F., & Saka, M. P. (2009). An adaptive harmony search method for structural optimization. *Journal of Structural Engineering, 137,* 419–431.

Hosseini, S. D., Akbarpour Shirazi, M., & Karimi, B. (2014). Cross-docking and milk run logistics in a consolidation network: A hybrid of harmony search and simulated annealing approach. *Journal of Manufacturing Systems, 33*(4), 567–577. doi:10.1016/j.jmsy.2014.05.004

Huang, Y.-F., Lin, S.-M., Wu, H.-Y., & Li, Y.-S. (2014). Music genre classification based on local feature selection using a self-adaptive harmony search algorithm. *Data & Knowledge Engineering, 92,* 60–76. doi:10.1016/j.datak.2014.07.005

Inbarani, H. H., Bagyamathi, M., & Azar, A. T. (2015). A novel hybrid feature selection method based on rough set and improved harmony search. *Neural Computing & Applications, 26*(8), 1859–1880. doi:10.1007/s00521-015-1840-0

Javadi, M. S., Esmaeel Nezhad, A., & Sabramooz, S. (2012). Economic heat and power dispatch in modern power system harmony search algorithm versus analytical solution. *Scientia Iranica*, *19*(6), 1820–1828. doi:10.1016/j.scient.2012.10.033

Javaheri, H., & Goldoost-Soloot, R. (2012). Locating and Sizing of Series FACTS Devices Using Line Outage Sensitivity Factors and Harmony Search Algorithm. *Energy Procedia*, *14*, 1445–1450. doi:10.1016/j.egypro.2011.12.1115

Jeddi, B., & Vahidinasab, V. (2014). A modified harmony search method for environmental/economic load dispatch of real-world power systems. *Energy Conversion and Management*, *78*, 661–675. doi:10.1016/j.enconman.2013.11.027

Jin, H., Xia, J., Wang, Y.-q. (2015). Optimal sensor placement for space modal identification of crane structures based on an improved harmony search algorithm. *J Zhejiang Univ-Sci A (Appl Phys & Eng)*, *16*(6), 464-477.

Karimi, Z., Abolhassani, H., & Beigy, H. (2012). A new method of mining data streams using harmony search. *Journal of Intelligent Information Systems*, *39*(2), 491–511. doi:10.1007/s10844-012-0199-2

Kaveh, A., & Ahangaran, M. (2012). Discrete cost optimization of composite floor system using social harmony search model. *Applied Soft Computing*, *12*(1), 372–381. doi:10.1016/j.asoc.2011.08.035

Kaveh, A., & Javadi, M. S. (2014). Shape and size optimization of trusses with multiple frequency constraints using harmony search and ray optimizer for enhancing the particle swarm optimization algorithm. *Acta Mechanica*, *225*(6), 1595–1605. doi:10.1007/s00707-013-1006-z

Khalili, M., Kharrat, R., Salahshoor, K., & Sefat, M. H. (2014). Global Dynamic Harmony Search algorithm: GDHS. *Applied Mathematics and Computation*, *228*, 195–219. doi:10.1016/j.amc.2013.11.058

Khazali, A. H., & Kalantar, M. (2011). Optimal reactive power dispatch based on harmony search algorithm. *International Journal of Electrical Power & Energy Systems*, *33*(3), 684–692. doi:10.1016/j.ijepes.2010.11.018

Kong, X., Gao, L., Ouyang, H., & Li, S. (2015a). A simplified binary harmony search algorithm for large scale 0–1 knapsack problems. *Expert Systems with Applications*, *42*(12), 5337–5355. doi:10.1016/j.eswa.2015.02.015

Kong, X., Gao, L., Ouyang, H., & Li, S. (2015b). Solving large-scale multidimensional knapsack problems with a new binary harmony search algorithm. *Computers & Operations Research*, *63*, 7–22. doi:10.1016/j.cor.2015.04.018

Kougias, I. P., & Theodossiou, N. P. (2013). Multiobjective pump scheduling optimization using harmony search algorithm (HSA) and polyphonic HAS. *Water Resources Management*, *27*(5), 1249–1261. doi:10.1007/s11269-012-0236-5

Kulluk, S., Ozbakir, L., & Baykasoglu, A. (2012). Training neural networks with harmony search algorithms for classification problems. *Engineering Applications of Artificial Intelligence*, *25*(1), 11–19. doi:10.1016/j.engappai.2011.07.006

Kumar, V., Chhabra, J. K., & Kumar, D. (2014). Parameter adaptive harmony search algorithm for unimodal and multimodal optimization problems. *Journal of Computational Science*, *5*(2), 144–155. doi:10.1016/j.jocs.2013.12.001

Layeb, A. (2013). A hybrid quantum inspired harmony search algorithm for 0–1 optimization problems. *Journal of Computational and Applied Mathematics*, *253*, 14–25. doi:10.1016/j.cam.2013.04.004

Lee, S., & Mun, S. (2014). Improving a model for the dynamic modulus of asphalt using the modified harmony search algorithm. *Expert Systems with Applications*, *41*(8), 3856–3860. doi:10.1016/j.eswa.2013.12.021

Li, J., & Duan, H. (2014). Novel biological visual attention mechanism via Gaussian harmony search. *International Journal for Light and Electron Optics*, *125*(10), 2313–2319. doi:10.1016/j.ijleo.2013.10.075

Li, Y., Li, X., & Gupta, J. N. D. (2015). Solving the multi-objective flowline manufacturing cell scheduling problem by hybrid harmony search. *Expert Systems with Applications*, *42*(3), 1409–1417. doi:10.1016/j.eswa.2014.09.007

Luo, Q., Wu, J., Sun, X., Yang, Y., & Wu, J. (2012). Optimal design of groundwater remediation systems using a multi-objective fast harmony search algorithm. *Hydrogeology Journal*, *20*(8), 1497–1510. doi:10.1007/s10040-012-0900-0

Luo, Q., Wu, J., Yang, Y., Qian, J., & Wu, J. (2014). Optimal design of groundwater remediation system using a probabilistic multi-objective fast harmony search algorithm under uncertainty. *Journal of Hydrology (Amsterdam)*, *519*, 3305–3315. doi:10.1016/j.jhydrol.2014.10.023

Mahdavi, M., & Abolhassani, H. (2009). Harmony K-means algorithm for document clustering. *Data Mining and Knowledge Discovery*, *18*(3), 370–391. doi:10.1007/s10618-008-0123-0

Mahdavi, M., Fesanghary, M., & Damangir, E. (2007). An improved harmony search algorithm for solving optimization problems. *Applied Mathematics and Computation*, *188*(2), 1567–1579. doi:10.1016/j.amc.2006.11.033

Maheri, M. R., & Narimani, M. M. (2014). An enhanced harmony search algorithm for optimum design of side sway steel frames. *Computers & Structures*, *136*, 78–89. doi:10.1016/j.compstruc.2014.02.001

Manahiloh, K. N., Nejad, M. M., & Momeni, M. S. (in press). Optimization of design parameters and cost of geosynthetic-reinforced earth walls using harmony search algorithm. *Int. J. of Geosynth. and Ground Eng.*

Manjarres, D., Del Ser, J., Gil-Lopez, S., Vecchio, M., Landa-Torres, I., Salcedo-Sanz, S., & Lopez-Valcarce, R. (2013). On the design of a novel two-objective harmony search approach for distance- and connectivity-based localization in wireless sensor networks. *Engineering Applications of Artificial Intelligence*, *26*(2), 669–676. doi:10.1016/j.engappai.2012.06.002

Merzougui, A., Hasseine, A., & Laiadi, D. (2012). Application of the harmony search algorithm to calculate the interaction parameters in liquid–liquid phase equilibrium modeling. *Fluid Phase Equilibria*, *324*, 94–101. doi:10.1016/j.fluid.2012.03.029

Miguel, L. F. F., Miguel, L. F. F., Kaminski, J. Jr., & Riera, J. D. (2012). Damage detection under ambient vibration by harmony search algorithm. *Expert Systems with Applications*, *39*(10), 9704–9714. doi:10.1016/j.eswa.2012.02.147

Morsali, R., Jafari, T., Ghods, A., & Karimi, M. (2014). Solving unit commitment problem using a novel version of harmony search algorithm. Front. *Energy*, *8*(3), 297–304.

Mukhopadhyay, A., Roy, A., Das, S., & Abraham, A. (2008). Population-variance and explorative power of harmony search: An analysis. *Second National Conference on Mathematical Techniques Emerging Paradigms for Electronics and IT Industries (MATEIT 2008)*. doi:10.1109/ICDIM.2008.4746793

Mun, S., & Cho, Y.-H. (2012). Modified harmony search optimization for constrained design problems. *Expert Systems with Applications*, *39*(1), 419–423. doi:10.1016/j. eswa.2011.07.031

Murren, P., & Khandelwal, K. (2014). Design-driven harmony search (DDHS) in steel frame optimization. *Engineering Structures*, *59*, 798–808. doi:10.1016/j. engstruct.2013.12.003

Nekkaa, M., & Boughaci, D. (2016). Hybrid harmony search combined with stochastic local search for feature selection. *Neural Processing Letters*, *44*(1), 199–220. doi:10.1007/s11063-015-9450-5

Niu, Q., Zhang, H., Wang, X., Li, K., & Irwin, G. W. (2014). A hybrid harmony search with arithmetic crossover operation for economic dispatch. *International Journal of Electrical Power & Energy Systems*, *62*, 237–257. doi:10.1016/j.ijepes.2014.04.031

Omran, M. G. H., & Mahdavi, M. (2008). Global-best harmony search. *Applied Mathematics and Computation*, *198*(2), 643–656. doi:10.1016/j.amc.2007.09.004

Pandi, V. R., & Panigrahi, B. K. (2011). Dynamic economic load dispatch using hybrid swarm intelligence based harmony search algorithm. *Expert Systems with Applications*, *38*(7), 8509–8514. doi:10.1016/j.eswa.2011.01.050

Papa, J. P., Scheirer, W., & Cox, D. D. (2016). Fine-tuning Deep Belief Networks using Harmony Search. *Applied Soft Computing*, *46*, 875–885. doi:10.1016/j.asoc.2015.08.043

Paqaleh, M. A., Rashidinejad, M., & Kasmaei, M. P. (2010). An implementation of harmony search algorithm to unit commitment problem. *Electrical Engineering*, *92*(6), 215–225. doi:10.1007/s00202-010-0177-z

Pires, R. G., Pereira, D. R., Pereira, L. A. M., Mansano, A. F., & Papa, J. P. (2016). Projections onto convex sets parameter estimation through harmony search and its application for image restoration. *Natural Computing*, *15*(3), 493–502. doi:10.1007/s11047-015-9507-4

Purnomo, H. D., & Wee, H.-M. (2014). Maximizing production rate and workload balancing in a two-sided assembly line using Harmony Search. *Computers & Industrial Engineering*, *76*, 222–230. doi:10.1016/j.cie.2014.07.010

Rastgou, A., & Moshtagh, J. (2014). Improved harmony search algorithm for transmission expansion planning with adequacy–security considerations in the deregulated power system. *International Journal of Electrical Power & Energy Systems*, *60*, 153–164. doi:10.1016/j.ijepes.2014.02.036

Razfar, M. R., Zinati, R. F., & Haghshenas, M. (2011). Optimum surface roughness prediction in face milling by using neural network and harmony search algorithm. *International Journal of Advanced Manufacturing Technology*, *52*(5-8), 487–495. doi:10.1007/s00170-010-2757-5

Sakthivel, V., Elias, E. (2015). Design of low complexity sharp MDFT filter banks with perfect reconstruction using hybrid harmony-gravitational search algorithm. *Engineering Science and Technology, an International Journal*, *18*(4), 648-657..

Salcedo-Sanz, S., Manjarrés, D., Pastor-Sánchez, Á., Del Ser, J., Portilla-Figueras, J. A., & Gil-López, S. (2013). One-way urban traffic reconfiguration using a multi-objective harmony search approach. *Expert Systems with Applications, 40*(9), 3341–3350. doi:10.1016/j.eswa.2012.12.043

Samiee, M., Amjady, N., & Sharifzadeh, H. (2013). Security constrained unit commitment of power systems by a new combinatorial solution strategy composed of enhanced harmony search algorithm and numerical optimization. *International Journal of Electrical Power & Energy Systems, 44*(1), 471–481. doi:10.1016/j.ijepes.2012.07.069

Segura, T. G., Yepes, V., Alcalá, J., & Pérez-López, E. (2015). Hybrid harmony search for sustainable design of post-tensioned concrete box-girder pedestrian bridges. *Engineering Structures, 92*, 112–122. doi:10.1016/j.engstruct.2015.03.015

Shivaie, M., Ameli, M. T., Sepasian, M. S., Weinsier, P. D., & Vahidinasab, V. (2015). A multistage framework for reliability-based distribution expansion planning considering distributed generations by a self-adaptive global-based harmony search algorithm. *Reliability Engineering & System Safety, 139*, 68–81. doi:10.1016/j.ress.2015.03.001

Sinsuphan, N., Leeton, U., & Kulworawanichpong, T. (2013). Optimal power flow solution using improved harmony search method. *Applied Soft Computing, 13*(5), 2364–2374. doi:10.1016/j.asoc.2013.01.024

Sirjani, R., & Bade, M. G. (2015). A global harmony search algorithm for finding optimal capacitor location and size in distribution networks. *J. Cent. South Univ, 22*(5), 1748–1761. doi:10.1007/s11771-015-2693-5

Sivasubramani, S., & Swarup, K. S. (2011). Multi-objective harmony search algorithm for optimal power flow problem. *International Journal of Electrical Power & Energy Systems, 33*(3), 745–752. doi:10.1016/j.ijepes.2010.12.031

Taleizadeh, A. A., Niaki, S. T. A., & Seyedjavadi, S. M. H. (2012). Multi-product multi-chance-constraint stochastic inventory control problem with dynamic demand and partial back-ordering: A harmony search algorithm. *Journal of Manufacturing Systems, 31*(2), 204–213. doi:10.1016/j.jmsy.2011.05.006

Tuo, S., Zhang, J., Yong, L., Yuan, X., Liu, B., Xu, X., & Deng, F. A. (2015). A harmony search algorithm for high-dimensional multimodal optimization problems. *Digital Signal Processing, 46*, 151–163. doi:10.1016/j.dsp.2015.08.008

Valian, E., Tavakoli, S., & Mohanna, S. (2014). An intelligent global harmony search approach to continuous optimization problems. *Applied Mathematics and Computation*, *232*, 670–684. doi:10.1016/j.amc.2014.01.086

Wang, C. M., & Huang, Y. F. (2010). Self-adaptive harmony search algorithm for optimization. *Expert Systems with Applications*, *37*(4), 2826–2837. doi:10.1016/j.eswa.2009.09.008

Wang, G.-G., Gandomi, A. H., Zhao, X., & Chu, H. C. E. (2015a). Hybridizing harmony search algorithm with cuckoo search for global numerical optimization. *Soft Computing*, *20*(1), 273–285. doi:10.1007/s00500-014-1502-7

Wang, L., & Li, L. P. (2013). An effective differential harmony search algorithm for the solving non-convex economic load dispatch problems. *International Journal of Electrical Power & Energy Systems*, *44*(1), 832–843. doi:10.1016/j.ijepes.2012.08.021

Wang, Y., Liu, Y., Feng, L., & Zhu, X. (2015b). Novel feature selection method based on harmony search for email classification. *Knowledge-Based Systems*, *73*, 311–323. doi:10.1016/j.knosys.2014.10.013

Zheng, L., Diao, R., & Shen, Q. (2015a). Self-adjusting harmony search-based feature selection. *Soft Computing*, *19*(6), 1567–1579. doi:10.1007/s00500-014-1307-8

Zheng, Y.-J., Zhang, M.-X., & Zhang, B. (2015b). Biogeographic harmony search for emergency air transportation. *Soft Computing*, *20*(3), 967–977. doi:10.1007/s00500-014-1556-6

Zinati, R. F., & Razfar, M. R. (2012). Constrained optimum surface roughness prediction in turning of X20Cr13 by coupling novel modified harmony search-based neural network and modified harmony search algorithm. *International Journal of Advanced Manufacturing Technology*, *58*(1-4), 93–107. doi:10.1007/s00170-011-3393-4

Chapter 2
Applying an Electromagnetism–Like Algorithm for Solving the Manufacturing Cell Design Problem

Jose M. Lanza-Gutierrez
*Universidad Politecnica de Madrid,
Spain*

Ricardo Soto
*Pontificia Universidad Católica de
Valparaíso, Chile*

Broderick Crawford
*Pontificia Universidad Católica de
Valparaíso, Chile*

Juan A. Gomez-Pulido
University of Extremadura, Spain

Nicolas Fernandez
*Pontificia Universidad Católica de
Valparaíso, Chile*

Carlos Castillo
*Pontificia Universidad Católica de
Valparaíso, Chile*

ABSTRACT

Group technology has acquired a great consideration in the last years. This technique allows including the advantages of serial production to any manufacturing industry by dividing a manufacturing plant into a set of machine-part cells. The identification and formation of the cells are known as the Manufacturing Cell Design Problem (MCDP), which is an NP-hard problem. In this paper, the authors propose to solve the problem through a swarm intelligence metaheuristic called ElectroMagnetism-like (EM-like) algorithm, which is inspired by the attraction-repulsion mechanism

DOI: 10.4018/978-1-5225-2322-2.ch002

of particles in the context of the electromagnetic theory. The original EM-like algorithm was designed for solving continuous optimization problems, while the MCDP is usually formulated by assuming a binary approach. Hence, the authors propose an adaptation of this algorithm for addressing the problem. Such adaptation is applied for solving a freely available dataset of the MCDP, obtaining competitive results compared to recent approaches.

INTRODUCTION

Group Technology (GT) is a manufacturing technique, which has acquired a special consideration in the last two decades. This is because it allows including the advantages of serial production to any manufacturing industry, generating additional economic and productivity benefits to practical environments (Ham, Hitomi, & Yoshida, 2012; Goldengorin, Krushinsky, & Pardalos, 2013).

This technique consists in dividing a manufacturing plant into a set of machine-part cells or manufacturing units by following the idea *"similar things should be made in the same way"* (Kusiak, 1987). The content of a cell is characterized by having some similarities, *e.g.*, materials, manufacturing processes, functions, and/or tools. The idea is to group machines and parts into cells with the purpose of minimizing the flow between them (Selim, Askin, & Vakharia,1998).

The independence of cells is difficult in practice. The reason is that it is usual that some parts need to be processed in more than one machine and these machines could be assigned to different cells. The identification and formation of cells is known as the Manufacturing Cell Design Problem (MCDP), which is an NP-hard optimization problem (Garey & Johnson, 1979).

Because of the relevance of this manufacturing technique, many techniques were applied for solving the problem (Papaioannou & Wilson, 2010; Chattopadhyay, Sengupta, Ghosh, Dan, & Mazumdar, 2013). Some authors addressed the MCDP by assuming exact techniques, such as branch-and-cut and branch-and-bound algorithms. However, this type of solving methods is not recommended for addressing NP-hard problems, because computational times rise exponentially with the problem dimension. Instead, approximate methods should be assumed, such as metaheuristics, which were successfully considered in the literature for solving NP-hard problems from different fields (Dasgupta & Michalewicz, 2013).

In this paper, the authors solve the MCDP by assuming a swarm intelligence metaheuristic, concretely the ElectroMagnetism-like (EM-like) algorithm, which was proposed by Birbil and Fang (2003). This population-based algorithm is inspired by the attraction-repulsion mechanism of particles in the context of the electromagnetic theory. The original EM-like algorithm was designed for solving continuous optimization problems. However, the MCDP is usually formulated by assuming a discrete scope. Hence, the authors propose a binarization approach of the EM-like algorithm for solving the problem. The metaheuristic is applied for solving a set of 50 known MCDP instances getting competitive results compared to recent techniques.

The remainder of this work is structured as follows. In the second section, the related work is discussed. In the third section, the MCDP is described, including a problem example. In the fourth section, the EM-like algorithm is introduced. In the fifth section, the experimental results are discussed. Finally, conclusions and future works are left for the last section.

BACKGROUND

There are two principal lines of research for papers addressing the MCDP. On the one hand, works considering exact techniques and on the other hand, authors assuming approximate techniques.

Beginning with the first line, there are authors considering different types of exact algorithms. Linear programming approaches were assumed by Purcheck (1975), Oliva-Lopez and Purcheck (1979), and Elbenani and Ferland (2012). Linear quadratic models were considered by Kusiak and Chow (1987) and Boctor (1991). Dynamic programming was assumed by Steudel and Ballakur (1987). Goal programming was assumed by Sankaran and Rodin (1990) and Shafer and Rogers (1991). Constraint programming and boolean satisfiability were considered by Soto et al. (2012). Mixed integer linear programming models were proposed by Krushinsky and Goldengorin (2012) and Fahmy (2015).

The authors in this first line guaranteed to find the optimal solution by analyzing the complete search space. This fact means that computational costs are commonly high for large instances. Based on this shortcoming, in the last years some authors considered approximate methodologies for solving the problem.

Following the second line, some authors considered heuristics. Waghodekar and Sahu (1984) proposed a heuristic approach based on the similarity coefficient of the product type. Khator and Irani (1987) presented a new heuristic for identifying clusters called the occupancy value method. Harhalakis, Nagi, and Proth (1990) designed a twofold heuristic algorithm for minimizing inter-cell material movement. Askin and Chiu (1990) presented a mathematical model for solving the problem through a heuristic graph partitioning procedure. Miltenburg and Zhang (1991) compared nine different algorithms, demonstrating that there was no algorithm that performed better on all problems. Hung, Yang, and Lee (2011) assumed a fuzzy relational clustering algorithm. Batsyn, Bychkov, Goldengorin, Pardalos, and Sukhov (2013) introduced a new pattern-based approach within the linear assignment model to design heuristics for combinatorial optimization problems.

In the last decades, metaheuristics acquired a great relevance, combining basic heuristic methods and effectiveness exploring the search space. In this line, the following contributions might be cited. Adenso-Dıaz, Lozano, Racero, and Guerrero (2001), Chung, Wu, and Chang (2011), and C. C. Chang, Wu, and Wu (2013) considered a Tabu search algorithm. Banerjee and Das (2012) developed a predator-prey genetic algorithm. Elbenani, Ferland, and Bellemare (2012) applied a genetic algorithm and large neighborhood search. Kao and Lin (2012), Kao and Chen (2014), and Kashan, Karimi, and Noktehdan (2014) considered a Particle Swarm Optimization (PSO). Paydar and Saidi-Mehrabad (2013) applied a hybrid genetic-variable neighborhood search algorithm. Brusco (2015) implemented an iterated local search method. Martins, Pinheiro, Protti, and Ochi (2015) assumed a hybrid iterated local search and variable neighborhood descent algorithm. Noktehdan, Seyedhosseini, and Saidi-Mehrabad (2016) applied a grouping version of the league championship algorithm. Thanh, Ferland, Elbenani, Thuc, et al. (2016) provided a computational study of hybrid metaheuristics. Zeb et al. (2016) implemented a hybridization of simulated annealing with a genetic algorithm.

The work presented in this paper is in the second line of research. The authors consider an approximate methodology for solving the MCDP, concretely the swarm intelligence EM-like metaheuristic. The following main contributions are provided along this work:

- As far as the authors know, the EM-like algorithm was not applied before for solving the MCDP.
- The original EM-like algorithm was designed for solving continuous optimization problems. Hence, the authors propose an adaptation of this metaheuristic for solving the discrete problem.
- The adapted EM-like algorithm is applied for solving a widely considered MCDP benchmark, getting competitive results compared to recent works as will be discussed below.

The reason why the EM-like metaheuristic was selected is because it was successfully applied for solving other optimization problems from different fields. P. C. Chang, Chen, and Fan (2009) solved the single machine scheduling problem. Roshanaei, Balagh, Esfahani, and Vahdani (2009) optimized the scheduling job shop production problem. Yurtkuran and Emel (2010) solved vehicle routing problems. Lee and Chang (2010) solved the fractional-order controller optimization. Naderi, Tavakkoli-Moghaddam, and Khalili (2010) optimized flow-shop scheduling problems. Lee and Lee (2012) designed nonlinear systems. Yan, Wan, and Xiong (2014) solved the two-stage assembly flow-shop scheduling problem. Zeng, Zhang, Kusiak, Tang, and Wei (2016) optimized wastewater pumping systems. Muhsen, Ghazali, Khatib, and Abed (2015) extracted the parameters of photovoltaic modules. Fathian, Jouzdani, Heydari, and Makui (2016) solved both location and transportation planning problems.

MANUFACTURING CELL DESIGN PROBLEM

The cell formation problem is modeled by considering an array-based clustering approach. Note that Table 1 includes the notation considered in this section. Let *A* be an incidence matrix of *m* machines and *p* parts, determining which part is processed by each machine. Each element of *A* has the value provided by the indicator function given by

$$a_{i,j} = \begin{cases} 1, & \text{if the j-th part is processed by the i-th machine} \\ 0, & \text{otherwise} \end{cases}, \qquad (1)$$

where $a_{i,j}$ is the value located at the position *(i, j)* of *A*, with i ∈ 1,2,…,m and j ∈ 1,2,…,p.

The objective of the MCDP is to group machines and parts into cells so that the number of parts transported between cells is minimized. Figure 1 shows an example of the incidence matrix *A* by considering *m* and *p* equaling 12. Analyzing this figure, it is found that the cell formation is not clear at a first step. However, given this initial matrix, it is possible to group machines and parts into two different cells. Figure 2 shows an equivalent incidence matrix, where machines and cells are organized as follows: machines 1 to 6 and parts 2, 3, 5, 7, 9, 11, 12 are in cell 1 and machines 7 to 12 and parts 1, 4, 6, 8, 10 are in cell 2.

Let *c* be the number of cells considered for grouping machines and parts. Let m_{max} be the maximum number of machines which could be assigned to any cell. Let *Y* be an incidence matrix, determining which machine is assigned to each cell. Each element of *Y* has the value provided by the indicator function expressed as

$$y_{i,k} = \begin{cases} 1, & \text{if the i-th machine is assigned to the k-th cell} \\ 0, & \text{otherwise} \end{cases}, \qquad (2)$$

Figure 1. Example of the incidence matrix A. Usual appearance of the matrix A, where the formation of groups is not clear

Part

	1	2	3	4	5	6	7	8	9	10	11	12
1	0	0	0	0	1	0	1	0	1	0	1	0
2	0	0	1	0	1	0	0	0	0	0	1	0
3	0	0	1	0	0	0	1	0	1	0	1	0
4	0	1	1	0	1	0	0	0	1	0	1	0
5	0	1	0	0	1	0	0	0	1	0	1	1
6	0	1	0	0	1	0	1	0	1	0	0	1
7	1	0	0	0	0	1	0	1	0	1	0	0
8	1	0	0	0	0	1	0	1	0	0	0	0
9	1	0	0	1	0	0	0	1	0	0	0	0
10	1	0	0	1	0	0	0	1	0	1	0	0
11	1	0	0	1	0	1	0	1	0	0	0	0
12	1	0	0	0	0	0	0	1	0	1	0	0

(Machine)

Figure 2. Example of the incidence matrix A. Appearance of the matrix A in Figure 1 after reorganizing its elements to form two groups

Part

	2	3	5	7	9	11	12	1	4	6	8	10
1	0	0	1	1	1	1	0	0	0	0	0	0
2	0	1	1	0	0	1	0	0	0	0	0	0
3	0	1	0	1	1	1	0	0	0	0	0	0
4	1	1	1	0	1	1	0	0	0	0	0	0
5	1	0	1	0	1	1	1	0	0	0	0	0
6	1	0	1	1	1	0	1	0	0	0	0	0
7	0	0	0	0	0	0	0	1	0	1	1	1
8	0	0	0	0	0	0	0	1	0	1	1	0
9	0	0	0	0	0	0	0	1	1	0	1	0
10	0	0	0	0	0	0	0	1	1	0	1	1
11	0	0	0	0	0	0	0	1	1	1	1	0
12	0	0	0	0	0	0	0	1	0	0	1	1

(Machine)

Table 1. Notation considered for modeling the MCDP

Symbol	Description
A	machine-part incidence matrix of size m x p.
$a_{i,j}$	value of the element of A placed on the position (i, j), with i $\in$ 1,2,...,m and j $\in$ 1,2,...,p.
c	number of cells.
M	number of machines.
m_{max}	maximum number of machines assigned to any cell.
p	number of parts.
Y	machine-cell incidence matrix of size m x c.
$y_{i,k}$	value of the element of Y placed on the position (i, k), with i $\in$ 1,2,...,m and k $\in$ 1,2,...,c.
Z	part-cell incidence matrix of size p x c.
$z_{j,k}$	value of the element of Z placed on the position (j, k), with j $\in$ 1,2,...,p and k $\in$ 1,2,...,c.

where $y_{i,k}$ is the value located at the position *(i, k)* of Y, with k $\in$ 1,2,...,c. Let Z be an incidence matrix determining which part is assigned to each cell. Each element of Z has the value provided by the indicator function given by

$$z_{j,k} = \begin{cases} 1, & \text{if the j-th part is assigned to the k-th cell} \\ 0, & \text{otherwise} \end{cases}, \tag{3}$$

where $z_{j,k}$ is the value located at the position *(j, k)* of Z . And let *f* be the fitness function of the optimization problem expressed as

$$f = \sum_{k=1}^{c}\sum_{i=1}^{m}\sum_{j=1}^{p} a_{i,j} z_{j,k}(1 - y_{i,k}), \tag{4}$$

Thus, given the incidence matrix A, the number of parts p, the number of machines m, the number of cells c, and the maximum number of machines per cell m_{max}, the objective is to get the matrix Y and Z to

$$\min(f), \tag{5}$$

subject to

Figure 3. Example of the output matrix obtained by optimizing the A matrix in Figure 1. Matrix Y obtained

Machine	Cell 1	Cell 2
1	1	0
2	1	0
3	1	0
4	1	0
5	1	0
6	1	0
7	0	1
8	0	1
9	0	1
10	0	1
11	0	1
12	0	1

Figure 4. Example of the output matrix obtained by optimizing the A matrix in Figure 1. Matrix Z obtained

Part	Cell 1	Cell 2
1	0	1
2	1	0
3	1	0
4	0	1
5	1	0
6	0	1
7	1	0
8	0	1
9	1	0
10	0	1
11	1	0
12	1	0

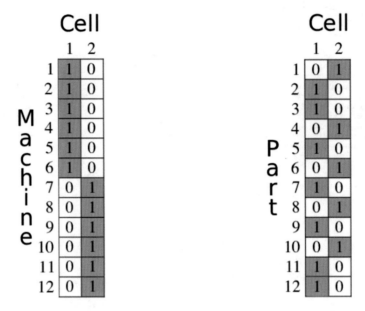

$$\sum_{k=1}^{c} y_{i,k} = 1, \forall i, \tag{6}$$

$$\sum_{k=1}^{c} z_{j,k} = 1, \forall j, \tag{7}$$

$$\sum_{i=1}^{m} y_{i,k} \leq m_{\max}, \forall k. \tag{8}$$

Note that Equation (6) ensures that each machine belongs to only one cell, Equation (7) guarantees that each part is assigned to only one cell, and Equation (8) delimits the maximum number of machines in a cell. Following the example proposed before in Figure 1 and assuming m_{max} equaling 6, a possible solution to the problem is shown in Figures 3 and 4, in which the output matrix *Y* and *Z* are included, respectively. Note that the two output matrix satisfy the constraints in Equations (6), (7), and (8).

ELECTROMAGNETISM-LIKE ALGORITHM

This population-based metaheuristic was proposed by Birbil and Fang (2003) and is inspired by the attraction-repulsion mechanism of particles in the context of the electromagnetism theory. Algorithm 1 shows the general scheme of the metaheuristic, which is composed of four main steps: initialization, local search, calculation of forces, and movement of particles. Next, it is discussed how the algorithm is adapted to solve the problem, focusing on these four main steps.

Initialization (Line 1 of Algorithm 1)

In this step, a population P of ps individuals (solutions) are generated as stated in Algorithm 2. To this end and for each individual in the population, each machine is randomly assigned to only one cell (lines 2 to 6 of Algorithm 2). Next, the part-cell incidence matrix of the individual is generated (lines 7 to 8 of Algorithm 2). To this end, one of the following procedures is randomly selected with the same probability:

- For each machine assigned to a cell, the parts processed by this machine are associated with the same cell in the case that the parts were not associated with any cell before.
- For each part processed by a machine, if the machine is assigned to a cell, then the part will be too. It includes a heuristic avoiding that a part is associated with several cells by following the rule: the cell selected will be where there are more machines processing the part.
- It generates an empty part-cell matrix.

For each part processed by a machine, if the machine is assigned to a cell, then the part will be too. It incorporates a heuristic avoiding that a part is associated with several cells by following the rule: the part is iteratively disassociated from a cell until it is associated with only one.

Algorithm 1: *General Scheme of the EM-Like Algorithm*

```
1: P, x^best = initialize(ps)          ◁ Step 1.
2: it = 1
3: while it < max_it do
4:         P, x^best = localSearch(iter_ls)      ◁ Step 2.
5:         F = calculateForces()       ◁ Step 3.
6:         P, x^best = movePopulation(F)          ◁ Step 4.
7:         it ← it + 1
8: end while
```

Algorithm 2: *EM-Like Algorithm. Step 1 – Initialization*

```
1: for h = 1 to ps do              ◁ For each solution in the popu-
lation.
2:          yʰᵢ,ₖ = 0, ∀i ∈ 1,2,…,m,  k ∈ 1,2,…,c
3:          for i = 1 to m do          ◁ Assign machines to cells.
4:                  k = randi(1, c)
5:                  yʰᵢ,ₖ = 1
6:          end for
7:          zʰⱼ,ₖ = 0, ∀j ∈ 1,2,…,p,  k ∈ 1,2,…,c
8:          Zʰ ← generatePartCellRelations(Yʰ)
9:          P[h] = Yʰ,Zʰ, calculateFitness(Yʰ,Zʰ)
10:          if isUnfeasible(P[h]) then
11:          h = h - 1              ◁ Discard the solution.
12:          end if
13: end for
14: xᵇᵉˢᵗ = bestSolution(P)          ◁ Return the best solution
found.
```

Next, the new solution is evaluated (line 9 of Algorithm 2). In the case that it does not satisfy the constraints, the solution is discarded (lines 10 to 12 of Algorithm 2). Finally, once all the individuals were generated, the best solution found x^{best} is returned (line 14 of Algorithm 2). Note that Algorithm 2 considers the following notation. Y^h is the machine-cell incidence matrix of the individual $h \in P$. $y^h_{i,k}$ denotes the value on the position (i, k) of Y^h as given by Equation 2, with $i \in 1,2,…,m$ and $k \in 1,2,…,c$. Z^h is the part-cell incidence matrix of the individual h, $z^h_{j,k}$ is the value on the position (j, k) of Z^h as given by Equation 3, with $j \in 1,2,…,p$. $isUnfeasible(\bullet)$ denotes if a solution satisfies the constraints. $randi(a, b)$ generates an integer random number between a and b, both included.

Local Search (Line 4 of Algorithm 1)

In this step, a local search is performed as described in Algorithm 3. To this end, each solution in the population is tried to be improved a number of attempts equaling $iter_{ls}$ (lines 1 to 2 of Algorithm 3). The procedure is as follows. Each machine of the solution is assigned to a random cell with a probability of 50% (lines 4 to 10 of Algorithm 3). Next, the part-cell incidence matrix is generated as described in the initialization step of Algorithm 1 (line 11 of Algorithm 3). The new solution is evaluated and in the case that it does not satisfy the constraints, the solution is restored to the previous values (lines 12 to 15 of Algorithm 3). Finally, once all the individuals were tried to be improved through the local search, the best solution found is returned (line 18 of Algorithm 3). Note that in Algorithm 3, *randd(a,b)* generates a double random number in the interval [*a*, *b*] and *f(•)* provides the fitness value of a solution.

Force Calculation (Line 5 of Algorithm 1)

In this step, the forces exerting on each particle are calculated as described in Algorithm 4. The charge $g^h \in \mathbb{R}$ of a solution h is calculated based on the Coulomb's law as given by (lines 2 to 4 of Algorithm 4)

$$g^h = e^{\left(cm \frac{f(P[h]) - f(P[x^{best}])}{\sum_{u=1}^{ps} \left(f(P[u]) - f(P[x^{best}]) \right)} \right)}. \tag{9}$$

Algorithm 3: *EM-Like Algorithm. Step 2 – Local Search*

```
1: for h = 1 to ps do ◁ For each solution in the population.
2:          for w = 1 to iter_ls do ◁ For each iteration of the lo-
cal search.
3:                    q = P[h]
4:                    for i = 1 to m do
5:                              if randd(0, 1) > 0.5 then
6:                                        y^h_i,k = 0, ∀k ∈ 1,2,...,c
7:                                        r = randi(1, c)
8:                                        y^h_i,r = 1 ◁ Assign the i-th
machine to the r-th cell.
9:                              end if
10:                   end for
11:                   Z^h = generatePartCellRelations(Y^h)
12:                   P[h] = Y^h, Z^h, calculateFitness(Y^h, Z^h)
13:                   if f(q) < f(P[h]) || isUnfeasible(P[h])
then
14:                             P[h] = q ◁ Return to the previous
solution.
15:                   end if
16:          end for
17: end for
18: x^best = bestSolution(P) ◁ Return the best solution found.
```

Algorithm 4: *EM-Like Algorithm. Step 3 – Force Calculation*

```
1: Fʰ = 0
2: for h = 1 to ps do          ◁ For each solution in the popu-
lation.
3:          gʰ = calculateCharges(h)
4: end for
5: for h = 1 to ps do          ◁ For each solution in the popu-
lation.
6:          Fʰ = 0
7:          for u = 1 to ps do          ◁ For each solution in the
population.
8:               if h ≠ u then
9:                    if f(P[u]) < f(P[h]) then
10:                        Fʰ = applyAttraction(u,h)
11:                    else
12:                        Fʰ = applyRepulsion(u,h)
13:                    end if
14:               end if
15:          end for
16: end for
```

Note that better solutions have higher charges than worse ones. Based on these charges, the total forces Fh exerted on each solution are calculated based on the machine-part incidence matrix (lines 5 to 16 of Algorithm 4). In this formulation, given any two solutions u and h, if it is supposed that u is better than h, then h is attracted towards u by following the expression given by

$$F^h = F^h + \left(Y^u - Y^h\right)\frac{g^u g^h}{\left(Y^u - Y^h\right)^2}, \tag{10}$$

and u is repealed from h by following the expression given by

$$F^u = F^u + \left(Y^h - Y^u\right)\frac{g^u g^h}{\left(Y^h - Y^u\right)^2}. \tag{11}$$

Algorithm 5: *EM-Like Algorithm. Step 4 – Movement of Particles*

```
1: Fʰ = 0
2: for h = 1 to ps do        ◁ For each solution in the popu-
lation.
3:          if h ≠ xᵇᵉˢᵗthen
4:                  q = P[h]
5:                  for i = 1 to m do        ◁ For each machine.
6:                          for k = 1 to c do        ◁ For each
cell.
7:                                  λ = randd(0, 1)
8:                                  if fʰᵢ,ₖ > 0.0 then
9:                                  yʰᵢ,ₖ = yʰᵢ,ₖ +
discretize(λfʰᵢ,ₖ(1-yʰᵢ,ₖ))
10:                                     else
11:                                             yʰᵢ,ₖ = yʰᵢ,ₖ -
discretize(λfʰᵢ,ₖyʰᵢ,ₖ)
12:                                     end if
13:                             end for
14:                     end for
15:                     Zʰ = generatePartCellRelations(Yʰ)
16:                     P[h] = Yʰ,Zʰ, calculateFitness(Yʰ,Zʰ)
17:                     if isUnfeasible(P[h]) then
18:                             P[h] = q ◁ Return to the previous
solution.
19:                     end if
20:             end if
21: end for
22: xᵇᵉˢᵗ = bestSolution(P) ◁ Return the best solution found.
```

In Algorithm 4, F^h is a matrix of size m x c in the domain of the real numbers, *calculateCharges(•)* calculates the charge of a particle as given by Equation 9, *applyAttraction(•)* updates the forces of a particle due to the attraction effect as given by Equation 10, and *applyRepulsion(•)* updates the forces of a particle due to the repulsion effect as given by Equation 11.

Particle Movement (Line 6 of Algorithm 1)

The forces acting on the solutions generate a global movement towards the best solutions found as stated in Algorithm 5. To this end and for each solution, excepting the best one, the machine-part matrix is modified by applying the forces (lines 5 to 14 of Algorithm 5). As this is a binary matrix and the forces are in the domain of the real numbers, a binarization technique is needed as discussed below. Note that positive forces cause a movement towards 1 values in the new machine-part matrix and negative forces cause a movement towards 0 values. Next, the part-cell incidence matrix is generated as described in the initialization step of Algorithm 1 (line 15 of Algorithm 5). The new solution is evaluated and in the case that it does not satisfy the constraints, the solution is restored to the previous values (lines 16 to 19 of Algorithm 5). Finally, the best solution found is returned. In Algorithm 5, *discretize($\bullet$)* provides the binary conversion of a given real number through the tangent approach. To this end, a real number in the interval [0, 1] is obtained as given by

$$rn' = \|\tanh(rn)\|, \tag{12}$$

where *rn* is the initial real number, *rn'* is the real number obtained in the interval [0, 1], and $\|\bullet\|$ is the absolute value of a number. Next, if *rn'* is lower than a randomly generated random number in the interval [0, 1], then the discretization function returns a 0 value and 1 otherwise.

EXPERIMENTAL RESULTS

The EM-like algorithm is applied for solving a dataset composed of 90 instances described as follows:

Group 1: 50 instances. Problems 1 to 10 proposed by Boctor (1991) with 5 different values of m_{max} (8 to 12) and a value of c equaling 2.
Group 2: 40 instances. Same problems as for group 1, but assuming 4 different values of m_{max} (6 to 9) and a value of c equaling 3.

The type of stop condition assumed is the same for all the instances, which is based on the number of iterations. The maximum number of iterations (max_{it}) for the first group is 50 and the maximum number of iterations for the second group is 10000. These values were experimentally obtained and are enough for analyzing the behavior of the algorithm. The reason why two different criteria are considered is due to the computation effort required for the two groups is notably different.

Before running the experiments, the EM-like algorithm was adequately configured through a parametric swap, obtaining the parameters $ps = 5$ and $iter_{ls} = 1000$. The results obtained while solving the first group are detailed in Table 2, where *opt*

Table 2. Results obtained by the EM-like algorithm for the first instance group

Problem	$m_{max} = 8$				$m_{max} = 9$				c = 2 $m_{max} = 10$				$m_{max} = 11$				$m_{max} = 12$			
	opt	best	avg	rpd	opt	best	avg	rpd	opt	best	avg	rpd	opt	best	avg	rpd	opt	best	avg	rpd
1	11	11	11	0	11	11	11	0	11	11	11	0	11	11	11	0	11	11	11	0
2	7	7	7	0	6	6	6	0	4	4	4	0	3	3	3	0	3	3	3	0
3	4	4	4	0	4	4	4	0	4	4	4	0	3	3	3	0	1	1	1	0
4	14	14	14	0	13	13	13	0	13	13	13	0	13	13	13	0	13	13	13	0
5	9	9	9	0	6	6	6	0	6	6	6	0	5	5	5	0	4	4	4	0
6	5	5	5	0	3	3	3	0	3	3	3	0	3	3	3	0	2	2	2	0
7	7	7	7	0	4	4	4	0	4	4	4	0	4	4	4	0	4	4	4	0
8	13	13	13	0	10	10	10	0	8	8	8	0	5	5	5	0	5	5	5	0
9	8	8	8	0	8	8	8	0	8	8	8	0	5	5	5	0	5	5	5	0
10	8	8	8	0	5	5	5	0	5	5	5	0	5	5	5	0	5	5	5	0

Table 3. Results obtained by the EM-like algorithm for the second instance group

	c = 3															
	m_{max} = 6				m_{max} = 7				m_{max} = 8				m_{max} = 9			
Problem	opt	best	avg	rpd	opt	best	avg	rpd	opt	best	avg	rpd	opt	best	avg	rpd
1	27	27	27	0	18	18	18	0	11	11	11	0	11	11	11	0
2	7	7	7	0	6	6	6	0	6	6	6	0	6	6	6	0
3	9	9	9	0	4	4	4	0	4	4	4	0	4	4	4	0
4	27	27	27	0	18	18	18	0	14	14	14	0	13	13	13	0
5	11	11	11	0	8	8	8	0	8	8	8	0	6	6	6	0
6	6	6	6	0	4	4	4	0	4	4	4	0	3	3	3	0
7	11	11	11	0	5	5	5	0	5	5	5	0	4	4	4	0
8	14	14	14	0	11	11	11	0	11	11	11	0	10	10	10	0
9	12	12	12	0	12	12	12	0	8	8	8	0	8	8	8	0
10	10	10	10	0	8	8	8	0	8	8	8	0	5	5	5	0

column denotes the known optimal value provided by Boctor (1991), *best* column shows the best solution found by the EM-like algorithm for 10 independent runs, *avg* column denotes the average solution found by the EM-like algorithm along executions, and *rpd* column is the Relative Percentage Deviation (RPD) of the average solution provided by the metaheuristic compared to the optimal one, which is given by

$$rpd = \frac{\left(avg - opt\right)}{opt} 100 \tag{13}$$

Analyzing Table 2, it is found that the algorithm is able to provide the optimal solution in each execution. Table 3 shows the results obtained while solving the second instance group. The notation considered in this table is the same as discussed for Table 2. Analyzing this table, it is found that the algorithm is able to provide the optimal solution in each solution as with the previous case. This could mean that the algorithm is robust while solving the problem. However, this situation could be due to a low benchmark complexity.

With the purpose of clarifying this situation, Table 4 compares the results obtained by the EM-like algorithm to the two metaheuristics discussed in Durán, Rodriguez, and Consalter (2010), while solving the same fist instance group, concretely PSO and Simulated Annealing (SA) algorithms. Note that *Percentage* column shows the number of times that an algorithm reaches the optimal solution on average term. Analyzing this table, it is found that the other metaheuristics do not reach the optimal solution for each instance of the benchmark as done by EM-like. Thus, PSO reaches the optimal solutions up to 42.00% and SA reaches the optimal solutions up to 68.00%. On the other hand, it is found that as the value of m_{max} increases, the benchmark complexity grows and the percentage of optimal solutions found by PSO and SA decreases. From these results, two main conclusions are reached:

- The algorithm is able to solve a non-trivial dataset from the literature, getting all the optimal solutions.
- The algorithm is robust while solving the problem because it reached the optimal solution in each execution.

Based on these statements, the algorithm can be recommended for solving the problem.

Finally, some implementation details, both the optimization problem and the solving methodology were encoded in Java and executed on an Intel Core i5 processor with 4GB of RAM running under Microsoft Windows 8.

Table 4. Comparing the results obtained by the EM-like algorithm to two other approaches for the first instance group

	c = 2 (best solution found)																			
	m_{max} = 8				m_{max} = 9				m_{max} = 10				m_{max} = 11				m_{max} = 12			
Problem	opt	EM	PSO	SA	opt	EM	PSO	SA	opt	EM	PSO	SA	opt	EM	PSO	SA	opt	EM	PSO	SA
1	11	11	11	11	11	11	11	11	11	11	11	11	11	11	11	11	11	11	11	11
2	7	7	7	7	6	6	6	6	4	4	5	10	3	3	4	4	3	3	4	3
3	4	4	5	5	4	4	4	4	4	4	5	4	3	3	4	4	1	1	3	4
4	14	14	15	14	13	13	13	13	13	13	13	13	13	13	13	13	13	13	13	13
5	9	9	10	9	6	6	8	6	6	6	6	6	5	5	5	7	4	4	5	4
6	5	5	5	5	3	3	3	3	3	3	3	5	3	3	4	3	2	2	4	3
7	7	7	7	7	4	4	5	4	4	4	5	4	4	4	5	4	4	4	5	4
8	13	13	14	13	10	10	11	20	8	8	10	15	5	5	11	11	5	5	6	7
9	8	8	9	13	8	8	8	8	8	8	8	8	5	5	5	8	5	5	8	8
10	8	8	9	8	5	5	8	5	5	5	7	5	5	5	7	5	5	5	6	5
Percentage	-	100%	40%	70%	-	100%	60%	90%	-	100%	50%	60%	-	100%	40%	40%	-	100%	20%	50%

CONCLUSION

In this paper, the authors proposed to solve the MCDP through the EM-like algorithm, which is a swarm intelligence metaheuristic inspired by the attraction-repulsion mechanism of particles in the context of the electromagnetic theory.

The original EM-like algorithm was designed for solving continuous optimization problems, while the MCDP is usually formulated by assuming a binary approach. Hence, the authors proposed an adaptation of this algorithm for addressing the problem. Such adaptation was applied for solving a freely available MCDP dataset composed of 90 instances.

As a result, the authors reached two main conclusions. On the one hand, the algorithm was able to solve a non-trivial dataset getting all the known optimal solutions. On the other hand, the algorithm was robust while solving the dataset, because it reached the optimal solution in each execution. Thus, the algorithm can be recommended for solving the problem.

As further works, it could be interesting to include a more complex benchmark, as well as other metaheuristics.

REFERENCES

Adenso-Díaz, B., Lozano, S., Racero, J., & Guerrero, F. (2001). Machine cell formation in generalized group technology. *Computers & Industrial Engineering*, *41*(2), 227–240. doi:10.1016/S0360-8352(01)00056-0

Askin, R. G., & Chiu, K. S. (1990). A graph partitioning procedure for machine assignment and cell formation in group technology. *International Journal of Production Research*, *28*(8), 1555–1572. doi:10.1080/00207549008942812

Banerjee, I., & Das, P. (2012). Group technology based adaptive cell formation using predator-prey genetic algorithm. *Applied Soft Computing*, *12*(1), 559–572. doi:10.1016/j.asoc.2011.07.021

Batsyn, M., Bychkov, I., Goldengorin, B., Pardalos, P., & Sukhov, P. (2013). Pattern-based heuristic for the cell formation problem in group technology. In M. V. Batsyn, V. A. Kalyagin, & P. M. Pardalos (Eds.), *Models, algorithms, and technologies for network analysis* (pp. 11–50). New York, NY: Springer. doi:10.1007/978-1-4614-5574-5_2

Birbil, S̹. I˙., & Fang, S. C. (2003). An electromagnetism-like mechanism for global optimization. *Journal of Global Optimization*, *25*(3), 263–282. doi:10.1023/A:1022452626305

Boctor, F. F. (1991). A linear formulation of the machine-part cell formation problem. *International Journal of Production Research*, *29*(2), 343–356. doi:10.1080/00207549108930075

Brusco, M. J. (2015). An iterated local search heuristic for cell formation. *Computers & Industrial Engineering*, *90*, 292–304. doi:10.1016/j.cie.2015.09.010

Chang, C. C., Wu, T. H., & Wu, C. W. (2013). An efficient approach to determine cell formation, cell layout and intracellular machine sequence in cellular manufacturing systems. *Computers & Industrial Engineering*, *66*(2), 438–450. doi:10.1016/j.cie.2013.07.009

Chang, P. C., Chen, S. H., & Fan, C. Y. (2009). A hybrid electromagnetism-like algorithm for single machine scheduling problem. *Expert Systems with Applications*, *36*(2, Part 1), 1259–1267. doi:10.1016/j.eswa.2007.11.050

Chattopadhyay, M., Sengupta, S., Ghosh, T., Dan, P. K., & Mazumdar, S. (2013). Neuro-genetic impact on cell formation methods of cellular manufacturing system design: A quantitative review and analysis. *Computers & Industrial Engineering*, *64*(1), 256–272. doi:10.1016/j.cie.2012.09.016

Chung, S. H., Wu, T. H., & Chang, C. C. (2011). An efficient tabu search algorithm to the cell formation problem with alternative routings and machine reliability considerations. *Computers & Industrial Engineering*, *60*(1), 7–15. doi:10.1016/j.cie.2010.08.016

Dasgupta, D., & Michalewicz, Z. (2013). *Evolutionary algorithms in engineering applications*. Berlin, Germany: Springer-Verlag Berlin Heidelberg.

Duran, O., Rodriguez, N., & Consalter, L. (2010). Collaborative particle swarm optimization with a data mining technique for manufacturing cell design. *Expert Systems with Applications*, *37*(2), 1563–1567. doi:10.1016/j.eswa.2009.06.061

Elbenani, B., & Ferland, J. A. (2012). An exact method for solving the manufacturing cell formation problem. *International Journal of Production Research*, *50*(15), 4038–4045. doi:10.1080/00207543.2011.588622

Elbenani, B., Ferland, J. A., & Bellemare, J. (2012). Genetic algorithm and large neighbourhood search to solve the cell formation problem. *Expert Systems with Applications*, *39*(3), 2408–2414. doi:10.1016/j.eswa.2011.08.089

Fahmy, S. A. (2015). Mixed integer linear programming model for integrating cell formation, group layout and group scheduling. In *Proceedings of IEEE international conference on industrial technology (ICIT'15)*. Seville, Spain: IEEE. doi:10.1109/ICIT.2015.7125452

Fathian, M., Jouzdani, J., Heydari, M., & Makui, A. (2016). Location and transportation planning in supply chains under uncertainty and congestion by using an improved electromagnetism-like algorithm. *Journal of Intelligent Manufacturing*, 1–18.

Garey, M. R., & Johnson, D. S. (1979). *Computers and intractability: a guide to the theory of np-completeness*. San Francisco, CA: Freeman.

Goldengorin, B., Krushinsky, D., & Pardalos, P. M. (2013). The problem of cell formation: Ideas and their applications. In B. Goldengorin, D. Krushinsky, P. M. Pardalos, & M. Panos (Eds.), *Cell formation in industrial engineering* (pp. 1–23). New York, NY: Springer. doi:10.1007/978-1-4614-8002-0_1

Ham, I., Hitomi, K., & Yoshida, T. (2012). *Group technology: applications to production management*. Hingham, MA: Kluwer.

Harhalakis, G., Nagi, R., & Proth, J. (1990). An efficient heuristic in manufacturing cell formation for group technology applications. *International Journal of Production Research*, *28*(1), 185–198. doi:10.1080/00207549008942692

Hung, W. L., Yang, M. S., & Lee, E. S. (2011). Cell formation using fuzzy relational clustering algorithm. *Mathematical and Computer Modelling*, *53*(910), 1776–1787. doi:10.1016/j.mcm.2010.12.056

Kao, Y., & Chen, C. C. (2014). Automatic clustering for generalised cell formation using a hybrid particle swarm optimisation. *International Journal of Production Research*, *52*(12), 3466–3484. doi:10.1080/00207543.2013.867085

Kao, Y., & Lin, C.-H. (2012). A pso-based approach to cell formation problems with alternative process routings. *International Journal of Production Research*, *50*(15), 4075–4089. doi:10.1080/00207543.2011.590541

Kashan, H. A., Karimi, B., & Noktehdan, A. (2014). A novel discrete particle swarm optimization algorithm for the manufacturing cell formation problem. *International Journal of Advanced Manufacturing Technology*, *73*(9), 1543–1556. doi:10.1007/s00170-014-5906-4

Khator, S., & Irani, S. (1987). Cell formation in group technology: A new approach. *Computers & Industrial Engineering*, *12*(2), 131–142. doi:10.1016/0360-8352(87)90006-4

Krushinsky, D., & Goldengorin, B. (2012). An exact model for cell formation in group technology. *Computational Management Science, 9*(3), 323–338. doi:10.1007/s10287-012-0146-2

Kusiak, A. (1987). The generalized group technology concept. *International Journal of Production Research, 25*(4), 561–569. doi:10.1080/00207548708919861

Kusiak, A., & Chow, W. S. (1987). Efficient solving of the group technology problem. *Journal of Manufacturing Systems, 6*(2), 117–124. doi:10.1016/0278-6125(87)90035-5

Lee, C. H., & Chang, F. K. (2010). Fractional-order PID controller optimization via improved electromagnetism-like algorithm. *Expert Systems with Applications, 37*(12), 8871–8878. doi:10.1016/j.eswa.2010.06.009

Lee, C. H., & Lee, Y. C. (2012). Nonlinear systems design by a novel fuzzy neural system via hybridization of electromagnetism-like mechanism and particle swarm optimisation algorithms. *Information Sciences, 186*(1), 59–72. doi:10.1016/j.ins.2011.09.036

Martins, I. C., Pinheiro, R. G., Protti, F., & Ochi, L. S. (2015). A hybrid iterated local search and variable neighborhood descent heuristic applied to the cell formation problem. *Expert Systems with Applications, 42*(22), 8947–8955. doi:10.1016/j.eswa.2015.07.050

Miltenburg, J., & Zhang, W. (1991). A comparative evaluation of nine well-known algorithms for solving the cell formation problem in group technology. *Journal of Operations Management, 10*(1), 44–72. doi:10.1016/0272-6963(91)90035-V

Muhsen, D. H., Ghazali, A. B., Khatib, T., & Abed, I. A. (2015). Extraction of photovoltaic module models parameters using an improved hybrid differential evolution/electromagnetism-like algorithm. *Solar Energy, 119*, 286–297. doi:10.1016/j.solener.2015.07.008

Naderi, B., Tavakkoli-Moghaddam, R., & Khalili, M. (2010). Electromagnetism-like mechanism and simulated annealing algorithms for flowshop scheduling problems minimizing the total weighted tardiness and makespan. *Knowledge-Based Systems, 23*(2), 77–85. doi:10.1016/j.knosys.2009.06.002

Noktehdan, A., Seyedhosseini, S., & Saidi-Mehrabad, M. (2016). A metaheuristic algorithm for the manufacturing cell formation problem based on grouping efficacy. *International Journal of Advanced Manufacturing Technology, 82*(1), 25–37. doi:10.1007/s00170-015-7052-z

Oliva-Lopez, E., & Purcheck, G. (1979). Load balancing for group technology planning and control. *International Journal of Machine Tool Design and Research*, *19*(4), 259–274. doi:10.1016/0020-7357(79)90015-5

Papaioannou, G., & Wilson, J. M. (2010). The evolution of cell formation problem methodologies based on recent studies (1997–2008): Review and directions for future research. *European Journal of Operational Research*, *206*(3), 509–521. doi:10.1016/j.ejor.2009.10.020

Paydar, M. M., & Saidi-Mehrabad, M. (2013). A hybrid genetic-variable neighborhood search algorithm for the cell formation problem based on grouping efficacy. *Computers & Operations Research*, *40*(4), 980–990. doi:10.1016/j.cor.2012.10.016

Purcheck, G. F. (1975). A linear–programming method for the combinatorial grouping of an incomplete power set. *Journal of Cybernetics, 5*(4), 51–58.

Roshanaei, V., Balagh, A. K. G., Esfahani, M. M. S., & Vahdani, B. (2009). A mixed-integer linear programming model along with an electromagnetism-like algorithm for scheduling job shop production system with sequence-dependent set-up times. *International Journal of Advanced Manufacturing Technology*, *47*(5), 783–793.

Sankaran, S., & Rodin, E. Y. (1990). Multiple objective decision making approach to cell formation: A goal programming model. *Mathematical and Computer Modelling*, *13*(9), 71–81. doi:10.1016/0895-7177(90)90079-3

Selim, H. M., Askin, R. G., & Vakharia, A. J. (1998). Cell formation in group technology: Review, evaluation and directions for future research. *Computers & Industrial Engineering*, *34*(1), 3–20. doi:10.1016/S0360-8352(97)00147-2

Shafer, S. M., & Rogers, D. F. (1991). A goal programming approach to the cell formation problem. *Journal of Operations Management*, *10*(1), 28–43. doi:10.1016/0272-6963(91)90034-U

Soto, R., Kjellerstrand, H., Duran, O., Crawford, B., Monfroy, E., & Paredes, F. (2012). Cell formation in group technology using constraint programming and Boolean satisfiability. *Expert Systems with Applications*, *39*(13), 11423–11427. doi:10.1016/j.eswa.2012.04.020

Steudel, H. J., & Ballakur, A. (1987). A dynamic programming based heuristic for machine grouping in manufacturing cell formation. *Computers & Industrial Engineering*, *12*(3), 215–222. doi:10.1016/0360-8352(87)90015-5

Thanh, L. T., Ferland, J. A., Elbenani, B., & Thuc, N. D. et al.. (2016). A computational study of hybrid approaches of metaheuristic algorithms for the cell formation problem. *The Journal of the Operational Research Society*, *67*(1), 20–36. doi:10.1057/jors.2015.46

Waghodekar, P., & Sahu, S. (1984). Machine-component cell formation in group technology: Mace. *International Journal of Production Research*, *22*(6), 937–948. doi:10.1080/00207548408942513

Yan, H. S., Wan, X. Q., & Xiong, F. L. (2014). A hybrid electromagnetism-like algorithm for two-stage assembly flow shop scheduling problem. *International Journal of Production Research*, *52*(19), 5626–5639. doi:10.1080/00207543.2014.894257

Yurtkuran, A., & Emel, E. (2010). A new hybrid electromagnetism-like algorithm for capacitated vehicle routing problems. *Expert Systems with Applications*, *37*(4), 3427–3433. doi:10.1016/j.eswa.2009.10.005

Zeb, A., Khan, M., Khan, N., Tariq, A., Ali, L., Azam, F., & Jaffery, S. H. I. (2016). Hybridization of simulated annealing with genetic algorithm for cell formation problem. *International Journal of Advanced Manufacturing Technology*, *86*(5), 1–12.

Zeng, Y., Zhang, Z., Kusiak, A., Tang, F., & Wei, X. (2016). Optimizing wastewater pumping system with data-driven models and a greedy electromagnetism-like algorithm. *Stochastic Environmental Research and Risk Assessment*, *30*(4), 1263–127. doi:10.1007/s00477-015-1115-4

KEY TERMS AND DEFINITIONS

Approximate Solving-Technique: Algorithm which sacrifices finding optimal solutions for the sake of getting approximate ones at a significant reduced time. It is suitable for tackling NP-hard problems. Some examples: heuristics and metaheuristics.

Continuous Optimization: It is opposed to discrete optimization. All the variables considered in a continuous problem are required to be continuous variables, i.e., to be chosen from a set of real values without gaps.

Discrete Optimization: It is opposed to continuous optimization. Some or all the variables considered in a discrete problem are restricted to be discrete variables. An example is combinatorial optimization; whose goal is to find an optimal object from a finite set of objects.

Exact Solving-Technique: Algorithm which guarantees to find the optimal solution for every finite size instance in bounded time. It is not suitable for solving

NP-hard problems because no polynomial time algorithm exists. Some examples: integer linear programming and finite domain constraint programming.

Heuristic: Traditional approximate technique which is specifically designed for solving a given problem. There are two main types: constructive and local search methods. Constructive methods generate solutions from scratch by adding elements to a solution until it is completed. Local search methods start from some initial solution, which is iteratively replaced by a better solution in its neighborhood.

Metaheuristic: Intelligence approximate method which combines basic heuristic methods and effectiveness exploring the search space. Some features: they are non-deterministic and non-problem high-level search strategies, it is usual to include mechanisms to avoid getting trapped in local optima, and they perform a dynamic balance between diversification and intensification.

Population-Based Algorithm: Solving method which performs search processes determining the evolution of a set of points in the search space. There are two main types: evolutionary algorithms and swarm intelligence algorithms.

Swarm Intelligence Algorithm: Approximate solving-technique inspired by the behavior of self-organized systems, where individuals interact with each others and with the environment, such as flocks of birds and colonies of ants. Some examples: Particle Swarm Optimization (PSO), Ant Colony Optimization (ACO), and Firefly Algorithm (FA).

Chapter 3
Stellar Mass Black Hole for Engineering Optimization

Premalatha Kandhasamy
Bannari Amman Institute of Technology, India

Balamurugan R
Bannari Amman Institute of Technology, India

Kannimuthu S
Karpagam College of Engineering, India

ABSTRACT

In recent years, nature-inspired algorithms have been popular due to the fact that many real-world optimization problems are increasingly large, complex and dynamic. By reasons of the size and complexity of the problems, it is necessary to develop an optimization method whose efficiency is measured by finding the near optimal solution within a reasonable amount of time. A black hole is an object that has enough masses in a small enough volume that its gravitational force is strong enough to prevent light or anything else from escaping. Stellar mass Black hole Optimization (SBO) is a novel optimization algorithm inspired from the property of the gravity's relentless pull of black holes which are presented in the Universe. In this paper SBO algorithm is tested on benchmark optimization test functions and compared with the Cuckoo Search, Particle Swarm Optimization and Artificial Bee Colony systems. The experiment results show that the SBO outperforms the existing methods.

DOI: 10.4018/978-1-5225-2322-2.ch003

INTRODUCTION

The objective of a heuristic approach is to generate a solution to the problem in a reasonable time frame and it is good enough to solve the problem within the search space. This solution may not be the best of all the actual solutions to the problem or it may approximate the exact solution. But it is valuable because it does not require a prohibitively long time for findings. An optimization is selecting the best solution with respect to certain criteria from the set of available solutions. Optimization problems consist of maximizing or minimizing a function by logically choosing input parameter values within a permissible set and computing the value of the function. Optimization means for a given defined domain finding the best available values of some objective function (Diewert, 2008). An optimization problem can be represented as Let $f: X \rightarrow R$ from some set S to the real numbers R Let X be a subset of the R^n, often specified by a set of constraints, inequalities or equalities that the members of X have to satisfy. The domain X of f is called the search space, while the elements of X are called candidate solutions or feasible solutions. The function f is said to be an objective function or fitness function. A feasible solution that minimizes or maximizes the objective function is called an optimal solution (Newman, 2008). An element x^* in X such that $f(x^*) \leq f(x)$ for all x in X for minimization and x^* is a global minimum point or such that $f(x^*) \geq f(x)$ for all x in X for maximization and x^* is global maximum point.

In domain X, f is said to have a local maximum point at the point x^* if there exists some $\varepsilon > 0$ such that $f(x^*) \geq f(x)$ for all x in X within distance ε of x^*. Likewise, the function has a local minimum point at x^* if $f(x^*) \leq f(x)$ for all x in X within distance ε of x^*. A global maximum point is always a local maximum point and global minimum point is always a local minimum points. A metaheuristic as an iterative generation process which guides a subordinate heuristic by combining intelligently different concepts and learning strategies are used in order to find efficiently near-optimal solutions (Osman & Laporte, 1996). A metaheuristic algorithm must be able to rapidly converge to the global optimum solution of the related objective function (Yang, 2006). Furthermore, the run-time required by a metaheuristic algorithm to reach to a global optimum solution must be at adequate levels for practical applications. The algorithmic structure of a metaheuristic algorithm is preferred to be simple enough to allow for its easy adaptation to different problems. The metaheuristic algorithm desired to has no algorithmic control parameters or very few algorithmic control parameters excluding the general parameters such as size of the population, total number of iterations and problem dimension.

Exploration and exploitation are two basic strategies during searching for the global optimum in metaheuristic optimization algorithms (Rashedi et al, 2009). The exploration process does well in enabling the algorithm to reach the best local solutions within the search space. The exploitation process succeeds the ability to reach the global optimum solution which is on the point around the local solutions obtained. Nature has rich source of inspiration and researchers have been motivated in many ways. At present, most of the new algorithms have been inspired by nature and they have been developed by enchanting inspiration from nature. In this work a novel stellar mass black hole optimization algorithm is developed for NP-hard problems based on the characteristics of stellar mass black hole. The sources of inspiration come from physical properties absorption, emission, coalescing and vanishing of black hole.

A black hole is a region of space where it's filled with so much matter. It can be formed when massive stars run out of fuel and collapse under their own mass, making such strong gravity that they vanish. While totally invisible, a black hole maintains a gravitational pull on surrounding matter. The rest of this paper is organized as follows. Section 1 presents the literature review of optimization algorithms. Section 2 explains the Nature-inspired Stellar mass black hole optimization. The experiment results of the SBO are analyzed and discussed with the PSO, ABC and CK in section 3.

Literature Review on Optimization Techniques

At present there are many optimization techniques available. The familiar methods are linear programming (Schrijver, 1998), the quadratic programming (Nocedal & Wright, 1999) the dynamic programming (Bertsekas, 2000) the simplex method (Wilson, 1975) and the gradient methods (Avriel, 2003) through which is possible to resolve certain types of optimization problems. In observation of these problems are too complex and require much time to resolve by deterministic methods. Metaheuristics are stochastic optimization. It finds a solution within a reasonable amount of time. They are generally iterative behavior. The same pattern is repeated until a end criterion is met at the beginning for optimization.

Simulated annealing based on the Metropolis algorithm that allows describing the evolution of a thermodynamic system. This probabilistic metaheuristic is inspired from the physical process of annealing the crystalline materials (Kirkpatrick 1983, Metropolis 1953). Simulated annealing process consists of heating a material at a high temperature and then it must get cooled slowly to enhance its crystal's size (Hastings, 1970). Atoms of heated material have a superior energy that causes them to change the positions and they can perform large random movements in the material. The atoms' energy and their movement capacity are reduced while using the slow cooling process. The various cooling momentary states make it possible to get homogeneous materials with good quality.

Tabu search algorithm introduced by (Fred & Glover, 1996). This metaheuristic is a mathematical optimization method used to solve combinatorial problems. It improves the performance of local search by relaxing its basic rule. First, at each step the aggravating moves can be accepted if there is no improvement in a move. From a given position, the tabu search algorithm explores the neighborhood of this position and chooses a new one that optimizes the objective function. Until the fixed criterions get satisfied, the search procedure is iteratively repeated. The algorithm isn't always efficient the addition of intensification and diversification processes that involves introduction of the new parameters.

The family of metaheuristic optimization was represented by the evolution strategies, inspired by evolution theory. This model is originally proposed by (Rechenberg, 1965); it is the first genuine metaheuristic and the first evolutionary algorithm. In its initial version, the algorithm manipulates iteratively a set of real variable vectors, using mutation and selection operators. Fogel et al. introduced evolutionary programming aimed to create a finite-state machine by successions of crossover and mutations (Fogel, 1996). This metaheuristic technique helps to predict future events based on previous observations. Genetic algorithms are stochastic search techniques and theoretical foundations were established by (Holland, 1975). Moreover, they are inspired by Darwin theory. There are two mechanisms for living species to evolve: natural selection and reproduction. The natural selection prefers species which are more adaptable to the surroundings. The reproduction is performed by crossovers and mutations within individuals' genes. Genetic programming is similar to genetic algorithms (Koza, 1992). Almost all techniques and results of genetic algorithms can also be applied to genetic programming.

Differential Evolution (DE) is stochastic, population-based optimization algorithm introduced by (Storn & Price, 1996). It is developed to optimize real parameter, real valued functions. Differential evolution is an evolutionary algorithm and it consolidates with Evolutionary Strategies and Genetic Algorithms. DE optimizes a problem by maintaining a population of candidate solutions and creating new candidate solutions by combining existing ones according to its simple formulae. It keeps the candidate solution with the best fitness on the optimization problem at hand.

Ant colony algorithms are born from a simple observation of insects. An especially ants, work out complex computational problems. The pheromones are primary factor that help in those ants communicate with each other indirectly owing to deposit of chemical substances. This indirect communication type is called stigmergy. If an obstacle is presented in ants' path, they will all tend, after a research phase, to follows the shortest way between nest and the obstacle (Goss, 1989). They are more attracted to the area where the pheromone trails rate is maximized. Ants that traveled by food source and reached too quickly to the nest are those that have taken the shorter way. Thereby, finally the shortest way has a greater possibility to be used by all ants than other ways. The first algorithms inspired from this analogy were introduced by (Colorni et al 1992, Dorigo et al 1996) to resolve the problem of business traveler.

Particulate Swarm Optimization is a metaheuristic technique proposed by (Kennedy & Eberhart, 1948). This method is inspired from animal's movement in swarms. The main employed example is the social behavior of bird flocking or fish schooling (Nelder & Mead 1965, Reynolds et al 1987), where every individual bird has the knowledge of only its nearest neighbor. It therefore uses not just its own memory, but also the information of nearest neighbors to decide its own movement. Simple rules, such as "maintain the same speed as others", "move in the same direction" and "stay close neighbors" are among key behaviors that maintain cohesion of the swarm and allow the implementation of complex and adaptive collective behaviors. The swarm's global intelligence is a direct consequence of local interactions between different particles. Therefore, system performance as a whole is greater than the performance sum of its different parts.

Artificial Bee Colony (ABC) algorithm is another population-based method presented by (Karaboga et al, 2007). What ABC algorithm does is that it imitates intelligent behavior of honey bees and applies three phases namely employed bee, onlooker bee and scout bee phases to find the best solution. Employed and onlooker bees does a local search in and around the neighborhood and choose food, based on the probabilistic and deterministic selection. They select food sources based on their and the nest mates' experience and modify their positions. In Scout phase, bees (scouts) fly and choose the food sources randomly unlike the previous mentioned phases. If the nectar amount found in the new source is higher than that of the previous one stored in their memory, then they memorize the new position and forget the previous one. Thus ABC balances intensification and diversification process with local and global search methods obtaining the best solution.

Cuckoo search is an optimization inspired by the brood parasitism of the cuckoo species by laying their eggs in the nests of other host birds (Yang & Deb, 2010). Some host birds can engage direct conflict with the intruding cuckoos. Host birds will either throw eggs away or simply abandon their nests and build new ones, if they discover the eggs are not their own. Each cuckoo egg represents a new solution and host birds egg in a nest represents a solution. In the easiest form, each nest has one egg. The aim is to employ the new and potentially better solutions (cuckoos) to replace not-so-good solutions in the nests. Cuckoo search idealized such breeding activities, and hence can be applied for various Engineering optimization problems.

NATURE-INSPIRED STELLAR MASS BLACK HOLE OPTIMIZATION

Preamble

In the late 1790s according to the statement of Newton's Laws, John Michell and Pierre-Simon Laplace separately suggested the existence of an invisible star (Michell & Laplace, 1998). The mass and size are calculated which is known as the event horizon, where an object needs to get an escape velocity that is greater than the speed of light. In 1915, the availability of black holes is predicted through the Einstein's theory of general relativity. In 1967 John Wheeler, an American theoretical physicist, applied the term "black hole" for the collapsed objects (Wheeler, 1994). The space and gravitational force of the black hole are highly compact in which any object can be prevented from escape including light. Around the black hole there is an event horizon which is a mathematically defined surface that marks the point of no return. There are number of black holes in the Universe which are non countable. A black hole is born while an object is unable to withstand the compressing force of its gravity. They form when there are massive stars collapsed together.

Generally the black holes are invisible, but can be identified due to material falling and being attracted by black holes. The hole is called "black" because it absorbs the entire substances that hit the horizon, reflecting nothing, just like a perfect blackbody in thermodynamics. In this way, the astronomers carefully observed the mass of black holes in the Universe. All the matters in a black hole are crushed into a region of immeasurably small volume known as the central singularity. The event horizon measures the closure of singularity of an object to get it safely. Once an object has passed the event horizon, it cannot be escaped. The object will be drawn by the black hole's gravitational pull and squashed into the singularity. The size of the event horizon is proportional to the mass of the black hole. The Schwarzschild and Kerr are the major types of black holes. The Schwarzschild black hole is popularly called as the simplest black hole, in which the core is idle. This type of black hole has only a singularity and an event horizon. The Kerr black hole is probably the most common form in nature. When the rotating star collapses, the core continues to rotate, and this carried over to the black hole.

The Kerr black hole has the following parts:

- **Singularity:** The collapsed core
- **Event horizon:** The opening of the hole
- **Ergosphere:** An egg-shaped region of distorted space around the event horizon
- **Static limit:** The boundary between the ergosphere and normal space.

Figure 1 (Rotating black hole (*Image credit: MesserWoland/wikimedia*)) shows the ergosphere of a rotating black hole accelerates the objects within its envelope, extracting energy from the hole. Two important surfaces are there around the rotating black hole. Event horizon is the first inner sphere and ergosphere is the second inner boundary of a region. The oval-shaped surface, touching the event horizon at the poles, is the outer boundary of the ergosphere. In the ergosphere a particle is enforced to rotate and may gain energy at the cost of the black hole rotational energy. When an object passes into the ergosphere, it can be expelled from the black hole by energy gaining. But, if an object crosses the event horizon, it is absorbed into the black hole and never gets escaped. Black holes have three properties which can be measured are mass, electric charge and angular momentum. The mass of the black hole is measured reliably by the movement of the other objects around it.

According to theory, there are three different types of black holes depending on their mass namely stellar, supermassive and miniature black holes as shown in Figure 2 (Different types of black holes based on the mass). These black holes are formed in various ways. Supermassive black holes, which are a mass equivalent to billions of suns, likely, exist in the centers of most galaxies. The miniature black hole has a mass much smaller than that of the Sun. The miniature black holes are formed after the big bang.

Figure 1. Rotating black hole
Source: MesserWoland/wikimedia

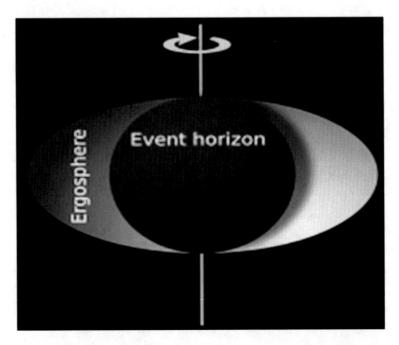

Figure 2. Different types of black holes based on the mass

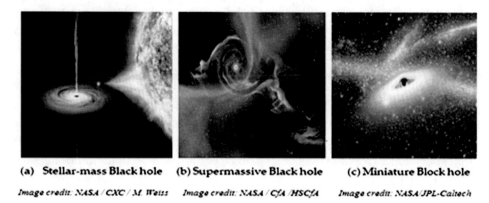

(a) Stellar-mass Black hole   (b) Supermassive Black hole   (c) Miniature Block hole

Image credit: NASA / CXC / M. Weiss   *Image credit: NASA / CfA /HSCfA*   *Image credit: NASA/JPL-Caltech*

Formation and Evolution of Stellar Mass Black Hole

The stellar mass black holes are formed during the gravitational collapse of heavy stars. When the massive stars are collapsed it produce the black holes up to 10^3 solar masses. Stellar mass black holes are born with big bang densities. Black holes are formed in high-energy collisions to get adequate density. They form due to huge massive star that runs out of nuclear fuel. Then the star explodes as a supernova. The rest of the substance is a black hole since the explosion blown as much of the stellar material away.

Growth

After the black hole formation, it continues to grow by absorbing the additional matter. Any black hole that continuously absorbs gases and interstellar dust from its direct surroundings and omnipresent cosmic background radiation. Merging with other objects such as stars or even other black holes is the possibility for a black hole. There is a rapid growth in stellar mass black holes by consuming nearby stars and gas, often in abundant supply near the galaxy center. The black hole may also grow by merging with other black holes that drift to the galactic center during collisions with other galaxies. A black hole may exist of any mass. The lower the mass, the higher the density of matter is in order to form a black hole.

Evaporation

In 1974, Hawking depicted that the black holes emit less amount of thermal radiation but they are not completely black (Hawking, 1974). A black hole is about to emit particles in a perfect black body spectrum. Because of loss in mass by the emission of photons and other particles the black holes are expected to shrunk and evaporate over time. The thermal spectrum temperature is proportional to the surface gravity of the black hole, which for a Schwarzschild black hole, is reciprocally proportional to the mass. If there is a smaller black hole the radiation effects may be very strong. Lower-mass black holes are expected to evaporate faster; for example, a black hole of smallest mass take less than 10-88 seconds to evaporate completely. Returning the energy to the Universe the black holes evaporate slowly. While emitting the particle the black hole loses its energy and becomes smaller. Smaller black holes emit more intense radiation than larger ones. The emission becomes more and more high and finally it get terminated.

Methodology

Mass of the black hole is increased after the black hole absorbs the matter. Based on the Black hole Stephen Hawking emission, its mass is reduced. By pulling the gas of companion star orbits around region the stellar mass black holes start growing. Mostly there is gas and dust in the diet of known black holes. Black holes can swallow the material torn from nearby stars. A black hole gathers any mass than it grows in mass and slightly in size. The mass decreases via a complicated process called black hole evaporation, or "Hawking Radiation," named for Stephen Hawking (Hawking & Penrose, 1970). Hawking radiation is a black body radiation that is predicted to be released by black holes, due to quantum effects near the event horizon. The characteristics of stellar mass black hole are:

- The mass of a black hole grows when it absorbs matter
- A black hole also grows by colliding and merging with other black holes
- During radiation a black hole loses energy and its mass is reduced.
- Smaller black holes radiates more than larger ones
- The radiation becomes more and more high, and the black hole is no more.

Based on the above properties the new optimization technique is devised which incorporates both diversification and intensification in the search space. The individuals succeed to get new characteristics that give them a survival. It resembles an evolutionary technique. The cumulative changes that occur in a population over time is referred as evolution. The perpetual mystery in the black holes is that they appear to exist on radically different size scales. The stellar mass black holes are peppered throughout the Universe generally 10 to 24 times as massive as the Sun. The scientists estimate that there are as many as ten million up to a billion, such black holes are only in the Milky Way. For the optimization problem the initial population of black holes with m dimensions is considered as candidate solution for the problem. Each black hole is considered as a fitness value according to the solution of the problem. Table 1 shows the comparison of social strategies with SBO.

Evolution

Schwarzschild radius is the distance from the surface (or event horizon) of the black hole to the center (or singularity). This radius is the size that any object would compress enough to form a black hole; it varies between only centimeters across to several kilometers across (Chaisson & McMillan, 2008). The Schwarzschild radius increases when the mass of the original object increases but the actual radius does not. It is interesting to mention that the irreducible mass is related to the area A of the event horizon by $M = \sqrt{\dfrac{A}{16\pi}}$

One way to grow a more massive black hole is for a seed black hole in a dense galactic nucleus to swallow up gas and normal stars. It keeps on growing by absorbing mass from its surroundings. By absorbing other stars and merging with other black holes, super massive black holes of millions of solar masses may form. If two black holes merge together then their event horizons are contiguous. Figure 3 (Growth of Black hole) shows the growth of a black hole and collision of two black holes (Hehl, 1998).

The mass of black hole is directly proportional to its growth rate. The higher mass black hole has a higher absorption level which is given in Equation 1:

$$\rho_i = \frac{f_i}{\sum_{i=1}^{N} f_i} \tag{1}$$

where

f_i - Fitness value of black hole i in the population $1 \le i \le N$
N - Number of black holes in the population.

The most abnormal behavior that a black hole possesses is its ability to radiate the energy. With respect to this process lose the mass is called as Hawking radiation (Hamilton, 1998). According to the Hawking's radiation theory of black holes, it is found that the energy lost from a black hole is inversely proportional to its mass. Larger mass black holes doesn't radiate much energy because of they have low temperatures. Smaller mass black holes emit more energy; hence have higher

Figure 3. Growth of Black hole

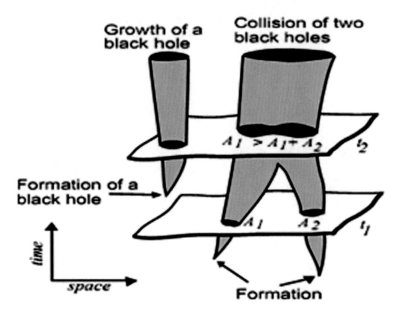

Table 1. Comparison of social strategies with SBO

Social Strategy	SBO
Black hole	Feasible solution to the problem
Black hole mass	Fitness value
Black holes in the universe	Population of feasible solution
Emission and Absorption of a black hole	Stochastic operators
Progression of populations to suit the Universe	Iteratively applying a stochastic operators on a set of feasible solutions

temperatures and frequency for their energy emission. Therefore, the subsequent implication of the inverse thermal/mass relationship is that black holes may suffer from thermal radiation runaway effects as their mass gets smaller through their end of life, it indicates that they lose a mass faster and they become smaller.

The black hole with the lowest mass has the higher radiation. The radiation level ε_i of individual black hole is given in Equation 2:

$$\varepsilon_i = 1 - \rho_i \tag{2}$$

The mass of the black hole is updated by using the following Equation:

$$b_{id}\left(t+1\right)=b_{id}\left(t\right)+\Delta a_{id}\left(t\right)-\Delta e_{id}\left(t\right) \tag{3}$$

where

$b_{i,d}$ - Value of ith Black hole in d^{th} dimension
$\Delta a_{i,d}$ - Growth at dimension d in i^{th} Black hole
$\Delta e_{i,d}$ - Radiation at dimension d in i^{th} Black hole
t –Time epoch

A spinning black hole permits the matter to orbit closer in the black hole and draws space around it. The researchers discover important clues about the growth of these objects over time by computing the spin of distance black hole. However, the black holes grow primarily while the collision and merge occurs in the galaxy, then the material accumulation takes place in a stable disk, due to steady supply of new material of the disk results in rapid spinning black holes. In dissimilarity, when many small accretion episodes enable the growth of black holes, they accumulate material from random directions. Based on the characteristics the growth of ith black hole in d^{th} dimension is given in Equation 4:

$$\Delta a_{id}\left(t\right)=\begin{cases}\alpha\left(\rho_i b_{id}\left(t\right)+\rho_{i+1}b_{id+1}\left(t\right)\right) & i=1\\\alpha\left(\rho_{i-1}b_{id-1}\left(t\right)+\rho_i b_{id}\left(t\right)+\rho_{i+1}b_{id+1}\left(t\right)\right) & 1<i<N\\\alpha\left(\rho_{i-1}b_{id-1}\left(t\right)+\rho_i b_{id}\left(t\right)\right) & i=N\end{cases} \tag{4}$$

where $0\leq\alpha\leq1$ and ρ_i is growth level of ith Black hole

The larger black holes have less powerful radiation than the smaller ones. The emissivity of black hole is measured by the proportion of the actual emitted radiance from a black hole which is given in Eq. (5):

$$\Delta e_{i,d}=\beta\varepsilon_i b_{i,d} \tag{5}$$

where $0\leq\beta\leq1$ and ε_i is radiation level of ith Black hole

Death of Black Hole

The Hawking Radiation enables the black holes to emit their energy. Generally it is accepted if the black holes radiate more mass than they take in, they will eventually evaporate [34]. Hamilton also says that many large black holes have the potential to "outlive" the universe. The process for evaporation is simple: the black hole radiates which causes the mass to decrease; as the mass decreases, radiation increases; as the radiation increases, the black hole evaporates faster and finally the black hole is no more (Gottesman, 1997). The black holes with very poor fitness value are removed from the population.

Stellar Mass Black Hole Optimization

```
Initialize a population of N candidate solutions Bₖ
  while not (termination criterion)
     for each Bₖ find fitness fₖ, growth rate ρₖ and radiation
rate εₖ
     for each Bₖ, update the mass using equation (3)
             Rank the solutions
             Replace fraction ofworst black holes with new black
holes
             Collide the nearest black holes and generate black
holes for left outs in the population
     Keep the best solution
Next generation
```

Collision of Black Holes

Scientists believe that the interaction of two black holes may have any one of the two events. The first is that much more massive black hole is formed when they combine together. The second is that due to spin, the two black holes interact and back away from each other sending one dashing away. The total mass would be the combined mass of the two black holes. If the two black holes b_p and b_q are too closer then they merge together and forms the new black hole b_k using the formula (6):

$$b_{kd} = rand\left(\right) \times \left(b_{pd} + b_{qd}\right) \tag{6}$$

Discussion of SBO algorithm

- The population size N is a tuning parameter. The optimization performance of SBO suffers when N is too small or too large. Typical implementations of SBO the value of N is somewhere between 20 and 200.
- The initial population of candidate solutions B_k is usually generated in random.

- The termination criterion is problem-dependent, like in any other evolutionary algorithm. In most applications the termination criterion is a generation count limit or a function evaluation limit.
- Smaller mass black holes emit more energy finally at end of their lives. So the black holes with lowest fitness value are replaced by the new black holes. It causes diversity in the solution.
- If the two black holes are nearer then it gets merge together and form a new black hole, it avoids premature convergence.
- The population size is fixed only then it generate the black holes for the left outs.
- In our experiments, absorption rate $\alpha = 0.5$ is employed and emission rate $\beta = 0.9$ is used through empirical analysis.

EXPERIMENTAL ANALYSIS

Table 2 shows the various benchmark functions used for testing the successes of SBO. The results obtained from SBO are compared with PSO, ABC and CK (Karaboga et al, 2009a). The dimensions of the benchmark functions vary between 2 and 30. The global minimum values of each of the benchmark functions are obtained by using different initial population at every turn of 20 epochs. The population size is 50. The stopping criterion is up to the maximum iteration 2,000,000 or the optimal check reached.

The setting values of algorithmic control parameters of the mentioned algorithms are given below:

- **PSO Settings:** $c_1 = c_2 = 1.80$ and $\omega = 0.60$ have been used as recommended in (Civicioglu & Besdok, 2011).
- **ABC Settings:** limit = $50D$ has been used as recommended in (Civicioglu & Besdok, 2011).
- **CK Settings:** $\lambda = 1.50$ and $p_a = 0.25$ have been used as recommended in (Osman & Laporte, 1996).
- **SBO Settings:** $\alpha = 0.5$ & $\beta = 0.9$

The best optimum values, mean of the best optimum values, the standard deviation value of mean optimum values and the mean iteration of the function evaluation values are computed by analyzing the recorded global minimum values during experiments and are shown in Tables 3-6 respectively.

Table 2. Benchmark optimization test functions

No	Function	Min.	Range	D	C	Formulation
F1	Ackley	0	[-32,32]	30	MN	$f(x) = -a\exp\left(-b\sqrt{\dfrac{1}{d}\sum_{i=1}^{d}x_i^2}\right) - \exp\left(\dfrac{1}{d}\sum_{i=1}^{d}\cos(cx_i)\right) + a + \exp(1)$
F2	Beale	0	[-4.5, 4.5]	5	UN	$f(x) = (1.5 - x_1 + x_1x_2)^2 + (2.25 - x_1 + x_1x_2^2)^2 + (2.625 - x_1 + x_1x_2^3)^2$
F3	Bohachevsky 1	0	[-100,100]	2	MS	$f_1(x) = x_1^2 + 2x_2^2 - 0.3\cos(3\pi x_1) - 0.4\cos(4\pi x_2)$
F4	Bohachevsky 2	0	[-100,100]	2	MN	$f_2(x) = x_1^2 + 2x_2^2 - 0.3\cos(3\pi x_1)\cos(4\pi x_2) + 0.3$
F5	Bohachevsky 3	0	[-100,100]	2	MN	$f_3(x) = x_1^2 + 2x_2^2 - 0.3\cos(3\pi x_1 + 4\pi x_2) + 0.3$
F6	Booth	0	[-10,10]	2	MS	$f(x) = (x_1 + 2x_2 - 7)^2 + (2x_1 + x_2 - 5)^2$
F7	Branin	0.397887	[-5, 0]x[0,15]	2	MS	$f(x) = a(x_2 - bx_1^2 + cx_1 - r)^2 + s(1-t)\cos(x_1) + s$
F8	Colville	0	[-10,10]	4	UN	$f(x) = 100(x_1^2 x_2)^2 + (x_1 - 1)^2 + (x_3 - 1)^2 + 90(x_3^2 - x_4)^2 + 10.1\left((x_2 - 1)^2 + (x_4 - 1)^2\right) + 19.8(x_2 - 1)(x_4 - 1)$
F9	Dixonprice	0	[-10,10]	30	UN	$f(x) = (x_1 - 1)^2 + \sum_{i=2}^{d} i(2x_i^2 - x_{i-1})^2$

continued on following page

Table 2. Continued

No	Function	Min.	Range	D	C	Formulation
F10	Easom	-1	[-100,100]	2	UN	$f(x) = -\cos(x_1)\cos(x_2)\exp(-(x_1-\pi)^2-(x_2-\pi)^2)$
F11	Goldstein- Price	3	[-2,2]	2	MN	$f(x) = \left[1+(x_1+x_2+1)^2\left(19-14x_1+3x_1^2-14x_2+6x_1x_2+3x_2^2\right)\right]\cdot\left[30+(2x_1-3x_2)^2\left(18-32x_1+12x_1^2+48x_2-36x_1x_2+27x_2^2\right)\right]$
F12	Griewank	0	[-600,600]	30	MN	$f(x) = \sum_{i=1}^{d}\frac{x_i^2}{4000} - \prod_{i=1}^{d}\cos\left(\frac{x_i}{\sqrt{i}}\right)+1$
F13	Hartman3	-3.86278	[0,1]	3	MN	$f(x) = -\sum_{i=1}^{4}c_i\exp\left[-\sum_{j=1}^{3}a_{ij}(x_j-p_{ij})^2\right]$
F14	Hartman6	-3.32237	[0,1]	6	MN	$f(x) = -\sum_{i=1}^{4}c_i\exp\left[-\sum_{j=1}^{6}a_{ij}(x_j-p_{ij})^2\right]$
F15	Hump camel 6	-1.0316	[-5,5]	2	MN	$f(x) = 4x_1^2-2.1x_1^4+\frac{1}{3}x_1^6+x_1x_2-4x_2^2+4x_2^4$
F16	Matyas	0	[-10,10]	2	UN	$f(x) = 0.26(x_1^2+x_2^2)-0.48x_1x_2$
F17	Michalewicz	-1.8013	[0,10]	2	MS	$f(x) = -\sum_{i=1}^{d}\sin(x_i)\sin^{2m}\left(\frac{ix_i^2}{\pi}\right)$

continued on following page

Table 2. Continued

No	Function	Min.	Range	D	C	Formulation
F18	Perm	0	[-D,D]	4	MN	$f(x)=\sum_{i=1}^{d}\left(\sum_{j=1}^{d}(j^i+\beta)\left(\left(\frac{x_j}{j}\right)^i-1\right)\right)^2$
F19	Powell	0	[-4,5]	24	UN	$f(x)=\sum_{i=1}^{d/4}\left[\begin{array}{l}(x_{4i-3}+10x_{4i-2})^2+5(x_{4i-1}-x_{4i})^2+\\(x_{4i-2}-2x_{4i-1})^4+10(x_{4i-3}-x_{4i})^4\end{array}\right]$
F20	Powersum	0	[0,D]	4	MN	$f(x)=\sum_{k=1}^{n}\left[\left(\sum_{i=1}^{n}x_i^k\right)-b_k\right]^2$
F21	Rastrigin	0	[-5.12,5.12]	30	MS	$f(x)=\sum_{i=1}^{n}\left[x_i^2-10\cos(2\pi x_i)+10\right]$
F22	Rosenbrock	0	[-30,30]	30	UN	$f(x)=\sum_{i=1}^{n-1}\left[100(x_{i+1}-x_i^2)^2+(x_i-1)^2\right]$
F23	Schaffer	0	[-100,100]	2	MN	$f(x)=0.5+\dfrac{\sin^2\left(\sqrt{x_1^2+x_2^2}\right)-0.5}{\left(1+0.001(x_1^2+x_2^2)\right)^2}$
F24	Shubert	-186.731	[-10,10]	2	MN	$f(x)=\left(\sum_{i=1}^{5}i\cos((i+1)x_1+i)\right)\left(\sum_{i=1}^{5}i\cos((i+1)x_2+i)\right)$

continued on following page

Table 2. Continued

No	Function	Min.	Range	D	C	Formulation
F25	Sphere	0	[-100,100]	30	US	$f(x) = \sum_{i=1}^{n} x_i^2$
F26	Step	0	[-100,100]	30	US	$f(x) = \sum_{i=1}^{n} \left(\lfloor x_i + 0.5 \rfloor \right)^2$
F27	Sum squares	0	[-10,10]	30	US	$f(x) = \sum_{i=1}^{n} i x_i^2$
F28	Trid	-50	[-D², D²]	6	UN	$f(x) = \sum_{i=n}^{n} \left(x_i - 1 \right)^2 - \sum_{i=2}^{n} x_i x_{i-1}$
F29	Quartic	0	[-1.28,1.28]	30	US	$f(x) = \sum_{i=1}^{n} i x_i^4 + random(0,1)$
F30	Zakharov	0	[-5,10]	10	UN	$f(x) = \sum_{i=1}^{n} x_i^2 + \left(\sum_{i=1}^{n} 0.5 i x_i \right)^2 + \left(\sum_{i=1}^{n} 0.5 i x_i \right)^4$

Min: Global Optimum, D: Dimension, C: Characteristics, U: Unimodal, M: Multimodal, S: Separable, N: Non-Separable.

Table 3. The Best optimum values obtained from SBO, PSO, ABC and CK

No	SBO	PSO	ABC	CK
F1	0.0000000000000008	0.0000000000000080	0.0000000000000222	0.0000000000000044
F2	0.0000000045955946	0.0000000000000000	0.0000000000000004	0.0000000000000000
F3	0.0000000000000000	0.0000000000000000	0.0000000000000000	0.0000000000000000
F4	0.0000000000000000	0.0000000000000000	0.0000000000000000	0.0000000000000000
F5	0.0000000000000000	0.0000000000000000	0.0000000000000000	0.0000000000000000
F6	0.0000000000000000	0.0000000000000000	0.0000000000000000	0.0000000000000000
F7	0.3978873687229315	0.3978873577297382	0.3978873577297382	0.3978873577297382
F8	0.0000000000000000	0.0000000000000000	0.0000874954660480	0.0000000000000000
F9	0.0000000000000000	0.6666666666666665	0.0000000000000014	0.6666666666666665
F10	-0.9999999999999999	-1.0000000000000000	-1.0000000000000000	-1.0000000000000000
F11	2.9999999999999215	2.9999999999999192	2.9999999999999210	2.9999999999999192
F12	0.0000000000000000	0.0000000000000000	0.0000000000000000	0.0000000000000000
F13	-3.8627893041522300	-3.8627821478207558	-3.8627821478207558	-3.8627821478207558
F14	-3.3227554926190700	-3.3219951715842431	-3.3219951715842426	-3.3219951715842431
F15	-1.0316291524942800	-1.0316284534898774	-1.0316284534898774	-1.0316284534898774
F16	0.0000000000000000	0.0000000000000000	0.0000000000000000	0.0000000000000000
F17	-1.8320436836719732	-1.8210436836776824	-1.8210436836776824	-1.8210436836776824
F18	0.0000000000000000	0.0000088339092326	0.0011011688503096	0.0000000085822797
F19	0.0000000000000000	0.0000211010308969	0.0002717789268690	0.0000000797695218
F20	0.0000000000000000	0.0000000000427674	0.0003305515663585	0.0000000509883999
F21	0.0000000000000000	13.9294167236679410	0.0000000000000000	0.0003806178377204
F22	0.0000000000000000	0.0000700595196601	0.0002227389995635	0.0000000000000000
F23	0.0000000000000000	0.0000000000000000	0.0000000000000000	0.0000000000000000
F24	-186.7309091409600210	-186.7309088310239800	-186.7309088310239800	-186.7309088310239800
F25	0.0000000000000000	0.0000000000000000	0.0000000000000003	0.0000000000000000
F26	0.0000000000000000	0.0000000000000000	0.0000000000000000	0.0000000000000000
F27	0.0000000000000000	0.0000000000000000	0.0000000000000003	0.0000000000000000
F28	-50.0338354523580000	-50.0000000000001710	-50.0000000000000570	-50.0000000000002270
F29	0.0000000028478791	0.0022391455486327	0.0059038261927937	0.0013909553459754
F30	0.0000000000000000	0.0000000000000000	0.0000000000000083	0.0000000000000000

Table 4. The Mean optimum values obtained from SBO, PSO, ABC and CK

No	SBO	PSO	ABC	CK
F1	0.0000000000000008	0.0000000000000080	0.0000000000000300	0.0000000000000044
F2	0.0000000699521289	0.0000000000000000	0.0000000000000008	0.0000000000000000
F3	0.0000000000000000	0.0000000000000000	0.0000000000000000	0.0000000000000000
F4	0.0000000000000000	0.0000000000000000	0.0000000000000000	0.0000000000000000
F5	0.0000000000000000	0.0000000000000000	0.0000000000000001	0.0000000000000000
F6	0.0000000000000000	0.0000000000000000	0.0000000000000000	0.0000000000000000
F7	0.3978873835217430	0.3978873577297382	0.3978873577297382	0.3978873577297382
F8	0.0000000000000000	0.0000000000000000	0.0216852782176882	0.0000000000000000
F9	0.0000000000000000	32.7000000000000030	0.0000000000000023	0.6666666666666663
F10	-0.9801304643033723	-1.0000000000000000	-1.0000000000000000	-0.3000000000000000
F11	2.9999999999999225	2.9999999999999205	2.9999999999999223	2.9999999999999201
F12	0.0000000000000000	0.0092269113767599	0.0000000000000000	0.0000000000000000
F13	-3.8628977494333400	-3.8627821478207536	-3.8627821478207536	-3.8627821478207536
F14	-3.3280327407667764	-3.2684932669902809	-3.3219951715842422	-3.3219951715842422
F15	-1.0316291524942800	-1.0316284534898774	-1.0316284534898774	-1.0316284534898774
F16	0.0000000000000000	0.0000000000000000	0.0000000000000001	0.0000000000000000
F17	-1.8320436836719732	-1.8210436836776824	-1.8210436836776824	-1.8210436836776824
F18	0.0000000000000000	0.0013823741082140	0.0204750133573142	0.0000528002823306
F19	0.0000000000000000	0.0000517665237642	0.0004486249518229	0.0000001506204011
F20	0.0000000000000000	0.0001616061328810	0.0022337034076446	0.0000029552286077
F21	0.0000000000000000	28.0080704889407630	0.0000000000000000	1.2828840539586595
F22	0.0000000000000000	2.3638709258458954	0.0609538747914428	0.0000000000000000
F23	0.0000000000000000	0.0000000000000000	0.0000000000000000	0.0000000000000000
F24	-186.7309890708511175	-186.7309088235984100	-186.7309088310239500	-186.7309088310239800
F25	0.0000000000000000	0.0000000000000000	0.0000000000000004	0.0000000000000000
F26	0.0000000000000000	0.0000000000000000	0.0000000000000000	0.0000000000000000
F27	0.0000000000000000	0.0000000000000000	0.0000000000000004	0.0000000000000000
F28	-50.5487614657409665	-50.0000000000001920	-49.9999999999999080	-50.0000000000001920
F29	0.0122237014923000	0.0047745343217586	0.0129825734203320	0.0021879618606472
F30	0.0000000000000000	0.0000000000000000	0.0000000000000488	0.0000000000000000

Table 5. The standard deviation of mean optimum values obtained from SBO, PSO, ABC and CK

No	SBO	PSO	ABC	CK
F1	0.0000000000000000	0.0000000000000000	0.0000000000000025	0.0000000000000000
F2	0.0000000566742933	0.0000000000000000	0.0000000000000002	0.0000000000000000
F3	0.0000000000000000	0.0000000000000000	0.0000000000000000	0.0000000000000000
F4	0.0000000000000000	0.0000000000000000	0.0000000000000000	0.0000000000000000
F5	0.0000000000000000	0.0000000000000000	0.0000000000000001	0.0000000000000000
F6	0.0000000000000000	0.0000000000000000	0.0000000000000000	0.0000000000000000
F7	0.0000000000000004	0.0000000000000000	0.0000000000000000	0.0000000000000000
F8	0.0000000000000000	0.0000000000000000	0.0145332859252275	0.0000000000000000
F9	0.0000000000000000	98.5965196353833020	0.0000000000000005	0.0000000000000005
F10	0.0000002651028946	0.0000000000000000	0.0000000000000000	0.4701623459816272
F11	0.0000000000000007	0.0000000000000009	0.0000000000000013	0.0000000000000009
F12	0.0000000000000000	0.0105600444455998	0.0000000000000000	0.0000000000000000
F13	0.0000000000000023	0.0000000000000023	0.0000000000000021	0.0000000000000023
F14	0.0000000000000010	0.0606851636993409	0.0000000000000005	0.0000000000000009
F15	0.0000000000000000	0.0000000000000000	0.0000000000000000	0.0000000000000000
F16	0.0000000000000000	0.0000000000000000	0.0000000000000000	0.0000000000000000
F17	0.0000000000000000	0.0000000000000000	0.0000000000000000	0.0000000000000000
F18	0.0000006893838249	0.0013347446743983	0.0149596386587757	0.0000448197610402
F19	0.0000000000000000	0.0000216470469136	0.0000666092006811	0.0000000545404714
F20	0.0000000000000000	0.0002478983088702	0.0015077135883540	0.0000029262253023
F21	0.0000000000000000	7.8693037959886158	0.0000000000000000	1.0406975037000643
F22	0.0000000000000000	0.0018352361800625	0.0024604768149038	0.0005667706273508
F23	0.0000000000000000	0.0000000000000000	0.0000000000000000	0.0000000000000000
F24	0.0000000000000021	0.0000000332053694	0.0000000000000160	0.0000000000000000
F25	0.0000000000000000	0.0000000000000000	0.0000000000000001	0.0000000000000000
F26	0.0000000000000000	0.0000000000000000	0.0000000000000000	0.0000000000000000
F27	0.0000000000000000	0.0000000000000000	0.0000000000000001	0.0000000000000000
F28	0.0000000002911607	0.0000000000000219	0.0000000000000818	0.0000000000000237
F29	0.0000111765635760	0.0018352361800625	0.0024604768149038	0.0005667706273508
F30	0.0000000000000000	0.0000000000000000	0.0000000000000430	0.0000000000000000

The comparison of SBO, PSO, ABC and CK are given in the Tables 7-10 for the best optimum, mean optimum, standard deviation of mean optimum and mean iteration of the function evaluation respectively. SBO performs better for 26 benchmark optimization test functions except F2, F7, F10 and F11 which is shown in Table 6. The best optimum obtained for the benchmark functions by PSO is 16, ABC is 11 and CK is 17. Table 7 shows the mean of optima values obtained for 20 different turns by SBO, PSO, ABC and CK. It reveals that SBO gives the best mean values for 25 functions, PSO for 15, ABC for 9 and CK for 17 functions. SBO gives the best standard deviation of mean optimum values for 23 functions 18, 14 and 19 for PSO, ABC and CK respectively which are shown in Table 8. Table 9 shows the mean iteration of the function evaluation value obtained from SBO, PSO, ABC and CK. It shows that SBO gives minimum number of mean iteration for 21 functions, PSO for 6, ABC for 2 and CK for 1 function.

Figure 4 (Mean absolute error of algorithms) shows the overall evaluation is done by the Mean Absolute Error (MAE) values acquired by the algorithms. It is one of the widely used natural measures of average error magnitude. In the mean absolute error calculation, the absolute differences between the values found by the algorithms

Figure 4. Mean absolute error of algorithms

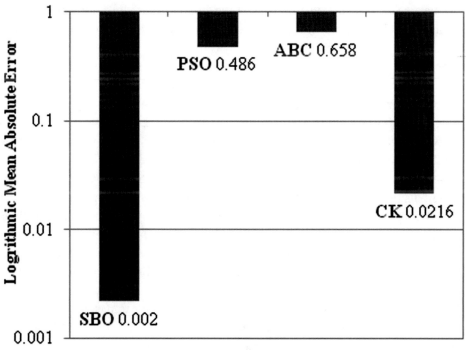

and the optimum of the corresponding functions were computed. Next, the total absolute errors were found for every algorithm. Eventually, the mean absolute error is calculated by dividing the total absolute error by the total number of test functions. Since there is a major difference between the mean absolute error values of the ABC algorithm, the graph in Figure 4 demonstrates the logarithmic error values obtained for the algorithms. It is understood that the SBO has the smallest mean absolute error. It means that when the results of all functions are evaluated together, the SBO algorithm outperforms the conventional evolutionary algorithms PSO, ABC and CK.

CONCLUSION

In this work a novel Stellar mass Black hole Optimization (SBO) is proposed and the performance is analyzed on the benchmark optimization test functions with PSO, ABC and CK. This optimization algorithm is realized from the properties of stellar mass black hole gravity's relentless pull. A black hole is a region of space-time from which nothing can escape, even light. The surface area of the event horizon / mass of a black hole can increase by absorbing matter. The two black holes can join to make a bigger black hole and one black hole can never split in two. During radiation the black hole's mass has decreased by the mass of the emitted particle, and the area of the event horizon has getting smaller. This algorithm considers the stellar mass black hole evolution through its properties absorption, radiation, coalescing and vanishing. SBO incorporates diversification by introducing new black holes in the population and intensification through combining the nearest black holes in the population. These properties avoid premature convergence. It has only few parameters to set. To analyze the performance of SBO it is experimented on benchmark optimization test functions and the results are demonstrated with state-of-art evolutionary algorithms PSO, ABC and CK. The experiment results show that the proposed SBO outperforms the PSO, ABC and CK.

SAME The number of benchmark functions that the SBO, PSO, ABC and CK algorithms provide equal values for the minimum *best optimum* parameter, *DIFF.* The number of benchmark functions that the SBO, PSO, ABC and CK algorithms provide different values for the minimum *best optimum* parameter.

SAME The number of benchmark functions that the SBO, PSO, ABC and CK algorithms provide equal values for the minimum *mean optimum* parameter, *DIFF.* The number of benchmark functions that the SBO, PSO, ABC and CK algorithms provide different values for the minimum *mean optimum* parameter.

SAME The number of benchmark functions that the SBO, PSO, ABC and CK algorithms provide equal values for the minimum *standard deviation of mean optimum* parameter, *DIFF.* The number of benchmark functions that the SBO, PSO,

Table 6. The mean iteration of the function evaluation value obtained from SBO, PSO, ABC and CK

No	SBO	PSO	ABC	CK
F1	18.70	287,335.00	676,613.60	747,320.00
F2	913341.60	21,550.00	1,209,937.00	64,115.00
F3	33.60	8,027.50	3,900.00	38,740.00
F4	34.70	8,505.00	10,288.75	43,420.00
F5	34.00	11,332.50	841,851.80	40,860.00
F6	776.65	16,192.50	1,068,879.25	46,005.00
F7	96884.25	7,277.50	6,492.00	42,735.00
F8	2000.45	109,8730.00	1,098,706.45	199,765.00
F9	529165.00	293,197.50	1,143,382.95	1,037,135.00
F10	843.80	7,817.50	68,610.80	17,545.00
F11	1078629.00	945,452.50	858,664.10	762,760.0
F12	36.45	212,505.00	43,0470.80	450,290.00
F13	113081.40	13,525.00	572,035.85	51,450.00
F14	115821.60	184,805.00	69,249.85	696,830.00
F15	6461.14	10,640.00	6,922.20	40,345.00
F16	537.35	24,962.50	1,079,579.85	41,055.00
F17	59733.80	8,127.50	73,930.25	33,565.00
F18	248709.20	12,51,597.50	886,792.15	1,954,575.00
F19	543.75	19,99,887.50	1,999,517.50	1,957,870.00
F20	544.70	1,395,240.00	1,036,051.25	1,879,165.00
F21	899.95	712,470.00	102,052.35	1,993,640.00
F22	28.95	1,999,950.00	965,998.00	1,497,570.00
F23	1036268.00	246,82.50	51,913.50	260,375.00
F24	26.70	640,845.00	504,695.75	955,790.00
F25	1114737.00	205,107.50	989,217.85	408,885.00
F26	2000.00	56,950.00	11,070.00	88,350.00
F27	235.15	197,022.50	1,004,375.15	393,375.00
F28	544.05	170,175.00	920,208.35	228,320.00
F29	2857.30	1,882,150.00	1,080,681.00	1,713,795.00
F30	538.70	123,570.00	1,945,944.40	221,570.00

Table 7. Comparison of the performances of the SBO, PSO, ABC and CK algorithms for the best optimum value

	SBO	PSO	ABC	CK
SAME	26 (for the functions of: F1, F3, F4, F5, F6, F8, F9, F12, F13, F14, F15, F16, F17, F18, F19, F20, F21, F22, F23, F24, F25, F26, F27, F28, F29, F30)	16 (for the functions of: F2, F3, F4, F5, F6, F7, F8, F10, F11, F12, F16, F23, F25, F26, F27, F30)	11(for the functions of: F3, F4, F5, F6, F7, F10, F12, F16, F21, F23, F26)	17 (for the functions of: F2, F3, F4, F5, F6, F7, F8, F10, F11, F12, F16, F22, F23, F25, F26, F27, F30)
DIFF.	4 (for the functions of: F2,F7,F10,F11)	14 (for the functions of: F1, F9, F13, F14, F15, F17, F18, F19, F20, F21, F22, F24, F28, F29)	19 (for the functions of: F1, F2, F8, F9, F11, F13, F14, F15, F17, F18, F19, F20, F22, F24, F25, F27, F28, F29, F30)	13 (for the functions of: F1, F9, F13, F14, F15, F17, F18, F19, F20, F21, F24, F28, F29)

Table 8. Comparison of the performances of the SBO, PSO, ABC and CK algorithms for the mean optimum value

	SBO	PSO	ABC	CK
SAME	25 (for the functions of: F1, F3, F4, F5, F6, F8, F9, F12, F13, F14, F15, F16, F17, F18, F19, F20, F21, F22, F23, F24, F25, F26, F27, F28, F30)	15 (for the functions of: F2, F3, F4, F5, F6, F7, F8, F10, F12, F16, F23, F25, F26, F27, F30)	9 (for the functions of: F3, F4, F6, F7, F10, F12, F21, F23, F26)	17 (for the functions of: F2, F3, F4, F5, F6, F7, F8, F11, F12, F16, F22, F23, F25, F26, F27, F29, F30)
DIFF.	5 (for the functions of: F2, F7, F10, F11, F29)	15 (for the functions of: F1, F9, F11, F12, F13, F14, F15, F17, F18, F19, F20, F21, F22, F24, F29)	21 (for the functions of: F1, F2, F5, F8, F9, F11, F13, F14, F15, F16, F17, F18, F19, F20, F22, F24, F25, F27, F28, F29, F30)	13 (for the functions of: F1, F9, F10, F13, F14, F15, F17, F18, F19, F20, F21, F24, F28)

Table 9. Comparison of the performances of the SBO, PSO, ABC and CK algorithms for the standard deviation of mean optimum value

	SBO	PSO	ABC	CK
SAME	23 (for the functions of: F1, F3, F4, F5, F6, F8, F9, F11, F12, F15, F16, F17, F18, F19, F20, F21, F22, F23, F25, F26, F27, F29, F30)	18 (for the functions of: F1, F2, F3, F4, F5, F6, F7, F8, F10, F15, F16, F17, F23, F25, F26, F27, F28, F30)	14 (for the functions of: F3, F4, F6, F7, F10, F12, F13, F14, F15, F16, F17, F21, F23, F26)	19 (for the functions of: F1, F2, F3, F4, F5, F6, F7, F8, F12, F15, F16, F17, F22, F23, F24, F25, F26, F27, F30)
DIFF.	7 (for the functions of: F2, F7, F10, F13, F14, F24, F28)	12 (for the functions of: F9, F11, F12, F13, F14, F18, F19, F20, F21, F22, F24, F29)	16 (for the functions of: F1, F2, F5, F8, F9, F11, F18, F19, F20, F22, F24, F25, F27, F28, F29, F30)	11 (for the functions of: F9, F10, F11, F13, F14, F18, F19, F20, F21, F28, F29)

Table 10. Comparison of the performances of the SBO, PSO, ABC and CK algorithms for the mean iteration of the function evaluation value

	SBO	PSO	ABC	CK
SAME	21 (for the functions of: F1, F3, F4, F5, F6, F8, F10, F12, F15, F16, F18, F19, F20, F21, F22, F24, F26, F27, F28, F29, F30)	6 (for the functions of: F2, F9, F13, F17, F23, F25)	2 (for the functions of: F7, F14)	1 (for the functions of: F11)
DIFF.	9 (for the functions of: F2, F7, F9, F11, F13, F14, F23, F25, F28)	24 (for the functions of: F1, F3, F4, F5, F6, F7, F8, F10, F11, F12, F14, F15, F16, F18, F19, F20, F21, F22, F24, F26, F27, F28, F29, F30)	28 (for the functions of F1, F2, F3, F4, F5, F6, F8, F9, F10, F11, F12, F13, F15, F16, F17, F18, F19, F20, F21, F22, F23, F24, F25, F26, F27, F28, F29, F30)	29 (for the functions of: F1, F2, F3, F4, F5, F7, F6, F8, F9, F10, F12, F13, F14, F15, F16, F17, F18, F19, F20, F21, F22, F23, F24, F25, F26, F27, F28, F29, F30)

ABC and CK algorithms provide different values for the minimum *standard deviation of mean optimum* parameter.

SAME The number of benchmark functions that the SBO, PSO, ABC and CK algorithms provide equal values for the *mean iteration of the function evaluation* parameter, *DIFF*. The number of benchmark functions that the SBO, PSO, ABC and CK algorithms provide different values for the *mean iteration of the function evaluation* parameter.

REFERENCES

Avriel, M. (2008). *Nonlinear Programming: Analysis and Methods*. Dover Publishing.

Bertsekas. (2000). Dynamic Programming and Optimal Control. Athena Scientific.

Chaisson & McMillan. (n.d.). Astronomy Today: Stars and Galaxies. *Benjamin-Cummings*.

Civicioglu, P., & Besdok, E. (2011). A conceptual comparison of the Cuckoo-search, particle swarm optimization, differential evolution and artificial bee colony algorithms. *Artificial Intelligence Review*, *39*(4), 315–346. doi:10.1007/s10462-011-9276-0

Colorni, , Dorigo, & Maniezzo. (1992). An Investigation of some Properties of an Ant Algorithm. *Proc. of the Parallel Problem Solving from Nature Conference*, 509 – 520.

Dorigo, M., Maniezzo, V., & Colorni, A. (1996). Ant System: Optimization by a colony of cooperating agents. *IEEE Trans. on Systems, Man, and Cybernetics – Part B.*, *26*(1), 29–41. doi:10.1109/3477.484436 PMID:18263004

Erwin Diewert, W. (2008). Cost functions. In *The New Palgrave Dictionary of Economics*. Palgrave McMillan.

Fogel, Owens, & Walsh. (1996). *Artificial Intelligence through Simulated Evolution*. John Wiley.

Fred, G. (1996). Future Paths for Integer Programming and Links to Artificial Intelligence. *Computers & Operations Research*, *13*, 533–549.

Goss, S., Aron, S., Deneubourg, J. L., & Pasteels, J. M. (1989). Self-organized shortcuts in the Argentine ant. *Naturwissenschaften*, *76*(12), 579–581. doi:10.1007/BF00462870

Gottesman, D. (1996). *Stabilizer codes and quantum error correction,quant-ph/9705052* (PhD Thesis). Cal Tech.

Hamilton, A. J. S. (1998). The Evolving Universe. Kluwer Academic.

Hastings, W. K. (1970). Monte Carlo Sampling Methods Using Markov Chains and Their Applications. *Biometrika, 57*(1), 197–109. doi:10.1093/biomet/57.1.97

Hawking & Penrose. (1970). The Singularities of Gravitational Collapse and Cosmology. *Proc. of the Royal Society A: Mathematical, Physical and Engineering Sciences, 314*(1519), 529 – 548.

Hawking, S. W. (1974). Black hole explosions? *Nature, 248*(5443), 30–31. doi:10.1038/248030a0

Hehl, F., Kiefer, C., & Metzler, R. (1998). *Black Holes: A General Introduction.* Lecture Notes in Physics.

Holland, J. H. (1975). *Adaptation in Natural and Artificial Systems: An Introductory Analysis with Applications to Biology, Control, and Artificial Intelligence.* Ann Arbor, MI: University of Michigan Press.

Karaboga, D., & Basturk, B. (2007). A powerful and efficient algorithm for numerical function optimization: Artificial bee colony (abc) algorithm. *Journal of Global Optimization, 39*(3), 459–471. doi:10.1007/s10898-007-9149-x

Karaboga, D., & Basturk, B. (2009a). A comparative study of artificial bee colony algorithm. *Applied Mathematics and Computation, 214*(1), 108–132. doi:10.1016/j.amc.2009.03.090

Kennedy, J., & Eberhart, R. C. (1995). Particle swarm optimization. *Proc. of IEEE International Conference on Neural Networks,* 1942 – 1948. doi:10.1109/ICNN.1995.488968

Kirkpatrick, S., Gelatt, C. D., & Vecchi, M. P. (1983). Optimization by Simulated Annealing. *Science, 220*(4598), 671–679. doi:10.1126/science.220.4598.671 PMID:17813860

Koza, J. R. (1992). *Genetic Programming: on the Programming of Computers by Means of Natural Selection.* MIT Press.

Metropolis, N., Rosenbluth, A. W., Rosenbluth, M. N., Teller, A. H., & Teller, E. (1953). Equations of State Calculations by Fast Computing Machines. *The Journal of Chemical Physics, 21*(6), 1087–1092. doi:10.1063/1.1699114

Michell, J., & Laplace, P. S. (1998). Black Holes: A General Introduction. Lecture Notes in Physics, 514, 3 – 34.

Nelder, J. A., & Mead, R. (1965). A Simplex Method for Function Minimization. *J. Computing.*, *7*(4), 308–313. doi:10.1093/comjnl/7.4.308

Newman. (2008). Indirect utility function. New York: The New Palgrave Dictionary of Economics.

Nocedal, J., & Wright, S. J. (1999). *Numerical Optimization, Springer Series in Operations Research and financial engineering.* Springer.

Osman & Laporte. (1996). Metaheuristics: A bibliography. *Ann. Oper. Res., 63*(5), 511 – 623.

Rashedi, E., Nezamabadi-Pour, H., & Saryazdi, S. (2009). GSA: A gravitational search algorithm. *Inform. Science.*, *179*(13), 2232–2248. doi:10.1016/j.ins.2009.03.004

Rechenberg. (1965). *Cybernetic Solution Path of an Experimental Problem.* Ministry of Aviation, Royal Aircraft Establishment.

Reynolds, C. W. (1987). Flocks, herbs, and schools: A distributed behavioral model. *Comput. Graph.*, *21*(4), 25–34. doi:10.1145/37402.37406

Schrijver. (1998). Theory of Linear and Integer Programming. John Wiley & Sons.

Storn, R., & Price, K. (1996). Minimizing the real functions of the ICEC'96 contest by Differential Evolution. *IEEE Conference on Evolutionary Computation*, 842 – 844. doi:10.1109/ICEC.1996.542711

Wheeler, J. A. (2000). *Exploring Black Holes: Introduction to General Relativity.* Addison Wesley.

Wilson, E. O. (1975). *Sociobiology: The new synthesis.* Belknap Press.

Yang & Deb. (2010). Engineering optimisation by Cuckoo search. *Int. J. Math. Modell. Numerical Optimization, 1*, 330 – 343.

Yang, X. S. (2008). *Nature-Inspired Metaheuristic Algorithms.* Luniver Press.

Section 2
Bio–Inspired Computational Techniques

Bio-Inspired computational techniques usually take motivation from various biological systems or processes existing in nature. The motivating features of biological systems or processes include adaptability and robustness that attracts to mimic them to develop computational techniques based upon them. Artificial Immune Systems, Viral Systems, foraging behaviour of mammals, hunting strategy adopted by predators etc. form the basis of some interesting biology-inspired computational techniques.

Chapter 4
Recent Advances in Artificial Immune Systems:
Models, Algorithms, and Applications

Florin Popentiu Vladicescu
Academy of Romanian Scientists, Romania

Grigore Albeanu
"Spiru Haret" University, Romania

ABSTRACT

The designers of Artificial Immune Systems (AIS) had been inspired from the properties of natural immune systems: self-organization, adaptation and diversity, learning by continual exposure, knowledge extraction and generalization, clonal selection, networking and meta-dynamics, knowledge of self and non-self, etc. The aim of this chapter, along its sections, is to describe the principles of artificial immune systems, the most representational data structures (for the representation of antibodies and antigens), suitable metrics (which quantifies the interactions between components of the AIS) and their properties, AIS specific algorithms and their characteristics, some hybrid computational schemes (based on various soft computing methods and techniques like artificial neural networks, fuzzy and intuitionistic-fuzzy systems, evolutionary computation, and genetic algorithms), both standard and extended AIS models/architectures, and AIS applications, in the end.

DOI: 10.4018/978-1-5225-2322-2.ch004

INTRODUCTION

The designers of Artificial Immune Systems had been inspired from the properties of natural immune systems: self-organization, adaptation and diversity, learning by continual exposure, knowledge extraction and generalization, clonal selection, networking and meta-dynamics, knowledge of self and non-self etc. They already had and continuously have to solve technical issues like knowledge representation, the development of suitable evolutionary algorithms, the identification of adequate metrics to differentiate various entities, the development of specialized algorithms tailored on some particular problem, and the design and implementation of AIS simulation frameworks.

The aim of this chapter, along its sections, is to describe the principles of artificial immune systems, the most representational data structures (for the representation of antibodies and antigens), suitable metrics (which quantifies the interactions between components of the AIS) and their properties, AIS specific algorithms and their characteristics, some hybrid computational schemes (based on various soft computing methods and techniques like artificial neural networks, fuzzy and intuitionistic-fuzzy systems, evolutionary computation, and genetic algorithms), both standard and extended AIS models/architectures, and AIS applications, in the end.

Details on the following classes of algorithms are given: (1) clonal selection class: Clonal Selection Algorithm (clonAlg); (2) self and non-self discrimination class: Negative Selection Algorithm (NSA); (3) Immune network theory class: Artificial Immune Network Algorithm (aiNET), Optimization Artificial Immune Network Algorithm (opt-aiNET); and 4) Danger theory class: Dendritic Cell Algorithm (DCA).

Variations of immune algorithms proposed by authors include IF-GAIN (intuitionistic-fuzzy general artificial immune algorithm), the usage of Pompeiu-Hausdorf (Danet, 2012). distance in Positive Selection type algorithms, particular architectures of AIS oriented to some real world applications.

New applications of artificial immune models are included with strong interest on software testing and learning in virtual environments. The work ends with concluding remarks on main ideas on AIS design and applications.

PRINCIPLES OF ARTIFICIAL IMMUNE SYSTEMS

Developing competitive algorithms for solving classification or optimization problems, using ideas inspired from immunology, asks for a deep understanding of both the mechanism discovered by immunologists and the models of AIS proposed by computer scientists. The next subsections describes the elements of the natural immune system and the proposed theories, the basics of artificial immune systems, and the design of computing processes as artificial immune algorithms.

Systemic Models of Immunity

The neutralization of pathogens is an important task not only for human body, but also for plants, invertebrates and vertebrates. It is already known the multilayer structure of the vertebrates and human immunity system: physical layer (skin and mucous membranes), innate layer (based on non-specific defense mechanisms: secretions, chemical signals etc.), and adaptive layer (based on specific mechanisms which are invaders oriented).

However, the plant immunity is assured by only two interacting systems: the recognizer system (based on Pattern Recognition Receptors (PRRs) located on the surface of plant cells – the physical layer), and the innate immunity system (composed by NB-LRR (Nucleotide-Binding site plus Leucine-Rich Repeat) proteins assuring the resistance on specific diseases, according to Twycross and Aickelin (2007).

A four-phase process is running in order to assure the plant immunity:

1. The pathogen recognition and sending the initial response (IR);
2. The pathogen spreading by effectors and suppressing the response;
3. The pathogen is recognized by NB-LRR protein and the immunity specialized effectors – the *Avirulence* protein (Avr) - is initiated (both *direct recognition* of Avr proteins by NB-LRR proteins, band *indirect recognition*: in this case, NB-LRR proteins are activated by products of the action of Avr proteins on the host based on guarding-activation scheme);
4. The selection mechanism will improve the plant immunity.

Plants also possess an array of mechanisms suited to protect them against herbivores such as insects and mammals. The recognition of self produces a response. However, the recognition of non-self does not produce a response. Moreover, the hermaphroditic plants (most flowering species) have developed recognition mechanisms to prevent inbreeding (by a self-incompatibility system).

Studies of invertebrate immune systems have demonstrated the existence of characteristics specific to vertebrates even the invertebrates have no adaptive immune system, as Twycross and Aickelin (2007) presented. An immune response to a pathogen is active after the recognition of an associated molecule called an *antigen* (Timmis et al, 2008). Hence, both invertebrate and vertebrate immune systems have evolved different mechanisms that provide antigen-specific memory and protection. Two different types of responses to antigens are possible: *humoral response* (by producing of antibodies through plasma cells) and *cell-mediated response* (depending on the specific action of Lymphocytes rather than antibodies).

According to immunologists, the main elements of the human immune system are (Broere et al, 2011; Dasgupta, 1999; Dasgupta and Nino, 2009; Zimmermann, 2014):

1. *Lymphocytes* (TCells: TKillers/THelpers and BCells);
2. *Memory Cells* (the immunological memory);
3. The *Major Histocompatibility Complex* (MHC);
4. *Antigen Presenting Cells* (APC) or macrophages, and
5. *Antibodies* (produced by BCells as immune response to an APC presented antigen).

The main function of MHC molecules is to bind to peptide fragments derived from pathogens in order to be recognized by the appropriate TCells. THelpers are specialized in recognition of antigens (in order to prevent infections/faults) and TKillers are able to destroy the infectious structures. Recently, The researchers proved that Natural Killer cells (NKCells) play a major role in the host-rejection of both tumors and virally infected cells (by herpes viruses and adenoviruses). NKCells are neither TCells nor BCells. More specific details on NKCells can be found in the paper of Lotze and Thomson (2010).

The lymphocytes BCells are involved in the humoral immune response, and the lymphocytes TCells are involved in the cell-mediated immune response. NKCells are critical in first line immunological defenses, according to Spits et al (2012). Therefore, the innate immune system should act as a *controller* of the immune system of plants, invertebrates, and vertebrates.

The most important rules of the controller have to model the following principles:

1. The immune system provides the body protection by *discriminating self from non-self* (pathogens: viruses, bacteria, altered self, etc.);
2. The *immature to mature evolution* of some constituents of the immune system;
3. Innate immune system *antigen presenting cells* (APCs), especially *dendritic cells*, are the principal controllers of the immune system;
4. *The immune system is a protector*, and the innate immune system has a central role in the generation of protection;
5. The immune system is a *maintenance* or *homeostatic system*; the function of the immune system is *tissue homeostasis*: all cells are able to signal the neighbors, when necessary.

These principles have been motivated by some considerations like CST (clonal selection theory), NST (negative selection theory), INT (immune network theory), and DT (danger theory), to be described below.

The clonal selection theory introduced by Burnet (1957, 1959) can explain how immunological memory permits a rapid response upon a second exposure to an antigen. Clones of BCells created and transformed by somatic hyper-mutation will introduce the diversity into the BCell population. There are produced two types of cells: plasma and memory cells. Plasma cells produce antibodies (which are antigen-specific) and, in a successful immune response, lead to the removal of the antigen. Memory cells remain within the body and assure, when necessary, a rapid secondary response.

As Timmis et al (2008) and Dasgupta et al (2011) described, the negative selection principle deals with the system's ability to detect unknown pathogens while not reacting to the self cells based on a censoring process (only TCells that do not bind to self-proteins are allowed to leave the thymus and circulate through the body in order to assure the protection against foreign antigens, while TCells that react against self cells are destroyed).

The immune network theory, proposed by Jerne (1974), is based on the hypothesis that the immune system maintains a network of B-cells interconnected (when their affinities exceed a certain threshold) in order to recognize antigens, and making use of stimulation/suppression operations in order to stabilize the network. Even this theory was refined; the idiotypic network theory is no longer widely accepted by immunologists (see (Langman and Cohn (1986), Timmis et al (2008)).

A popular immunity model among immunologists is based on danger theory and was firstly described by Matzinger (2002): antigen presenting cells (APCs) are activated by danger/alarm signals from injured cells, such as those exposed to pathogens, toxins, mechanical damage, and so forth, as Dasgupta et al (2011) emphasized. However, the exact nature of the danger signal is unclear as Matzinger (2002) mentioned. It is also difficult to discriminate danger from non-danger.

Basics of Artificial Immune Systems

According to Freitas & Timmis (2003), artificial immune systems (AISs) design will permit to solve practical problems using algorithms inspired from biological immune systems, and not for simulating biological phenomena. In this view, AISs follow a particular design depending on the problem to be solved, and the behavior of the system depends on a specific immune algorithm. However, any artificial immune system considers antigen and antibody models, affinity measures, and evolutionary algorithms inspired from biological immune processes.

Due to the pattern matching nature of the recognition process, the models for antigen and antibody will present common features at least at subset (ordered subset, subsequence, substring or chain) level.

Tarakanov et al (2003) presented a formal description of such models. Their "formal protein" model has an algebraic structure based on quaternions and is able to compute the free energy of every protein. Formal immune networks were defined over formal B-cells/T-cells, and free formal proteins. The evolution of these formal cells may use specific rewriting systems like attributive grammars in order to compute a "formal immune response" (see also Jerne (1984), the Nobel lecture).

Other proposals made use of sets of features (numerical, and/or categorical) in order to use metric spaces techniques, or string processing algorithms. An overview on representations of the following types: binary strings (common to genetic inspired approaches), strings over general finite alphabets, real-valued arrays (elements of a vector space), and hybrid representations (structures or records of relational databases with fields of various types) was presented by Dasgupta and Nino (2009). See also Brusic and Petrovsky (2003) for more considerations on data models for immune-informatics.

Variable length arrays/structures are used to model immune entities in artificial immune systems, as proposed for some specific immune algorithms; see Brownlee (2005). According to the above types of representation, depending on the selected representation, and the requirements of the problem under analyze, a *shape space* is necessary to be designed (item representation, topological operators etc.).

Detection, recognition and the classification are usual activities performed during decision process in artificial immune systems and use specific instruments like similarity measures or distance models. In the following, we review common similarity measures.

A common shape space in uses binary sequences of length N. Let x and y be two binary sequences of length N, and:

- a be the proportion of 1s that the variables share in the same positions (positive matching),
- b be the proportion of 1s in the first variable and 0s in second variable in the same positions,
- c be the proportion of 0s in the first variable and 1s in second variable in the same positions, and
- d be the proportion of 0s that both variables share in the same positions (interpreted as negative matching, when the binary variable describes the absence of a feature or attribute, in this case the d quantity is not used for computing an affinity index).

Since a, b, c and d are proportions then $a+b+c+d=1$. These quantities define "affinity" measures when the binary sequences are used to model antigens/antibodies/cells/proteins, as below:

1. **Hamming Distance $d_H(x,y)$:** The number of "non-matching" positions (*xor* operator when x and y are binary models) – "small" distance determines "large" affinity;
2. **Jaccard's Affinity Index (1912):** $S_J = a / (a+b+c) = a/(1-d)$;
3. **Sokal and Michener's Affinity Index (1958):** $S_{SM} = (a+d) / (a+b+c+d) = (a+d)$;
4. **Sokal and Sneath's Affinity Index (1963):** $S_{SS} = 2(a+d)/(2a+b+c+2d) = 2(a+d)/(a+d+1)$;
5. **Rogers and Tanimoto's Affinity Index (1960):** $S_{RT} = (a+d)/(a+2(b+c)+d) = (a+d) /(1 +b+c)$;
6. **Rusel and Rao's Affinity Index (1940):** $S_{RR}= a / (a+b+c+d) = a$;
7. **Kulczynski's Affinity Index (1927):** $S_K = (a/(a+b)+a/(a+c))/2$;
8. **Yule's Affinity Index (1900):** $S_Y = (ad-bc)/(ad+bc)$.

It is easy observed, for the binary shape space, that if $x = y$ then $d_H(x, y) = 0$, and all affinity measures are computed as one (unity).

Other representation uses sequence of positive integer values, as shown by Harmer et al (2002), associated to biochemical or physical structures. Given two sequences x and y, these can be compared using a sliding window of size N (the positions inside the window being denoted by $\{(X_i, Y_i), i = 1, 2, …, N\}$, and one of the following landscape-affinity measures:

1. The *difference-matching index* $S_{dif} = \sum\{abs(X_i-Y_i), i=1, 2, …, N\}$, where *abs* denote the absolute value or modulus;
2. The *slope matching index* $S_{slope} = \sum\{abs[(X_{i+1}-X_i)-(Y_{i+1}-Y_i)], i=1, 2, …, N-1\}$;
3. The *physical matching index* $S_{physical} = \sum\{(X_i-Y_i), i=1, 2, …, N\}+3 \min\{abs(X_i-Y_i), i = 1, 2, …, N\}$.

Let us consider a general string representation over a general alphabet U, x and y be two strings and N contiguous positions from x and y denoted by $\{(X_i, Y_i), i = 1, 2, …, N\}$. An affinity measure among x and y can be defined by the *Levenshtein distance*: the minimum number of single-character edits (by insertion, deletion or substitution) for changing x into y, when consider only the window of size N (Levenshtein, 1966).

Another matching rule is the *r* contiguous block (rcb) matching rule (Percus et al. (1993), see (Dasgupta and Nino, 2009): let be *x* and *y* are equal-length strings over a finite alphabet, then x and y are similar if x and y agree in at least r contiguous locations.

Affinity measures can also use the degree of similarity of every symbol X_i with elements in U (in a fuzzy modeling). Let $s(X_i, a)$ be the similarity degree of X_i with a (a in U). The influence (weight) of X_i is defined by $h(X_i) = \sum \{s(X_i, a)$, all a in U$\}$ (also an Euclidian alternative can be considered: $h(X_i) = \mathrm{sqrt}(\sum \{s^2(X_i, a)$, all a in U$\}))$. Let p_i be the impact of the symbols on the ith position $p_i = \sum \{abs(s(X_i, a) - s(Y_i, a))$, a in U$)$, $d_X(x, y) = \sum \{p_i h(X_i), i = 1, 2, ..., N\}$, $d_Y(x, y) = \sum \{p_i h(Y_i), i = 1, 2, ..., N\}$. The affinity measure can be defined by $d(x,y) = (d_X(x, y) + d_Y(x,y))/2$, inspired by the value difference metric of Hamaker and Boggess (2004).

The analysis is simpler when the shape space is modeled by real-valued metric space, endowed with a distance like: Euclidean (d_2), Minkowski (d_1), general d_k-distance, or Chebyshev (d_∞), where $d_k = \mathrm{pow}(\sum\{abs(X_i-Y_i)^k; i=1, 2, ..., N\}, 1/k)$, and $pow(u,v)$ stands for u^v, k is a natural number, and $d_\infty(x,y) = \max\{abs(X_i-Y_i), i = 1, 2, ..., N\}$. The affinity will be measured taking into account the distance between the antigen and antibody/cell/protein assuring the immune response.

Artificial Immune Computing Processes

Computing in immunological frameworks imposes not only representational schemes, and affinity metrics, but also processing algorithms applied to populations of antigens and various cells assuring artificial immune functions.

Two main challenging problems should be implemented by artificial immune systems: differentiation between self (the system under protection) and non-self (the invaders/intruders/pathogens), and differentiation between danger and not danger.

Depending on the application field, the self test should be implemented by some logically evaluated function: *self*(x) is *true* when x is not an intruder, and *false,* otherwise. A database of non-self entities (the signature file of antivirus software or non-trusted IP addresses / domains), or a database of specific behavior of non-self entities should be maintained. Some examples of non-self entities consist of opening communication ports or trying to access locations (memory, files, external connections) which are not permitted (unknown by the system under protection, or listed in a signature database).

Self and non-self, from computational point of view, are treated like static components. However, when consider aspects related to dangerous theories, the dynamic aspect should be considered. Firstly, we consider the differentiation concerning self and non-self entities. The dynamic evolution of the self is modeled as an expert system with capability of *insert/delete* rules of behavior.

The process of differentiation between self and non-self has two main phases: positive selection (PS) and negative selection (NS). When a population of Tcells are generated, if one TCell fails to recognize any of the MHC molecules it is removed, only the MHC recognizers are kept. This is the PS phase. However, if there are TCells recognizing combinations of MHC and self-peptides, these are removed; only non-recognizers are kept. This is the filtering process of the NS phase. A first computational model of self/non-self discrimination was proposed by Forrest et al. (1994): the "NSA - negative selection algorithm". Based on an initial database of self-entities, a random generator, and a monitoring scheme, two subroutines are designed and serial connected in order to fulfill the NSA objective. Let S be the data base on self-entities. Using a random generation scheme, a new data base D of detectors is built, according to the rule R1. The monitoring step analyses input samples and classifies them in "self" or "non-self", according to the rule R2.

R1. While not enough detectors then generate a random candidate and if not match self-samples from S then add to the database D.

R2. For every new input sample x, if x matches any detector then x belongs to "non-self", otherwise x belongs to the "self" class.

The monitoring rule can be implemented using a crisp approach (where matching is applied as in previous subsection), a fuzzy approach (using fuzzy entities as introduced by Zadeh(1965)), or an intuitionistic-fuzzy approach (Atanassov 1986; Mahapatra, 2009), through linguistic variables associated to the attributes of entities stored in a specific database. Let **low**, **medium**, and **high** be linguistic variables, and (a, b, c) be attributes of a sample x to be monitored. An example of fuzzy monitoring rule is: *if (a is**low**or**medium**) and (b is**high**) and (c is**medium**) then x is "non-self"*. A truth level *t* is computed when a pure fuzzy approach is used (as Gonzales (2003) described), or a pair of values (f, t) can be obtained in an intuitionistic-fuzzy – based methodology, where *f* stands for the degree of non-membership and *t* is the membership degree to the "non-self" intuitionistic-fuzzy set *(t+f ≤ 1)*.

Also, positive selection algorithms (PSAs) can be designed to be used for pattern recognition, classification, and clustering. In this case, the detectors work for the recognition of "self" entities, using distance inter items, or distance to the "cluster centroid" when appropriate. A possible extension to cluster classification is based on inter-cluster distance based on the definition introduced by Pompeiu and Haussdorf.

Other processing methods are inspired from clonal selection theory of Burnet (1959) which describes the response of BCells to antigens. Clonal selection algoritms (CSAs) are particular evolutionary algorithms, also population based, that provide a collection of suitable antibodies in order to solve a given optimization problem. The model of both antigens and antibodies consists of a set of attributes which are represented as a n-dimensional array. The affinity measure is based on a similarity formula.

In order to describe a generic CSA (example: clonAlg of De Castro and Zuben (2000)), let be AB - the generic data collection of antibodies, Ag - a generic antigen, f – the affinity data: f_i = affinity(x_i, Ag), where x_i is a generic antibody from AB, and n – the number of the antibodies having the highest affinity, C_i the set of clones of the antibody x_i, C_i^* - the set of mature clones of the antibody x_i. The main steps of the clonAlg are:

1. Create AB = initial random population of antibodies;
2. While not stop_condition do for each antigen Ag execute steps 2.1 to 2.4
   a. affinity_evaluation(Ag, AB, f);
   b. selection_and_cloning(AB, n, C);
   c. hypermutation(C, C*);
   d. diversification(AB).

During affinity evaluation, for every x_i in AB the affinity of x_i with Ag is computed and stored in f_i. In step 2.2, the antibodies with highest affinity are selected (n of them), every selected antibody is multiplied (cloned) with a rate directly proportional to its affinity and C is the collection of all generated clones which are mutated in step 2.3 with a rate inversely proportional to their affinity and stored in C*. The diversification process will add the best clones of C* to AB, and replace from AB those antibodies with lowest affinity by randomly generated new antibodies.

The clonAlg computational process can be adapted to a specific problem in order to recognize patterns or to optimize multimodal functions.

Another computational processes inspired from immune systems address the immune networks (INs). Immune networks can be viewed as graphs whose nodes are antibodies, the edges describe the interaction between antibodies, and arrows are used to show the external stimulation of antigens. Two categories of IN model were developed by researchers: *continuous models* – described by differential equations useful to modelling a biological phenomenon, and *discrete functional models* – suitable to solve computational problems. In the following we are interested in discrete models and we will identify them as *artificial immune networks* (AINs). The first AIN model was proposed by Hunt and Cooke (1996) where the nodes are BCells interacting according to their affinities (computing by a Hamming based metric). Timmis and Neal (2001) use real-valued vectors to model BCells and antigens, the Euclidean metric in order to measure the BCells affinity and the interaction between an antibody and an antigen, and a network affinity threshold (NAT) to select only strongest connections to be considered for computing the stimulation level of antibodies. Their computational model was called AINE, and the explosion in BCells population was experienced. The RAIN (resource-limited AIN) computing process was proposed to eliminate the drawbacks of AINE by Timmis et al. (2000).

The network nodes are *artificial recognition balls* (ARBs) that contain a number of identical BCells. The model is endowed with a resource pool (of BCells) with a centralized control, the ARBs are competing in order to gain resources, according to the following steps:

1. Create an initial network of BCells;
2. For each antigen do
    a. For each network cell determine the stimulation level;
    b. Eliminate those network cells with low stimulation level (via the resource allocator);
    c. Select the most stimulated cells and reproduce them according to their stimulation level;
    d. Mutate each clone inversely proportional to its stimulation level;
    e. Select mutated clones to be incorporated into the network.
3. Repeat step 2 until a stopping criterion met.

An alternative approach to RAIN is aiNET proposed by De Castro and Von Zuben (2001) using the affinity concept in the place of stimulation concept: if the affinity between two antibodies is over a specified threshold then only one antibody will be kept in network.

Opt-aiNET is a variant of aiNET proposed by De Castro and Timmis (2002) for solving optimization problems. A fitness function is used to evaluate each BCell (encoded as real-valued vector in a Euclidian space) based on the objective function to be optimized. Opt-aiNET maintains a memory set of BCells associated to good values of the objective function and the network evolves until it reaches a stable state:

1. Initially, create a random population P of BCells;
2. Repeat steps 2.1 to 2.9 until a stopping condition is satisfied:
    a. Compute the fitness of every BCells in P and normalize the vector of all BCells fitness;
    b. For each BCell in P generate a number of clones and add new clones to P;
    c. Mutate every clone from P proportional to the parent fitness and add the mutated cell to P;
    d. Reevaluate the fitness of all members of P (including mutated clones);
    e. Remove from P the clones with lowest fitness;
    f. Compute average fitness of the BCells stored in P;
    g. Remove from P those BCells whose affinities are below a suppression threshold (based on network connections);
    h. Determine the set of memory BCells;
    i. Add new randomly generated BCells into the network.

Opt-aiNet is an immune network based procedure that uses a Gaussian mutation approach that is inversely proportional to the normalized fitness of each parent cell. Other mutation strategies can be used to improve the cells variability.

Nasraoui et al. (2002) extended AINE model in order to deal with uncertainty and fuzziness inherent in the matching process between antibodies and antigens, and called this model as fuzzyAINE. The fuzzyAINE process consists of the following steps:

1. Create: 1) an initial network; 2) the initial set of ARBs based on the input antigen data set. Every ARB, identified by *i,* has its own radius of influence σ_i, and the membership function associated to this ARB depends on the distance from antigen to the center of ARB according to a radial-basis-type model.
2. For each antigen do
    a. For each fuzzy ARB compute its stimulation level and update its influence radius;
    b. Allocate BCells to fuzzy ARB's based on stimulation level and remove those fuzzy ARBs with low stimulation level;
    c. Select most stimulated fuzzy ARBs and reproduce them in proportion to their stimulation level. The radius of influence of cloned ARBs is inherited from the corresponding parent;
    d. Mutate each fuzzy ARB inversely proportional to its stimulation level;
    e. Select mutated fuzzy ARBs to be included in the network;
    f. For each pair of ARBs do merge two ARBs in a single fuzzy ARB if and only if the affinity between the ARBs is less than a threshold. The merging strategy can use crossover operation based on center/radius of influence components.
3. Repeat step 2 until a stopping criterion met.

The above ideas were considered by Gonzales et al. (2005) in their GAIN (General Artificial Immune Network) algorithm having as input a set of antigens and producing as output a stable immune network consisting of BCells.

In order to make GAIN more robust to noise and outliers, intuitionistic-fuzzy (IF) aspects can be incorporated. The usage of Triangular Intuitionistic Fuzzy Numbers for modeling linguistic variables (very small, small, medium, large, very large) is a good choice. The intuitionistic-fuzzification is applied to all computed levels: affinity, stimulation, and suppression. The steps of the new IF-GAIN algorithm are:

1. Input A – the set of antigens;
2. Create: 1) B = the initial set of BCells; 2) L = the initial network of BCells;
3. For any *a* in A do
    a. For any *b* in B compute the affinity degree of *a* and *b*: affinity(*a*, *b*);

b. For any b in B compute the stimulation level stimulation_$f_A(b, a)$ as a function of the affinity(a, b);

c. For any b and b' in B compute the stimulation level stimulation_$f_B(b, b')$ and the suppression level suppression_$f_B(b, b')$.

d. For any b in B compute the total stimulation level $F(b)$ as an intuitionistic-fuzzy operator applied to all stimulation levels involving the vertex b of the network: the antigens connected to b ($_f_A$), other BCells b' which are connected to b (using both stimulation and suppression levels $_f_B$).

e. For any b in B such as affinity(a, b) is large do create f_cloning(b) clones of the BCell b, mutate them, and calculate the simulation level of all new generated BCells;

f. Add/Remove those BCells with large/low stimulation level and update the network L.

4. Repeat step 3 until a stopping criterion is met. Output B and L.

The summation operator used in step 3.4 works according to Mahapatra (2009), when triangular intuitionistic fuzzy numbers are used: if $x = (x_1, x_2, x_3; x', x'')$ and $y = (y_1, y_2, y_3; y', y'')$ are triangular intuitionistic-fuzzy numbers, then x+y, as triangular intuitionistic fuzzy number is obtained by $(x_1+y_1, x_2+y_2, x_3+y_3; x'+y', x''+y'')$, where the membership degree of x is given by $\mu_x(t) = \{(t-x_1)/(x_2-x_1)$ if t in $[x_1, x_2]; (x_3-t)/(x_3-x_2)$ if t in $[x_2, x_3]; 0$ otherwise$\}$, and the non-membership degree of x is given by $\nu_x(t) = \{(x_2-t)/(x_2-x')$ if t in $[x', x_2]; (t-x_2)/(x''-x_2)$ if t in $[x_2, x'']$, 1 otherwise$\}$.

The IF-GAIN algorithm is similar to GAIN, only improvements in noise (imprecision) and outliers' behavior are obtained. When applied to optimization problems the affinity operator will be connected to the objective function values.

The last immune computational type process is based on danger theory (DT) of Matzinger (2002) and integrates dendritic cells (DCs) into a Dendritic Cell Algorithm (DCA), as introduced by Greensmith (2007). The DT suggests that APCs (like THelper cells) activate an alarm signal providing the required costimulation (CSM) of antigens to respond. These signals are termed PAMPs (pathogenic associated molecular patterns) and act as biological signatures of potential intrusion. DCs belongs to the innate immune system that respond to some specific form of danger signals and can be of the following type: immature – collecting parts of the antigen and the signals; semi-mature – deciding on safe and tolerance state; mature – deciding on danger and reactive response state. According to Brownlee (2011), the classification of input patterns in normal or anomalous is the result of three asynchronous processes: 1) the migration of stimulated immature cells; 2) promoting migrating cells toward the safe or danger status depending on their accumulated response, and 3) labeling observed patterns as safe or dangerous based on the sub-population of cells that respond to each pattern.

As Brownlee (2011) said, DCA "is not specifically a classification algorithm", but a "data filtering method for use in anomaly detection problems". The DCA is a population based algorithm, with the population consisting of a set of interacting objects, each representing one cell. According to Greensmith (2007), the main components of a DC based algorithm are:

1. Individual DCs with the capability to perform multi-signal processing;
2. Antigen collection and presentation;
3. Sampling behavior and state changes;
4. A population of DCs and their interactions with signals and antigen
5. Incoming signals and antigen, with signals pre-categorized as PAMP, danger, safe or inflammation;
6. Multiple antigen presentation and analysis using 'types' of antigen;
7. Generation of anomaly coefficient for various different types of antigen.

The whole process is an iterative one and depends on various thresholds and parameters: migration threshold, P_w – the PAMP weight, D_w – the danger weight, S_w – the Safe weight, I – the inflammation signal, CSM output, and MCAV - mature context antigen value.

Applied initially for network intrusion detection, DCA shown good behavior in sensor networks and mobile robotics. The above components can be customized depending on the application field.

AIS ARCHITECTURES AND APPLICATIONS

According to the above considerations, the Artificial Immune Systems (AIS) should manage a database of antibodies and the kernel of AIS should provide both the computational algorithm and a mechanism to generate the problem's solution. This requirement is satisfied only by particular AIS which depends on the problem's nature. The computational algorithm (variants of NSA, PSA, CSA, AIN, DCA) applied over a particular representation of antibodies/antigens, with a particular metric or similarity measure, and a specific selection procedure, when adequate input date like: problem size, accuracy level, limits of resources (number of generations, number of function evaluations, size of AB global database etc.) will establish a design suitable to a specific project. The authors' experience on data analysis under various paradigms claims that only particular implementations are successful after specific calibration steps on various thresholds.

In the following let us describe some architectural models of AIS and their applications to real world problem solving.

A first architecture was proposed by Hofmeyr and Forrest (1999) and is called ARTIS (ARTificial Immune System). The utility of ARTIS was proved for network intrusion detection. ARTIS has the following characteristics: 1) two kinds of discrimination errors are supported: a false positive occurs when a self pattern is classified as anomalous, and a false negative occurs when a non-self pattern is classified as normal; 2) the ARTIS model, as a distributed environment, is a graph where each vertex contains a local set of detectors and detectors migrate between vertices via the edges; 3) Every detection node has a local sensitivity level in order to permit the detector activation when compared against an activation threshold; 4) ARTIS is based on NSA; 5) ARTIS uses memory-based detection; 6) ARTIS implements a form of costimulation; 7) the states of any detector are: randomly generated, immature, mature and naive, activated, memory, and death; the transition from one state to other is determined by decisions based on various computed levels and given thresholds.

The AIRS - the artificial immune recognition system - was proposed by Watkins et al (2004) as an artificial immune algorithm. It was compared by McEwan and Hart (2011) against of a deterministically variant in order to show the AIRS limits. AIRS was designed as supervised algorithm based on ARBs and used for classification problem domains. The AIRS computational process is related to RAIN and can be described as follows:

1. Initially create a memory pool (M) and an ARB Pool (P);
2. For each antigenic pattern do
   a. For each element of M determine their affinity to the antigenic pattern, and select highest affinity memory cell and clone it proportionally to its antigenic affinity to add to the set of ARBs (P);
   b. Mutate each ARB descendant of this highest affinity memory cell, and place each mutated ARB into P;
   c. Use a resource allocation mechanism to process every ARB. Compute the average stimulation of every ARB.
   d. Select a subpopulation of ARBs from P, and clone and mutate them in proportion to their stimulation level.
   e. Repeat from steps 2.3 until the average stimulation level is above a threshold.
   f. Update the memory set M with the best memory cell candidate.

A new class of AISs use databases. These systems use NSA and stores a collection of data records referred to as positive database (DB) in order to identify the "self". Esponda et al. (2004) propose the usage of negative representations such as negative database (NDB) which consists of all records that are not in DB.

In order to solve optimization problems, the opt-aiNet and its variants can be used. In order to increase the speed of convergence, some hybridizations were proposed, many of them adding support for crossover operations (genetic algorithms), recombination operators (evolutionary algorithms), fuzzification/defuzzification operators in order to manage imprecision and multiple local optimum situations. More real world applications can be found in the book of Dasgupta and Nino (2009). In the following some recent applications from software testing and learning in virtual environments will be described.

Many concepts in software testing comes from evolutionary theories: from an initial population, through evolutionary operators (mutation, crossover etc.) and selection (based on some fitness measure), after a number of steps, a final population is obtained. The lifecycle of any evolutionary algorithm for software testing starts with a number of suitable test cases, as initial population. According to Popentiu and Albeanu (2016), the evaluation metric is always based on a fitness function. In this context, let be n the total number of domain regions / testing paths, k be the number of regions/paths covered by a test, hence the test case associated fitness/ performance is k/n. The recombination and mutation operators applied to test case work as described, applied to sequences/strings and depending only on the test case structure (representation).

Clonal selection can be used to test generation (a large collection of test cases can be obtained by mutation operator). The size of collection, considered like detectors, can be reduced by simulate a negative selection to eliminate those detectors which are not able to detect faults. The remaining detectors will be cloned and mutated, evaluated and used to create a new population of detectors. In this way a mixed CSA + NSA strategy is obtained. Another application of AIS in software testing may consider the mutation testing and extend the already existing techniques.

For software testing optimization is considered the following set of attributes: *the maximum number of defect detection capability* (the detectability index), *the minimum test design efforts/cost* (mainly for the initial population*), the largest number of domain-data regions or control flow paths covered by the testing suite* etc. Hence the software testing optimization can be viewed and solved like a multiobjective optimization problem, or multiple criteria ranking problem. Both numeric and linguistic variable based algorithms can be used for test cases ranking, including intuitionistic-fuzzy approaches.

In some cases, the similarity index among test cases can be used. Based on the normalized matrix associated to the population P, according to the above attributes, a distance (Euclidian, Hamming, etc.) matrix D can be computed (d_{ij} is the distance between individuals i and j). Then the distance of an individual i in the population is the sum of distances on the row *i*, and the quality index of P can be given as the sum of all elements of D. In this way, is easy to extend the approach to a multi-population based algorithm, where populations evolve in parallel, and finally the most suited population of test cases should be selected.

According to Hunt & Cooke (1996), an artificial immune system for learning should be "an evolutionary learning mechanism which possesses a content address-able memory and the ability to «forget» little-used information".

As Albeanu et al. (2016) mentioned, the learning process can be implemented as an artificial neural network, but the AIS will be responsible to assure the immunity of the learning system against poor quality information from the environment. Therefore, the AIS for learning can be seen as a data analysis processing system of huge structured information. If the information is unstructured, a preprocessing module should scan and evaluate it.

Discriminating between bad information and knowledge to be stored and used to solve problems depends on the specific domain and should consider the most recent affinity metrics suitable for structured or unstructured texts. As pointed out by Albeanu et al. (2016), not all information is equally reliable, and it necessary to design, implement and operate an expert system which should quickly identify high value information and reject poor quality information. The following quality indices/metrics should be considered for storing in the system memory: *accuracy, consistency, security, timeliness, completeness, concise, reliability, accessibility, availability, objectivity, relevancy, usability, understandability, amount of data, believability, navigation, reputation, useful,* and *value-added,* according to Knight and Burn (2005). The discrimination is possible by a metric/an affinity measure over 20 parameters. Depending on the problem to be solved, the recognition/rejection procedure can evaluate individuals themselves, and/or individuals against already memorized knowledge.

The main components of an AIS for learning are: 1) *interface* (user interface, plugins); 2) *AIS kernel* responsible with detector generation taking into account basic rules (innate immunity) and adaptive rules (acquired immunity); and 3) *knowledge database* (KDB).

As pointed above, the entities stored in KDB depends on the knowledge representation approach taking into account: syntax (mathematical, logical, model, cases, rules, graphs, frames, symbols), semantics (specification of behaviors for human understanding), and reasoning (with certainty/uncertainty). The most common representations include: logic based (propositional/predicates), semantic networks (collection of nodes and links), frames (structured knowledge - similar to OOC, but without methods), production rules (procedural schemes), and Object Oriented Classes (OOC). The most used knowledge base oriented language is PROLOG (see

Yalcinalp (1991)) which is relational (by predicates), is based on logical implication and uses the backtracking mechanism for searching in KDB.

However, for structured knowledge (well stored/retrieved in object oriented databases) procedural programming in common/popular programming languages is a reliable choice. The recent developments both in object oriented systems, and unstructured information processing, mainly for WEB applications, provide new tracks in modern KDB developments for real world applications. The obtained results are valuable for AIS kernel development to use the internal structure of KDB and interpret/compile the specific queries.

FUTURE PERSPECTIVES

Some major challenging aspects of designing AIS for solving new problems by AIS computing approaches were identified and new solutions should be found. A particular AIS implementations are successful only after specific calibration steps on various thresholds. New ways for calibrating immune algorithms are required.

Also, discriminating between bad information and knowledge to be stored and used to solve problems depends on the specific domain and should consider suitable affinity metrics for structured or unstructured texts. Developments on new affinity metrics under new knowledge representations schemes should be addressed according to the specific domain.

It is important to choose from negative (N) and positive (A) approaches when use database oriented computing processes. The identification of the best approach depends on the application. A combination of N&P will improve the results.

Based on immune theories, and evolutionary strategies, real improvements of immune strategies can be obtained using hybrid approaches: neural networks, fuzzy methodologies, and intuitionistic-fuzzy numbers.

Due to the nature of artificial immune systems and their usage to solve real life problems which ask for pattern recognition, classification, or optimization, then comparative studies on the efficiency of AIS immune strategies against other nature inspired strategies are required. These are problem dependent and will be discussed in a future work.

CONCLUSION

The principles of artificial immune systems, the most representational data structures, suitable metrics, AIS specific algorithms, hybrid computational schemes, standard and extended AIS models/architectures, and AIS recent AIS applications had been covered from soft computing point of view.

Two new applications of artificial immune models are introduced with strong interest on software testing and learning in virtual environments. Also, some improvements in AIS computing processing area were proposed: the usage of Pompeiu-Hausdorff distance for inter-cluster (or ARBs) variability evaluation, and the IF-GAIN algorithm based in intuitionistic-fuzzy triangular numbers.

As a bio-inspired tool, an AIS can be used to solve many real world problems based both on intelligent information processing and KDB searching, under appropriate solutions of the challenging aspects presented above.

ACKNOWLEDGMENT

The authors would like to thank both the editor and the referees for their valuable comments which helped to improve the presentation. During this work, the authors were supported by their institutions in the framework of annual research programm.

REFERENCES

Albeanu, G., Madsen, H., & Popentiu-Vladicescu, F. (2016). Learning from Nature: Nature Inspired Algorithms. *The 12ᵗʰ International Scientific Conference eLearning and Software for Education.* doi:10.12753/2066-026X-16-158

Atanassov, K. T. (1986). Intuitionistic Fuzzy Sets. *Fuzzy Sets and Systems, 20*(1), 87–96. doi:10.1016/S0165-0114(86)80034-3

Broere, F., Apasov, S. G., Sitkovsky, M. V., & van Eden, W. (2011). T cell subsets and T cell-mediated immunity. In F. P. Nijkamp & M. J. Parnham (Eds.), *Principles of Immunopharmacology* (pp. 15–27). Springer. doi:10.1007/978-3-0346-0136-8_2

Brownlee, J. (2005). *Immunos-81. The Misunderstood Artificial Immune System.* Technical Report No. 3-01. Swinburne University of Technology.

Brownlee, J. (2011). *Clever Algorithms: Nature-Inspired Programming Recipes.* Retrieved from http://www.cleveralgorithms.com/

Brusic, V., & Petrovsky, N. (2003). Immunoinformatics - the new kid in town. In *Symposium on Immunoinformatics: Bioinformatic strategies for better understanding of immune function.* Wiley and Sons.

Burnet, F. M. (1957). A modification of Jerne's theory of antibody production using the concept of clonal selection. *Australian Journal of Science, 20*, 67–69.

Burnet, F. M. (1959). *The clonal selection theory of acquired immunity*. Vanderbilt University Press. doi:10.5962/bhl.title.8281

Danet, N. (2012). Some remarks on the Pompeiu-Hausdorff distance between order intervals. *ROMAI J., 8*(2), 51–60.

Dasgupta, D. (Ed.). (1999). *Artificial Immune Systems and Their Applications*. Springer-Verlag. doi:10.1007/978-3-642-59901-9

Dasgupta, D. (2010). *Artificial Immune Systems: A Bibliography*. Computer Science Department, University of Memphis. Retrieved from http://ais.cs.memphis.edu/files/papers/AIS-bibliography-March2010.pdf

Dasgupta, D., & Nino, L. F. (2009). *Immunological Computation, Theory and Applications*. CRC Press.

Dasgupta, D., Yu, S., & Nino, F. (2011). Recent Advances in Artificial Immune Systems: Models and Applications. *Applied Soft Computing, 11*(2), 1574–1587. doi:10.1016/j.asoc.2010.08.024

de Castro, L. N., & Timmis, J. (2002). An artificial immune network for multimodal function optimization. *Proceedings of IEEE Congress on Evolutionary Computation*, 699-704. doi:10.1109/CEC.2002.1007011

de Castro, L.N., & Timmis, J. (2002). *Artificial Immune System: A New Computational Approach*. Springer-Verlag.

de Castro, L. N., & Von Zuben, F. (2001). aiNET: An Artificial Immune Network for Data Analysis. In Data Mining: A Heuristic Approach. Idea Group Publishing.

de Castro, L. N., & Von Zuben, F. J. (2000). The clonal selection algorithm with engineering applications. *Proceedings of GECCO*, 36–39.

Esponda, F., Forrest, S., & Helman, P. (2004). *Enhancing Privacy through Negative Representations of Data*. UNM Computer Science Technical Report TR-CS-2004-18.

Forrest, S., Perelson, A. S., Allen, L., & Cherukuri, R. (1994). Self-nonself discrimination in a computer. *Proceedings of the IEEE Computer Society Symposium on Research in Security and Privacy*, 202–212. doi:10.1109/RISP.1994.296580

Freitas, A. A., & Timmis, J. (2003). Revisiting the Foundations of Artificial Immune Systems: A Problem-Oriented Perspective. In J. Timmis et al. (Eds.), *ICARIS 2003, LNCS 2787* (pp. 229–241). doi:10.1007/978-3-540-45192-1_22

Gonzalez, F. (2003). *A Study of Artificial Immune Systems Applied to Anomaly Detection*. (PhD Thesis). The University of Memphis.

Gonzalez, F., Galeano, J., & Veloza, A. (2005). A comparative analysis of artificial immune network models.*Proceedings of the 2005 Conference on Genetic and Evolutionary Computation,*361–368.

Greensmith, J. (2007). *The Dendritic Cell Algorithm* (PhD Thesis). University of Nottingham.

Hamaker, J. S., & Boggess, L. (2004). Non-euclidean distance measures in airs an artificial immune classification system.*Proceedings of the 2004 congress on evolutionary computation*, 1067–1073. doi:10.1109/CEC.2004.1330980

Harmer, P. K., Williams, P. D., Gunsch, G. H., & Lamont, G. B. (2002). An Artificial Immune System Architecture for Computer Security Applications. *IEEE Transactions on Evolutionary Computation*, 6(3), 252–280. doi:10.1109/TEVC.2002.1011540

Hofmeyr, S. A., & Forrest, S. (1999). Architecture for an Artificial Immune System. *Evolutionary Computation*, 7(1), 45–68. PMID:10199995

Hunt, J. E., & Cooke, D. E. (1996). Learning using an artificial immune system. *Journal of Network and Computer Applications*, 19(2), 189–212. doi:10.1006/jnca.1996.0014

Jerne, N. K. (1974). Towards a Network Theory of the Immune System. *Annals of Immunology*, 125C(1-2), 373–389. PMID:4142565

Jerne, N. K. (1984). *Nobel Lecture: The Generative Grammar of the Immune System*. Karolinska Institutet, Stockholm. Retrieved from http://www.nobelprize. org/mediaplayer/index.php?id=1653

Knight, S. A., & Burn, J. (2005). Developing a Framework for Assessing Information Quality on the World Wide Web. *Informing Science Journal*, 8, 159–172.

Langman, R. E., & Cohn, M. (1986). The complete idiotype network is an absurd immune system.*Immunology Today*, 7(4), 100–101. doi:10.1016/0167-5699(86)90147-7 PMID:25289798

Levenshtein, Vladimir, I. (1966). Binary codes capable of correcting deletions, insertions, and reversals. *Soviet Physics, Doklady*, 10(8), 707–710.

Lotze, M. T., & Thomson, A. W. (2010). *Natural Killer Cells. Basic Science and Clinical Application*. Elsevier.

Mahapatra, G. S. (2009). *Reliability Optimization in Fuzzy and Intuitionistic Fuzzy Environment*. Bengal Engineering and Science University.

Matzinger, P. (2002). The danger model: A renewed sense of self. *Science*, *296*(5566), 301–305. doi:10.1126/science.1071059 PMID:11951032

McEwan, Ch., & Hart, E. (2011). On clonal selection. *Theoretical Computer Science*, *412*(6), 502–516. doi:10.1016/j.tcs.2010.11.017

Nasaroui, O., Gonzalez, F., & Dasgupta, D. (2002). The Fuzzy Artificial Immune System: Motivations, Basic Concepts, and Application to Clustering and Web Profiling. *IEEE International Conference on Fuzzy systems*, 711-716. doi:10.1109/FUZZ.2002.1005080

Percus, J. K., Percus, O. E., & Perelson, A. S. (1993). Predicting the size of the T-cell receptor and antibody combining region from consideration of efficient self-nonself discrimination. *Proceedings of the National Academy of Sciences of the United States of America*, *90*(5), 1691–1695. doi:10.1073/pnas.90.5.1691 PMID:7680474

Popentiu-Vladicescu, F., & Albeanu, G. (2016). Nature-inspired approaches in software faults identification and debugging. *Procedia Computer Science*. doi:10.1016/j.procs.2016.07.315

Spits, H., Bernink, J., Peters, Ch., & Mjosberg, J. (2012). Role of human innate lymphoid cells in IMID. *Journal of Translational Medicine*, *10*(Suppl 3), I16. doi:10.1186/1479-5876-10-S3-I16

Tarakanov, A. O., Skormin, V. A., & Sokolova, S. P. (2003). *Immunocomputing: Principles and Applications*. New York: Springer-Verlag. doi:10.1007/978-1-4757-3807-0

Timmis, J., Hone, A., Stibor, T., & Clark, E. (2008). Theoretical advances in artificial immune systems. *Theoretical Computer Science*, *403*(1), 11–32. doi:10.1016/j.tcs.2008.02.011

Timmis, J., & Neal, M. (2001). A resource limited artificial immune system for data analysis. *Knowledge-Based Systems*, *14*(3-4), 121–130. doi:10.1016/S0950-7051(01)00088-0

Timmis, J., Neal, M., & Hunt, J. (2000). An Artificial Immune System for Data Analysis. *Bio Systems*, *55*(1), 143–150. doi:10.1016/S0303-2647(99)00092-1 PMID:10745118

Twycross, J., & Aickelin, U. (2007). Biological Inspiration for Artificial Immune Systems. *LNCS, 4628*, 300-311. doi:10.2139/ssrn.2831297

Watkins, A., Timmis, J., & Boggess, L. (2004). *Artificial Immune Recognition System (AIRS): An Immune-Inspired Supervised Learning Algorithm*. Kluwer. doi:10.1023/B:GENP.0000030197.83685.94

Yalcinalp, L. U. (1991). *Meta-programming for knowledge based systems in PRO-LOG* (PhD Thesis). Case Western Reserve University.

Zadeh, L. A. (1965). Fuzzy sets. *Information and Control, 8*(3), 338–353. doi:10.1016/S0019-9958(65)90241-X

Zimmermann, K. A. (2014). *Immune System: Diseases, Disorders & Function*. Retrieved from http://www.livescience.com/26579-immune-system.html

Chapter 5

Collective–Animal–Behaviour–Based Optimized Null Placement in Time–Modulated Linear Antenna Arrays

Gopi Ram
MITS Madanpalle, India

Durbadal Mandal
NIT Durgapur, India

Rajib Kar
NIT Durgapur, India

Sakti Prasad Ghoshal
NIT Durgapur, India

ABSTRACT

In this paper optimal design of time modulated linear antenna arrays (TMLAA) with optimal placement of nulls in the desired direction of elevation plane has been dealt with the approach based on evolutionary algorithm like collective animal behaviour (CAB). Analysis has been done in theoretical and practical environment. Firstly the current excitation weights of the linear array of isotropic elements have been optimized by CAB is applied to improve null performance of TMLAA by Radio Frequency (RF) switch in MATLAB environment. The nulls positions of a TMLAA can be reduced significantly by optimizing the static excitation amplitudes and proper design of switch-on time intervals of each element. The CAB adjusts the current excitation amplitude of each element to place deeper nulls in the desired directions. Secondly the obtained optimal current excitation weight of the array factor is practically implemented in computer simulation technology- microwave studio (CST- MWS) environment. The array of microstrip patch antenna has been designed to operate at 5.85 GHz.

DOI: 10.4018/978-1-5225-2322-2.ch005

INTRODUCTION

Microstrip patch antennas have very attractive features and advantages due to their robustness, easy to fabricate and their small size and low cost, ease of installation and integration with feed networks (Ballanis, 2005). One of the downbeat limitations of this type of antenna is that it has limited bandwidth of operation at which the antenna can perform comfortably. These characteristics become an important factor while designing the antenna. This is mainly used in wireless and mobile communication. Patch antenna consists of a substrate followed by a ground plane at the bottom of the substrate. A patch antenna is placed at the top of the substrate which is made up of a perfect electrical conductor. This is connected to the feed line from where the patch is being excited. Substrate is made up of a perfectly dielectric material and the most commonly used material is FR-4 (Stutzman & Thiele, 2012). There are many ways to operate one antenna in the multiple bands. One way may be the perturbation slots in the patch and the other way may is the fractal approach. Due to the recent improved technologies coming day by day in the real world the enabled communication devices have to have smaller size. The size of the antenna is a key factor for the design of any communication devices or any antenna enabled devices. Due to this the small size antenna has a very high demand for WLAN and Wi-MAX. This technology gives great freedom and flexibility to move around the wide coverage area with all-time connection with network. Different applications of communication require various different types of antenna to improve the transmission and the reception of the desired signal.

During the last couple of decade time modulated antenna arrays have turned into an emergent research domain for the antenna designers due to their benefits in excess of conventional array antennas. Shanks and Bickmore first time introduced the exploitation of the time modulation technique as an additional degree of freedom for the synthesis of antenna arrays (Schrank, 1983). Time-modulated antenna arrays can be used to achieve the desired radiation patterns by utilizing on-off switching of the array elements (Hardel, Yalapragada, Mandal, & Bhattacharjee, 2011; Yang, Gan, & Tan, 2005; Yang, Gan, & Qing, 2002; Yang, Gan, & Tan, 2003; Fondevila, Brégains, Ares, & Moreno, 2004; Yang, Gan, Quing, & Tan, 2005; Yang, Gan, & Tan, 2004; Yang, Gan, & Quing, 2003). This feature can aid to accomplish a better radiation pattern than those of the traditional antenna array synthesis methods (Haupt, 1997; Steyskal, Shore, & Haupt, 1986; Haupt 1988; Chung & Haupt, 1999; Mandal, Ghoshal & Bhattacharjee, 2009a; Mandal, Ghoshal & Bhattacharjee, 2009b; Chen, Jan, Lee, & Chen, 2011; Ram, Mandal, Kar, & Ghoshal, 2013). For the implementation of any practical antenna, the consideration of parameter is very important. The simulation software used here is computer simulation technology Microwave Studio (CST-MW), which is a computing package established on Finite

Integration Technique (FIT). CST-MW is the widely and simple to use electromagnetic field simulation software (Onol & Ergul, 2014; Jayasinghe, Anguera, & Uduwawala, 2013; Sorokosz, Zieniutycz, Pergol, & Mazur, 2011). It overtures discriminative, effectual simulation explication for the electromagnetic design and analysis. CST-MS is a powerful technique used in the range of low frequency to a very high frequency. After structure designing automatic meshing procedure is applied before a simulation is started. CST-MS works on Method on Demand which gives the choice of simulate or mesh type which suits for the particular problem. Patch antennas are low cost, have a low profile and are easily fabricated antenna. Due to simple structure it is widely used in telecommunication. It is widely used in cellular mobile communication. Also it is useful in designing of different types of antenna array like linear array, circular array and planar array. These days it is widely used in conformal array designing. An approach based on CAB (Ram, Mandal, Kar, & Ghoshal, 2013) algorithm is applied to introduce deeper nulls in the radiation pattern. Further, results obtained from CAB are implemented by the CST-MWS simulation software (CST, 2013) for the validation purpose. There are other research works carried out to improve the particular antenna elements (Onol & Ergul, 2014; Jayasinghe, Anguera, & Uduwawala, 2013; Pergol, Mazur, Zieniutycz, & Sorokosz, 2011). Evolutionary algorithms applied in the different field of engineering are also shown in (Kułakowski, Alonso, López, Ludwin, Haro, 2016).

The rest of the paper is ordered in the following manner: Section II explicates the theoretical analysis of TMLAA and the fitness function formulation; Section III explicates the computational results; Section IV deals with the discussion about the results and finally, the conclusion is presented in Section IV.

Design Equations

Consider a linear array of isotropic elements which are placed in the z axis, and are symmetric along the center of z-axis. All the array elements are controlled by the high speed radio frequency (RF) switch, which is used to switch ON-OFF the particular elements periodically. Figure 1(a) shows the geometry of linear array of isotropic elements and Figure 1(b) shows the designed structure of microstrip patch antenna. For broadside beams, the array factor is given by

$$AF(\theta, t) = 2\sum_{k=1}^{N} U_k(t) I_k \cos[(\frac{2k-1}{2}) K d \cos(\theta)] \tag{1}$$

where θ = angle of radiation of electromagnetic wave; d = inter-element spacing; K = propagation constant; $2N$ = total number of elements in the array; I_k = current excitation weight of kth element; Uk = switching function for which each element's switch ON time is $\tau_k (0 \leq \tau_k \leq T)$. Details of the ON-OFF time sequences for an array of N elements with M consecutive ON elements are shown below. The transmitted pulse width is T; the pulse repetition frequency is T_{prf} and the pulse repetition period is $T_p = T_{prf}$. This switching scheme implies that $T = T_p$, which is actually in the form of continuous time modulation. The time switching function $U_k(t)$ for the kth element within one pulse width T is expressed as given below (Hardel, Yala-pragada, Mandal, & Bhattacharjee, 2011) and (Ballanis, 2005).

$$U_1(t) = \begin{cases} 1, & 0 \leq t \leq \tau \\ 0, & otherwise \end{cases}$$

$$U_k(t) = \begin{cases} 1, & t_{1k} \leq t \leq t_{2k} \\ 1 & t_{3k} \leq t \leq t_{4k} \ (1 < k \leq N - M) \\ 0, & otherwise \end{cases}$$

$$U_k(t) = \begin{cases} 1, & t'_{1k} < t \leq t'_{2k} \\ 0, & otherwise \end{cases} (N - M < k \leq N)$$

Figure 1. (a) Geometry of a 2N-element linear isotropic array along the z-axis, (b) Structre of patch antenna

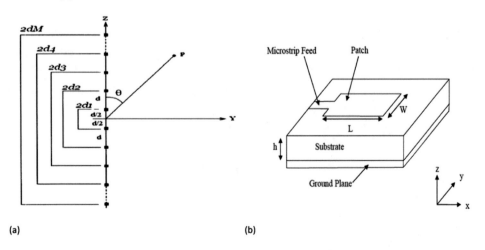

(a)   (b)

where M = Consecutive on elements; t_{1k}, t_{3k}, t'_{1k} and t_{2k}, t_{4k}, t'_{2k} are the ON and OFF time switching instants, respectively, and are given by

$$t_{1k} = Max[0, (k - M)\tau];$$

$$t_{2k} = k\tau;$$

$$t_{3k} = T - (k - 1)\tau;$$

$$t_{4k} = Min[T, T - (k - M - 1)\tau];$$

$$t'_{1k} = Max[0, (k - M)\tau];$$

$$t'_{2k} = Min[T, T - (k - M - 1)\tau].$$

The time step τ is given by

$$\tau = \frac{T}{2(N - M)}$$

From (1) the overall total radiation pattern is given by

$$AF_{Total}(\theta) = EP(\theta) \times AF(\theta, t) \tag{2}$$

Here, $EP(.)$ is the radiation pattern of individual array elements, $AF(.)$ is the array factor, and (θ, ϕ) are the elevation and azimuthal angle, respectively, of the spherical coordinate system.

For the design of microstrip antenna, following consideration has been made. The discussions presented so far have only considered an array consisting of isotropic radiators, mainly the array factor. However, an array with a more directive element patterns such as a patch antenna is considered for this design, and then the principle of pattern multiplication has to be utilized. Assuming that there is no mutual coupling between the patch antenna, and the theory of pattern multiplication describes that the total field of the array is the product of radiation pattern of a single element multiplied by the array factor (Ballanis, 2005). The resultant radiation pattern at the fundamental frequency is calculated as the product of the conventional array factor multiplied by the element pattern of the patch antenna.

In this antenna, the substrate has a thickness h=1.6 mm and a *relative* permittivity, ε_r = 4.4. 'c' is the speed of light in mm; f_r is the operating frequency (5.85 GHz for Wi-MAX application), ε_0 is the permittivity in vacuum, μ_0 is the permeability in the free space. Based on the above numerical values of parameters various patch parameters can be calculated by the following equations (Ballanis, 2005):

$$W = \frac{1}{2f_r\sqrt{\mu_0\varepsilon_0}}\sqrt{\frac{2}{\varepsilon_r+1}} \tag{3}$$

Effective permittivity is given by

$$\varepsilon_{reff} = \frac{\varepsilon_r+1}{2} + \frac{\varepsilon_r-1}{2}[1+12\frac{h}{W}] \tag{4}$$

$$\frac{\Delta L}{h} = 0.412\frac{(\varepsilon_{reff}+0.3)}{(\varepsilon_{reff}-0.258)}\frac{(\frac{w}{h}+0.264)}{(\frac{w}{h}+0.8)} \tag{5}$$

The length of the patch is given by

$$L = L_{eff} - 2\Delta L \tag{6}$$

L_g and W_g are the length and width of the ground plane calculation.

$$L_g = 6h + L \tag{7}$$

$$W_g = 6h + W \tag{8}$$

The calculation of inset feed is calculated as follows (Ballanis, 2005):

$$G_1 = \frac{-2 + \cos(k_0 W) + k_0 W * S_i(k_0 W) + \dfrac{\sin(k_0 W)}{k_0 W}}{120\pi^2} \tag{9}$$

$$G_{12} = \frac{1}{120\pi^2} \int_0^\pi \left[\frac{\sin(\dfrac{k_0 W}{2} \cos\theta)}{\cos\theta} \right]^2 J_0(k_0 L \sin\theta) \sin^3\theta\, \partial\theta \tag{10}$$

$$R_{in} = \frac{1}{2(G_1 + G_{12})} \tag{11}$$

$$y_0 = \frac{L}{\pi} \cos^{-1}\left(\sqrt{\frac{Z}{R_{in}}}\right) \tag{12}$$

where J_0 is the Bessel's function of first kind of zero order. k_0 is the propagation constant, R_{in} is the resonant input resistance, Z is the characteristic impedance, G_{12} is the mutual conductance, G_1 is the conductance of feed line conductance.

The objective function (OF) can be formulated as follows

$$OF = \frac{\left| \displaystyle\prod_{i=1}^m AF(null_i) \right|}{|AF|} \tag{13}$$

where 'm' denotes the number of null positions in the desired direction of the array factor (AF). In this paper all the possible combinations of the 2nd, 3rd nulls and 2nd, 3rd peak positions have been taken, that means $m = 1, 2$. $\left| \displaystyle\prod_{i=1}^m AF(null_i) \right|$ denotes the absolute of multiplication of the array factor values for the particular value of m. $\left| AF_{max} \right|$ denotes the absolute maximum value of the array factor in the entire elevation plane. From (13) it is clear that it is the minimization problem.

Computational Results

12-, 16-, and 20- elements with M consecutive ON elements as 10-, 14-, and 18-, respectively, with λ/2 spacing, are considered for TMLAA with $T_p = 12\,\mu s$, $16\,\mu s$, $20\,\mu s$, respectively. CAB is applied to get the deeper nulls. Control parameters of CAB (Ram, Mandal, Kar, & Ghoshal, 2013) are shown in Table 1. Table 2 shows the initial values of FNBW for TMLAA ($I_n = 1$) array.

Figures 2(a)-(b) and Figure 3(a) show the optimized deeper nulls in the array pattern obtained by CAB for time modulated isotropic antenna array over the 3rd null for 12-, 16-, and 20-element structures, respectively. Figure 3(b) and Figures 4(a)-(b) show the optimized deeper nulls in the array pattern obtained by CAB for time modulated isotropic antenna array over the 3rd peak for 12-, 16-, and 20-element structures, respectively. Figures 5(a)-(b) and Figure 6(a) show the optimized deeper nulls in the array pattern obtained by using CAB for time modulated isotropic antenna array at the 2nd and 3rd peaks for 12-, 16-, 20-element, respectively. Figure 6 (b) and Figures 7(a)-(b) show the optimized deeper nulls in the array pattern obtained by CAB for time modulated isotropic antenna array at the 2nd and 3rd nulls for 12-, 16-, and 20-element structures, respectively. Tables 3-6 show the improvements in the nulling performance of antenna arrays obtained by using CAB. So from the tables and figures it is clear that considerable achievement of deeper nulls in the time modulated isotropic over non-optimized uniformly excited time modulated linear antenna arrays has been achieved.

Table 1. Control parameters of CAB

Parameters	CAB
Population size	60
Iteration Cycle	100
$C_1 = C_2$	1.5
v_i^{min}, v_i^{max}	0.01, 1.0
Z	100

Table 2. Initial value of FNBW for TM-LAA ($I_n = 1$) array

N	FNBW (deg.)
12	19.08
16	14.4
20	11.48

Table 3. Optimized value of current excitation coefficients, initial value of null, final value of null, and FNBW obtained by using CAB for a null imposed at 3rd null

2N	$(I_1, I_2, ..., I_N)$	Non-optimized null value (dB)	Optimized null value (dB)	FNBW (deg.)
12	0.4412 0.6035 0.4118 0.6561 0.5584 0.8255	-58.32	-119.3	18
16	0.4491 0.8144 0.1733 0.7649 0.1631 0.4693 0.3334 0.1284	-52.71	-115.8	16.9200
20	0.3679 0.6121 0.3507 0.2528 0.5735 0.4291 0.0737 0.9152 0.4850 0.7620	-78.29	-94.79	10.44

Table 4. Optimized value of current excitation coefficients, initial value of null, final value of null, and FNBW obtained by using CAB for a null imposed at 3rd peak

2N	$(I_1, I_2, ..., I_N)$	Non-optimized peak value (dB)	Optimized peak value (dB)	FNBW (deg.)
12	0.2835 0.3604 0.7475 0.3659 0.1115 0.4262	-18.31	-89.54	21.22
16	0.7943 0.4909 0.4735 0.4974 0.5989 0.7579 0.2759 0.1256	-17.48	-99.73	15.48
20	0.3582 0.3391 0.6144 0.1616 0.9617 0.5576 0.7418 0.5574 0.2743 0.5603	-17.57	-95.92	11.16

Table 5. Optimized value of current excitation coefficients, initial value of null, final value of null, and FNBW obtained by using CAB for nulls imposed at 2nd and 3rd peak

2N	$(I_1, I_2, ..., I_N)$	Non-optimized peak values (dB)	Optimized peak values (dB)	FNBW (deg.)
12	0.0701 0.0982 0.3507 0.3373 0.2604 0.3646	-27.78, -18.31	-101.5, -67.61	16.56
16	0.4856 0.6721 0.0729 0.9031 0.2672 0.5329 0.1993 0.6998	-24.01, -17.48	-77.95, -114.4	15.12
20	0.2379 0.4655 0.1317 0.7437 0.5247 0.8385 0.7984 0.1098 0.7526 0.2744	-22.78, -17.57	-105.5, -80.53	11.52

Table 6. Optimized value of current excitation coefficients, initial value of null, final value of null, and FNBW obtained by using CAB for nulls imposed at 2ⁿᵈ and 3ʳᵈ null

N	$(I_1, I_2, ..., I_N)$	Non-optimized null values (dB)	Optimized null values (dB)	FNBW (deg.)
12	0.4304 0.6581 0.1092 0.4495 0.2239 0.2378	-66.42, -58.32	-95.88, -81.57	23.02
16	0.3773 0.4810 0.4122 0.4311 0.3859 0.5971 0.2541 0.6566	-53.74, -52.71	-98.43, -63.66	14.4
20	0.4692 0.2920 0.3728 0.7451 0.3376 0.1772 0.6451 0.7866 0.1955 0.7731	-47.63, -78.29	-62.20, -98.25	11.52

Figure 2. Power pattern obtained by using CAB for the (a) 12-element array at 3ʳᵈ nulls i.e. θ= 59.94 degree. (b) 16-element array at 3rᵈ null i.e. θ=68.04 degree

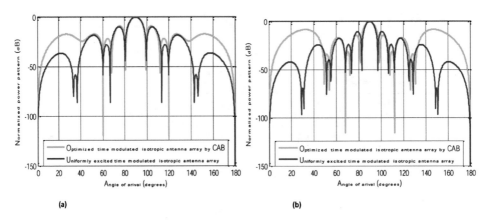

Figure 3. Power pattern obtained by using CAB for the (a) 20-element array at 3ʳᵈ null i.e. θ=72.54 degree, (b) 12-element array at 3rᵈ peak i.e. θ =51.84 degree

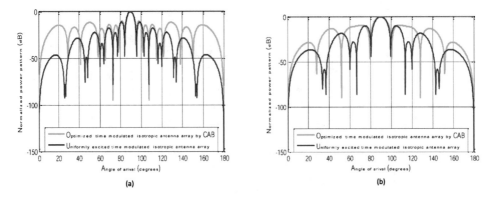

Figure 4. Power pattern obtained by using CAB for the (a)16-element array at 3rd peak i.e. θ =62.64 degrees, (b) 20-element array at $3r^d$ peak i.e. θ =68.58 degree

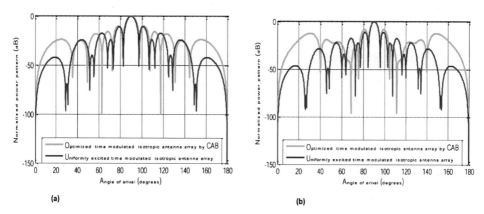

(a)　　　　　　　　　　　　　(b)

Figure 5. Power pattern obtained by using CAB for the (a) 12-element array at 2nd and 3rd peaks i.e. θ =63.54 degree and 51.84 degree respectively; (b) 16-element array at $2n^d$ and $3r^d$ peak i.e. θ=71.1 degree and 62.64 degree, respectively

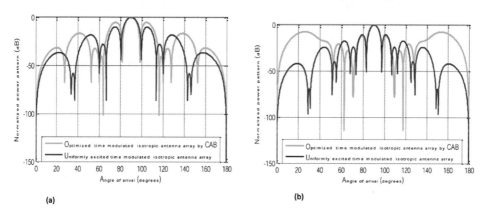

(a)　　　　　　　　　　　　　(b)

DISCUSSIONS

In this example, a simple patch antenna has been simulated in the Transient Solver in CST and it is designed to operate at 5.85 GHz. The substrate material used for this design is normal FR-4 with a thickness of 1.6 mm and a relativity permittivity of 4.4. Detailed geometry of the patch antenna and its bottom view are described in Figure 1 (b). The scattering parameters are often used to describe the antenna performance. The reflection coefficient Γ of an antenna is defined by the ratio of

Figure 6. Power pattern obtained by using CAB for the (a) 20-element at 2ⁿᵈ and 3ʳᵈ peaks i.e. θ =75.06 degree and 67.68 degree, respectively, (b) 12-element array at 2nᵈ and 3rᵈ nulls i.e. θ =66.42degree and 60.48 degree, respectively

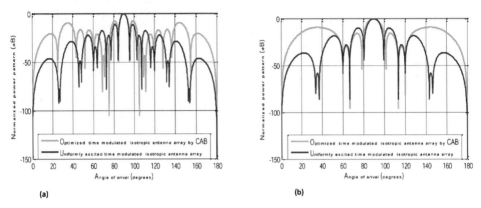

(a)　　　　　　　　　　　　　　　　(b)

Figure 7. Power pattern obtained by using CAB for the (a) 16-element array at 2ⁿᵈ and 3ʳᵈ nulls i.e. θ=73.26 degree and 68.04 degree, respectively, (b) 20-element array at 2nᵈ and 3rᵈ nulls i.e. θ=77.22 degree and 72.54 degree, respectively

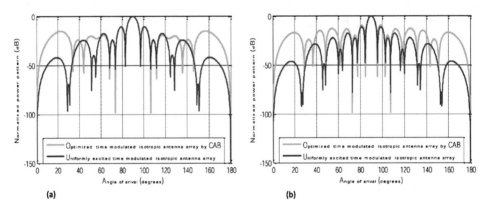

(a)　　　　　　　　　　　　　　　　(b)

the power reflected back to the total input power. The reflection coefficient in dB is expressed as $20\log|\Gamma|$.

Figures 8 (a)-(b) show the designed microstrip patch antenna, and far-field pattern of directivity of the devised microstrip patch antenna, respectively. The design parameters of microstrip patch antenna are given in Table 7. From the results it is clear that the resonant frequency of CST-MWS simulated microstrip patch antenna array is 5.86 GHz with a bandwidth of 335 MHz. Directivity obtained for the patch antenna is 6.392 dBi. Figures 9(a)-(b) show the far-field pattern of gain of the devised microstrip patch antenna, and the return loss curve for the same, respectively. The same figure shows the measured gain and return loss of the designed microstrip patch antenna as 3.683dB, -15.541 dB, repectively. Figures 10 (a)-(b) show VSWR for the same, and bandwidth curve, respectively. From the same table it is clear that VSWR is 1.377dB, and the bandwidth of the microstrip patch antenna is 0.3357 GHz. For the ideal matching there should not be any reflection and return loss, i.e., VSWR=1. This is impractical in real life scenario, so it is suggested that VSWR<2 gives rise to a reasonably good matching system. Figure 11 shows the far-field radiation pattern for the directivity of the linear array of microstrip patch antenna element. The calculated directivity of linear array of microstrip patch antenna element is 16.21 dB for 12 elements. Figures 12 (a)-(b) show the polar plot for the elevation angle of the desiged linear array of microstrip patch antenna element and array pattern, respectively, of linear array of microstrip patch antenna elements designed by using CST-MWS for 12 elements, respectively. From Figure 12(b) it is clear that the radiation pattern of MATLAB simulated 12-elements linear array of microstrip patch antenna element is approximately matching with that of the same linear array of microstrip patch antenna element simulated with CST-MWS as the results with the imposing null at 3rd peak position. So it proves and validates that optimized nulling value obtained by simulation results by using CAB in MATLAB platform and CST-MWS platform.

Table 7. Calculated value of the patch parameters

Parameter	Description of the Parameters	Numerical Value Obtained (mm)
W	Width if the patch antenna	15.5940
ε_{reff}	Effective permittivity	3.8381 unit
L_{eff}	Effective length	13.0881
ΔL	extended incremental length of the patch	0.7232
L	Length of the patch antenna	11.6417
L_g	Length of the substrate/ ground plane	21.2417
W_g	Width of the substrate/ ground plane	25.1940
h	Thickness of the substrate	1.6
mt	Thickness of the ground plane and patch antenna	0.4
Gp	Gap between feed line and the patch	0.3
Mf	Width of the patch	0.31

Figure 8. (a) Designed microstrip patch antenna, (b) Far-field radiation pattern for the directivity of the designed microstrip patch antenna

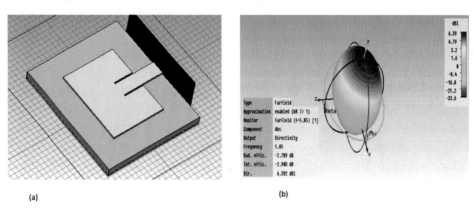

(a)   (b)

Figure 9. (a) Far-field radiation pattern for the gain of the designed microstrip patch antenna, (b) Return loss curve for the same

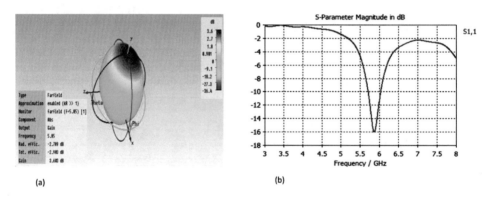

(a)   (b)

Figure 10. (a) VSWR for the designed microstrip patch antenna, (b) Bandwidth curve for the designed microstrip patch antenna

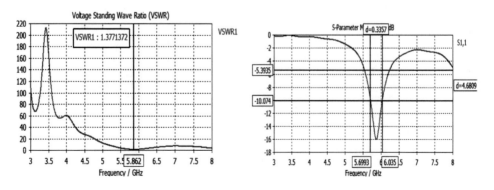

Figure 11. Far-field radiation pattern for the Directivity of the desigened linear array of 12-element microstrip patch antenna

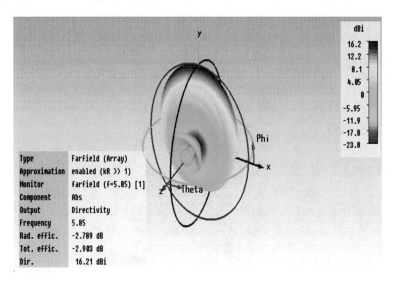

Figure 12. (a) Polar plot for elevation angle of the designed linear array of 12-element microstrip patch antenna. (b) array pattern of linear array of 12-element microstrip patch antenna designed in CST-MWS

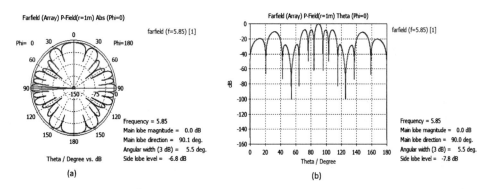

CONCLUSION

In this paper, the design of a non-uniformly excited symmetric time modulated linear antenna arrays (TMLAA) with uniform spacing ($\lambda / 2$) between the elements has been described using the optimization technique based on collective animal behavior (CAB). CAB is used to improve the null performance of the TMLAA. The results are validated for practical purpose using EM simulator. For the practical implementation and validation of the optimal result obtained by using CAB algorithm in MALTLAB environment, a linear array of microstrip patch antenna has been designed and is validated in CST-MWS. From the numerical results and Figure 12 (b) it is clear that results of optimized pattern and CST MWS simulated pattern are approximately matching. The FNBW of optimized radiation patterns of TMLAA remains approximately same as uniform TMLAA.

REFERENCES

Balanis, C. A. (2005). *Antenna theory: Analysis and design.* Academic Press.

Chen, L. C., Jan, M. R., Lee, Y. T., & Chen, H. C. (2011). A Particle Swarm Optimization with Improved Inertia Weight Algorithm Solution of Economic Dispatch With Valve Point Loading. *Journal of Marine Science and Technology, 19*(1), 43–51.

Chung, Y. C., & Haupt, R. L. (1999, July). Adaptive nulling with spherical arrays using a genetic algorithm. *Antennas and Propagation Society International Symposium*, 2000-2003. doi:10.1109/APS.1999.788352

CST-Microwave Studio. (2013). User's Manual. Author.

Fondevila, J., Brégains, J. C., Ares, F., & Moreno, E. (2004). Optimizing uniformly excited linear arrays through time modulation. *IEEE Antennas and Wireless Propagation Letters, 3*(1), 298–301. doi:10.1109/LAWP.2004.838833

Hardel, G. R., Yalapragada, N. T., Mandal, D., & Bhattacharjee, A. K. (2011). Introducing Dipper Nulls in Time modulated Linear symmetric Antenna Array Using Real Coded Genetic Algorithm. *IEEE Symposium on Computers and Informatics,* 249-254.

Haupt, R. L. (1988). Adaptive nulling in monopulse antennas. *IEEE Transactions on Antennas and Propagation, 36*(2), 202–208. doi:10.1109/8.1097

Haupt, R. L. (1997). Phase-only adaptive nulling with a genetic algorithm. *IEEE Transactions on Antennas and Propagation, 45*(6), 1009–1015. doi:10.1109/8.585749

Jayasinghe, J. W., Anguera, J., & Uduwawala, D. N. (2013). Genetic algorithm optimization of a high-directivity microstrip patch antenna having a rectangular profile. *Radioengineering, 22*(3).

Kułakowski, P., Vales-Alonso, J., Egea-López, E., Ludwin, W., & García-Haro, J. (2010). Angle-of-arrival localization based on antenna arrays for wireless sensor networks. *Computers & Electrical Engineering*, *36*(6), 1181–1186. doi:10.1016/j.compeleceng.2010.03.007

Mandal, D., Bhattacharjee, A. K., & Ghoshal, S. P. (2009, December). A novel particle swarm optimization based optimal design of three-ring concentric circular antenna array. In *Advances in Computing, Control, & Telecommunication Technologies, 2009. ACT'09. International Conference on* (pp. 385-389). IEEE. doi:10.1109/ACT.2009.101

Mandal, D., Ghoshal, S. P., & Bhattacharjee, A. K. (2009). Determination of the optimal design of three-ring concentric circular antenna array using evolutionary optimization techniques. *International Journal of Recent Trends in Engineering*, *2*(5), 110–115.

Onol, C., & Ergül, O. (2014). Optimizations of patch antenna arrays using genetic algorithms supported by the multilevel fast multipole algorithm. *Radioengineering*, *23*(4), 1005–1014.

Pergol, M., Mazur, W., Zieniutycz, W., & Sorokosz, L. (2011). Mutual Coupling Between IFF/SSR Microstrip Antennas with Reduced Transversal Size-Experimental Study. *Radioengineering, 20*(1).

Ram, G., Mandal, D., Kar, R., & Ghoshal, S. P. (2013). Optimized hyper beamforming of linear antenna arrays using collective animal behaviour. *The Scientific World Journal*. PMID:23970843

Schrank, H. E. (1983). Low sidelobe phased array antennas IEEE Antennas Propagat. *Soc. Newslett.*, *25*(2), 4–9.

Steyskal, H., Shore, R. A., & Haupt, R. (1986). Methods for null control and their effects on the radiation pattern. *IEEE Transactions on Antennas and Propagation*, *34*(3), 404–409. doi:10.1109/TAP.1986.1143816

Stutzman, W. L., & Thiele, G. A. (2012). *Antenna theory and design*. John Wiley & Sons.

Yang, S., Beng Gan, Y., & Qing, A. (2003). Moving phase center antenna arrays with optimized static excitations. *Microwave and Optical Technology Letters*, *38*(1), 83–85. doi:10.1002/mop.10977

Yang, S., Gan, Y. B., & Qing, A. (2002). Sideband suppression in time-modulated linear arrays by the differential evolution algorithm. *IEEE Antennas and Wireless Propagation Letters*, *1*(1), 173–175. doi:10.1109/LAWP.2002.807789

Yang, S., Gan, Y. B., Qing, A., & Tan, P. K. (2005). Design of a uniform amplitude time modulated linear array with optimized time sequences. *IEEE Transactions on Antennas and Propagation*, *53*(7), 2337–2339. doi:10.1109/TAP.2005.850765

Yang, S., Gan, Y. B., & Tan, P. K. (2003). A new technique for power-pattern synthesis in time-modulated linear arrays. *IEEE Antennas and Wireless Propagation Letters*, *2*(1), 285–287. doi:10.1109/LAWP.2003.821556

Yang, S., Gan, Y. B., & Tan, P. K. (2004). Comparative study of low sidelobe time modulated linear arrays with different time schemes. *Journal of Electromagnetic Waves and Applications*, *18*(11), 1443–1458. doi:10.1163/1569393042954910

Yang, S., Gan, Y. B., & Tan, P. K. (2005). Linear antenna arrays with bidirectional phase center motion. *IEEE Transactions on Antennas and Propagation*, *53*(5), 1829–1835. doi:10.1109/TAP.2005.846754

Chapter 6
An Incremental Evolutionary Approach to Tabu Search

Yoshinori Suzuki
Iowa State University, USA

Juan David Cortes
Iowa State University, USA

ABSTRACT

Based on recent viral transmission events in the swine species, we present a new framework to implement and execute tabu search (TS). The framework mimics the gradual evolutionary process observed when certain flu viruses move from one host population to another. It consists of three steps: (1) executing TS on a smaller subset of the original problem, (2) using one of its promising solutions as an initial solution for a marginally larger problem, and (3) repeating this process until the original problem is reached and solved. Numerical experiments conducted with randomly-generated vehicle routing instances demonstrate interesting results.

INTRODUCTION

Tabu search (TS) is one of the most widely used metaheuristics in practice and academic research, especially for solving difficult combinatorial problems (e.g., traveling-salesman, vehicle routing, sequencing, network-design, and spanning tree problems) (Toth & Vigo, 2003). Past studies have investigated the question of how

DOI: 10.4018/978-1-5225-2322-2.ch006

to improve the effectiveness (solution quality) and efficiency (solution speed) of TS by exploring a variety of diversification and intensification strategies, neighborhood definitions, tabu-list updating procedures, and termination criteria (Ho, Shiyou, Ni, & Wong, 2001; Gendreau & Potvin, 2010). To the best of our knowledge, however, none of these past studies have explored the question of how the TS performance can be improved by changing the nature (e.g., size) of the problem during the optimization run. Changing the problem characteristics during the optimization run can be potentially beneficial, as it can provide the information that would be difficult to obtain under the conventional TS execution method (where the nature of the problem is fixed), which may be used to enhance the TS performance. We investigate a new way of executing TS that changes the nature of the problem dynamically during the optimization run, and contrast its performance with that of a well-known TS procedure.

BASIC IDEA AND RELATED LITERATURE

General Idea

The basic idea of our approach (framework) is inspired by the viral transmission incidents observed between swine (pig) and avian (bird) flues several years ago. These incidents showed that while influenza A virus (bird flu) in its original form can hardly infect human beings, it can transform itself into a new form which can pose threats to humans if it goes through pigs. In other words, while moving directly from birds to humans is an infeasible path for the flu, moving indirectly from birds to humans through pigs is a feasible path (see Figure 1). This means that, although a virus residing in one environment (E_1) cannot move to a very different environment (E_M) directly, it may be able to eventually transform itself into a new form that can reside in E_M if, for example, it goes through an indirect transmission path: $E_1 \rightarrow E_2 \rightarrow ... \rightarrow E_m \rightarrow E_{m+1} \rightarrow ... \rightarrow E_M$, where E_m and E_{m+1} represent different, but similar, living environments (hosts populations) for the virus. Our approach is based on this idea of sequential (and gradual) viral transmission and evolution.

Related Literature

A limited number of studies have developed algorithms that involve the emulation of viral movements among host populations, most of which relied on the use of genetic algorithms (GAs). Arakawa et al. (1996) implemented a virus-based GA to the trajectory generation problem, particularly with application to robotics. The algorithm divides the population into several subpopulations (virus and host popu-

Figure 1. Viral transmission paths

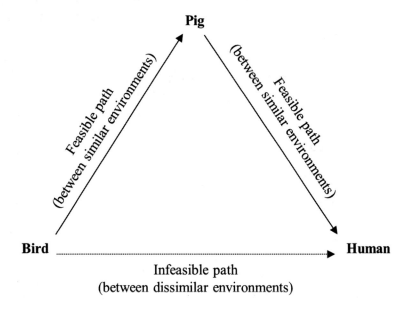

lations), wherein each virus subpopulation undergoes the processes of crossover, mutation, infection, selection, and cross-population migration. Chun et al. (1998) developed and compared an Immune algorithm (IA), an evolution strategy (ES), and a GA. Their approach, which heavily relies on stochastic transition and movements of viruses, is based on the genetic abilities of viruses to cope with invading antigens and the production of antibodies to exclude the antigens. Cortes et al. (2013) developed a virus-inspired algorithm, designed specifically for the elevator dispatching problem, in which each cell may be infected with a virus based on a probability, where the infection level of each cell depends on a given antigen level.

Some studies developed virus-like algorithms specifically for routing problems. Kanoh & Tsukahara (2010) proposed a variant of a GA for the capacitated vehicle routing problem (CVRP) which updates and maintains a population of k viruses (each of which is a single route) with a better likelihood of producing quality feasible solutions. Each of these k viruses has the ability to infect solutions to make part of them resemble the virus, so that, after several iterations, the method leads to improved solutions. Prins (2004) presented a viral-movement like hybrid GA for the distance-constrained CVRP that initially solves a problem by relaxing the vehicle capacity and maximum tour length constraints, and subsequently executes a second stage optimization run consisting of an optimal splitting procedure to generate competitive solutions with feasible tours. Suryadi & Kandi (2012) developed a viral systems algorithm emulating the cellular infection process to solve the traveling salesman problem. They proposed two moves (i.e. lytic replication and lysogenic replication) to change the locations (i.e., sequence) of the nodes within the solution.

While valuable in many respects, none of the above studies has developed a framework specifically for TS that mimics the viral infection process, nor proposed a framework that solves a given problem by emulating an indirect, gradual transformation process of certain flu viruses. This study fills this gap in the literature by investigating a new framework that combines TS and the aforementioned gradual viral transformation process. Given the widespread use of TS among researchers and practitioners, there should be considerable value in developing such a framework.

THE FRAMEWORK

Solution Strategy

First, we create a series of problems $\{P_1, P_2, P_3, ..., P_m, ..., P_M\}$, where P_M is the focal (original) problem to be solved (which is difficult to solve) and $P_1, P_2, ...$ represent the problems similar to, but less complex than, P_M (their problem size, denoted n, is smaller than that of P_M). The problems are numbered such that P_m has a smaller n than P_{m+1}. n of two adjacent problems (P_m and P_{m+1}) are similar, but those of P_1 and P_M are substantially different (i.e., P_1 is substantially easier to solve than P_M). Second, we solve P_1 to either optimality or near optimality (given that P_1 is easy to solve, this can be done, for example, by using enumeration). We denote the best solution found for P_1 as S_1. Third, we solve P_2 via the method that can perform an in-depth neighborhood search (TS) by using S_1 (or its slightly modified version) *as the initial solution*. Fourth, we repeat the above process (i.e., solve P_m by running TS which uses S_{m-1} as the initial solution) many times, successively moving from one problem to another, until we reach and solve the focal problem P_M.[1]

Note that, in essence, our framework performs the following set of actions: (*i*) generate an optimal (or near-optimal) solution to P_1, the simplified form of P_M (denoted S_1), (*ii*) transmit S_1 to a similar, but more complex, environment (P_2) and let it evolve within the new environment until it transforms itself into another form that performs well within this new environment (S_2), and (*iii*) repeat this transmission (evolution) process many times until the solution transforms itself into a form that performs well in the final environment (S_M) (see Figure 2 for the outline of our framework). Also note that, although executing the above framework may seem time-consuming, as it requires a series of TS runs, its actual run time may not be very long for two reasons. First, in most TS runs n is much smaller than that of P_M, so that these runs would not take long time. Second, since P_{m-1} and P_m are "similar" problems, meaning that the best solution found for P_{m-1} is a good candidate for the

Figure 2. Outline of the framework

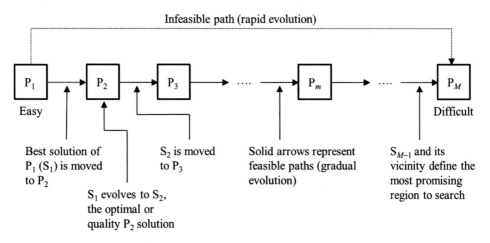

Infeasible path (rapid evolution)

Easy   Difficult

Best solution of S_2 is moved   Solid arrows represent S_{M-1} and its
P_1 (S_1) is moved   to P_3 feasible paths (gradual   vicinity define the
to P_2 evolution)   most promising
                                                                                  region to search

S_1 evolves to S_2,
the optimal or
quality P_2 solution

optimal solution of P_m, the TS run for P_m (which uses a proxy of the P_{m-1} best solution as the initial solution) should, in many cases, converge to quality solutions quickly.[2]

Diversification and Intensification

Although in the previous paragraph we argued that each TS run is expected to find quality solutions quickly in the vicinity of the initial solution, this does not mean that we merely focus on searching the areas near the initial solution in each TS run. Since the initial solution may not always be located near the optimal solution, and since it is known that diversification is a useful strategy for finding quality solutions, we perform multiple diversifications in each TS run. However, because executing many diversifications in each TS run can be time-consuming, we employ an approach which performs intensive (a larger number of) diversifications when n is small, but performs a limited number of diversifications as n grows larger. There are two reasons for this.

First, from the standpoint of finding quality solutions, we may not need to perform as many diversifications when m is large (i.e., when n is large) as when m is small (when n is small). Note that, given that the change in n from P_m to P_{m+1} must always be "gradual" (i.e., the difference in n between P_m and P_{m+1} is small; e.g., 2), the degree of change from, say, $n = 100$ to 102 (2% change) may be less "drastic" than that from $n = 10$ to 12 (20% change). This implies that, to find good solutions, more extensive search (more diversifications) may be needed when m is small than when it is large, as it may take more time for an initial solution to "evolve" into the form that fits well to the new environment when the difference between old and new environments is drastic than when it is moderate. Second, since it is less time-consuming to perform many diversifications (and intensifications) when n is small than when it is large, the above approach allows us to perform a large number of diversifications without significantly increasing the frameworks' overall run time.

Note that, given the diversification strategy above, our framework becomes conceptually similar to simulated annealing (SA). Recall that our framework first executes a series of small-scale TS runs, each of which performs many diversifications, to explore various parts of the P_M feasible region by using its small "replicas", and then executes a final TS run which performs a focused local search with limited diversifications around the area given by the initial solution (the most promising area identified by the series of small-scale TS runs). This approach is similar to that of SA, which initially performs an extensive search of a large solution space (by accepting many inferior-quality solutions) but gradually focuses on searching narrow, more promising areas.

Potential Advantage

Notice that standard TS methods generally rely on "unsystematic" diversification strategies to explore a large solution space; i.e., they attempt to improve the solution quality by moving the current solution to an arbitrarily or randomly-selected new region. This means that there is no guarantee that the diversification will move the solution to a *more-promising area* (that is more likely to contain an optimal solution). Hence, traditional diversification strategy may be viewed as a type of "trial and error", which can often be a time-consuming process with little or no rewards. Such strategy works only if we have sufficient time to perform a large (infinitely many) number of diversifications, but in practice decision makers have only limited time to solve a problem.

Our approach, in contrast, relies less on the use of "arbitrary" or "random" diversifications. Recall that our framework does not perform many diversifications in its final TS run, but instead performs an intensive local search of the small "promising" area (vicinity of the best solution found for P_{M-1}), which was identified by using a "systematic" procedure of solving $M - 1$ similar, but less complex, problems sequentially. This suggests that our framework relies less on "luck" but more on "evidence" derived from previous TS runs to identify the areas to explore in the final TS run. Therefore, unlike other (standard) TS methods, our framework may not suffer from the potentially inefficient search of the large P_M solution space based on the "trial and error" strategy.

APPLICATION TO THE VEHICLE-ROUGING PROBLEM

The above framework can be used to solve a variety of combinatorial problems. In this section, we develop a TS algorithm that solves the CVRP, and empirically test its performance.

Problem Definition

Let $G(V, A)$ be a complete graph, where $V = \{0, 1, 2, \ldots, n\}$ is the set of nodes, and A is the set of arcs connecting each pair of nodes. Customers are represented by nodes 1 to n, inclusive, and the depot by node 0. Distance (miles) of each arc (i, j) $\in A$ is denoted d_{ij}. Each customer $i \in V \setminus \{0\}$ has a nonnegative delivery demand D_i (pounds). A set of K identical vehicles, each with a capacity of Q (pounds), is available at the depot. The objective is to minimize the summed distance of all the arcs traversed by the vehicles. The constraints are that: (*i*) each vehicle route must start and end at the depot, (*ii*) each $i \in V \setminus \{0\}$ must be visited exactly once by one vehicle, and (*iii*) the sum of D_i's of all the customers visited by a single vehicle must not exceed Q. Following the standard practice, we use the string format to specify a CVRP solution. Under this format, a solution is given by a one-dimensional vector of $n + K + 1$ nodes with n customers and $K + 1$ depots (each sub-string in the vector which begins and ends with a zero represents a route).

Framework Application to the CVRP

To use our framework to solve the CVRP the following questions must be answered: (*i*) what is the proper size of P_1 (how small the value of n should be for P_1), (*ii*) what is the proper value of M (how many small replicas of the problem should be generated and solved), (*iii*) how small the difference of n should be between a given pair of adjacent problems P_m and P_{m+1}, (*iv*) how do we create P_{m+1} (which new customers should be added to P_m to define P_{m+1}), (*v*) how do we create the initial solution for P_{m+1} (where should we insert the new customers in the solution vector S_m to create the initial solution for P_{m+1}), and (*vi*) how do we set the TS termination criteria for each P_m. To answer these questions, we performed a series of preliminary experiments using the 50-node CVRP instance given in Christofides & Eilon (1969). The goal here was to determine the techniques and approaches that achieve the best performance. Details of these preliminary experiments, along with our findings, are discussed below (see Table 1 for the list of CVRP algorithms developed and tested in our preliminary experiments).

Table 1. Algorithms tested

Alg. No.	Node insertion	Simulated annealing	*pIncrease*	Tour addition	Tabu Tenure	Random number generation	Average solution value	Average run time (min)	Average optimality gap*
1	Random	–	1	–	$\sim U[\hat{c}_1,\hat{c}_2]$	Java Random	550.70	1.38	4.97%
2	Array angle	–	1	–	$\sim U[\hat{c}_1,\hat{c}_2]$	Java Random	544.35	1.37	3.76%
3	Array length	–	1	–	$\sim U[\hat{c}_1,\hat{c}_2]$	Java Random	546.56	1.60	4.18%
4	Array angle & length	–	1	–	$\sim U[\hat{c}_1,\hat{c}_2]$	Java Random	551.56	1.42	5.14%
5	Shortest Path	–	1	–	$\sim U[\hat{c}_1,\hat{c}_2]$	Java Random	536.35	1.54	2.24%
6	Shortest Path	ln P_M	1	–	$\sim U[\hat{c}_1,\hat{c}_2]$	Java Random	531.23	1.95	1.26%
7	Shortest Path	ln P_M	5	–	$\sim U[\hat{c}_1,\hat{c}_2]$	Java Random	530.09	2.92	1.04%
8	Shortest Path	Short in P_m, long in P_M	5	–	$\sim U[\hat{c}_1,\hat{c}_2]$	Java Random	529.45	2.05	0.92%
9	Shortest Path	Short in P_m Long In P_M	5	–	$\sim U[\hat{c}_1,\hat{c}_2]$	Java Random	533.25	2.05	1.65%
10	Shortest Path	Only in P_1 and P_M	5	–	$\sim U[\hat{c}_1,\hat{c}_2]$	Java Random	555.88	3.47	5.96%
11	Shortest Edge	Each P_m	5	–	$\sim U[\hat{c}_1,\hat{c}_2]$	Java Random	544.28	1.00	3.75%
12	Shortest Edge	–	1	–	$\sim U[\hat{c}_1,\hat{c}_2]$	Java Random	525.82	9.10	0.23%
13	Shortest Edge	–	$\lceil 0.1|\beta|\rceil$	–	$\sim U[\hat{c}_1,\hat{c}_2]$	Java Random	535.70	3.72	2.11%
14	Shortest Edge	–	$\lceil 0.1|\Omega|\rceil$	–	$\sim U[\hat{c}_1,\hat{c}_2]$	Java Random	527.51	7.39	0.55%
15	Shortest Edge	Each P_m (moves 0s)	1	–	$\sim U[\hat{c}_1,\hat{c}_2]$	Java Random	530.09	14.76	1.04%
16	Shortest Edge	–	Until S_m infeasible	–	$\sim U[\hat{c}_1,\hat{c}_2]$	Java Random	530.63	2.24	1.15%
17	Shortest Edge	–	Until S_m infeasible	If all tours infeasible beforeTS	$\sim U[\hat{c}_1,\hat{c}_2]$	Java Random	531.10	1.72	1.24%
18	Shortest Edge	–	Until S_m infeasible	If at least one tour infeasible after TS	$\sim U[\hat{c}_1,\hat{c}_2]$	Java Random	524.86	5.08	0.05%
19	Shortest Edge	–	Till all tours infeasible	If all tours infeasible before TS	$\sim U[\hat{c}_1,\hat{c}_2]$	Java Random	545.73	0.48	4.03%
20	Shortest Edge	–	Until S_m infeasible	If at least one tour infeasible after TS	$\sim U[\hat{c}_1,\hat{c}_2]$	Java Random	524.61	3.21	0.00%
21	Shortest Edge	–	Until S_m infeasible	If at least one tour infeasible after TS	$\sim U[\hat{c}_1,f(n)]$ $f\sim$ Exponential	Java Random	525.45	2.69	0.16%
22	Shortest Edge	–	Until S_m infeasible	If at least one tour infeasible after TS	$\sim U[\hat{c}_1,f(n)]$ $f\sim$ Logistics	Java Random	524.66	2.43	0.01%
23	Shortest Edge	–	Until S_m infeasible	If at least one tour infeasible after TS	$\sim U[\hat{c}_1,f(n)]$ $f\sim$ Logistics	Mersenne twister	524.76	2.49	0.03%
24	Shortest Edge	–	Until S_m infeasible	If at least one tour infeasible after TS	$\sim U[\hat{c}_1,f(n)]$ $f\sim$ Logistics	Mersenne twister 2	524.63	2.59	0.00%

*Gap when compared to the best known solution of 524.61 for the 50–customer instance.

Cardinality of P1

We evaluated different ways to create the first problem P_1 by varying the number of nodes (n) in P_1 (i.e., $|P_1|$). We experimented $|P_1| = 1$ to $|P_1| = 10$. Results showed that the better solutions almost always began with $|P_1| = 1$ (not including the depot).

Which Nodes/Arcs to Insert at Each Transition Phase

To determine which nodes to insert in each problem evolution phase ($P_m \rightarrow P_{m+1}$), we tested several methods. These methods include: (1) *random selection*, (2) *sweep method* (node with the smallest ray angle and ray length from the depot is added sequentially), (3) *shortest-path* method (node closest to the "last inserted" node is added sequentially), and (4) *shortest-edge* method (node having the shortest edge to any node in the current solution is inserted sequentially). For all methods, the new node was inserted into the position yielding the lowest insertion cost (the increment in solution value that is caused by inserting a node into a given position). Results showed that random selection and sweep method performed worse than the shortest-path or shortest-edge methods.

How Many Nodes to Insert at Each Transition Phase

We tested several approaches to determine the number of nodes to insert at each problem evolution phase (we denote this variable as *pIncrease*). The first approach inserts a fixed number of nodes to P_m at each evolution phase. We tested 1 and 5 for this fixed number. The second approach inserts a fixed percentage of the nodes in the set $\Omega = V \setminus \{\theta\}$ to P_m at each phase, where θ is the set of nodes already included in P_m (including the depot). The third approach, which is similar to the second approach, inserts $|\theta| \times y$ nodes of the set $\Omega = V \setminus \{\theta\}$ to P_m at each phase, where $0 \leq y \leq 1$ is a constant. Results of comparing the second and third approaches indicated that the former (with *pIncrease* = $\lceil 0.1|\Omega| \rceil$) outperformed the latter. This implies that it is more beneficial to insert a larger number of nodes when m is small, and to include fewer nodes as the problem becomes larger. The fourth approach inserts nodes continuously to P_m until at least one tour becomes infeasible. The fifth approach inserts nodes continuously to P_m until all tours become infeasible. Results showed that the fourth approach performs better than the fifth approach in term of the solution quality.

Vehicle Insertion (Tour Addition)

We tested several strategies to determine when to add new vehicles or tours (adds "0" to the solution vector) during the evolutionary process. The first is the method in which all tours are already included from the beginning; i.e., the initial solution S_1 of problem P_1 already has $K + 1$ zeros. The second is a method which starts with a single tour and adds a new tour to the solution each time a node insertion triggers capacity violation; i.e., add "0" to the solution if, after inserting customers and running TS at each evolution phase, at least one tour is infeasible (the process of inserting tour and running TS is repeated until the solution becomes feasible). The third is similar to the second, except that a new tour is added to the solution if, after inserting customers and running TS at each evolution phase, all tours are infeasible (if solution is neither feasible nor in the state where all tours are infeasible, the combined process of customer insertion and TS run is repeated). The fourth is a special version used only for algorithm 21, whose *pIncrease* strategy is to insert customers to the solution until all tours become infeasible. In this fourth strategy one tour is first inserted into the solution before running TS, and then repeats the process of adding a tour and running TS until the solution becomes feasible. Results showed that the second strategy is the best, while the first is the worst.

Tabu Tenure

We tested three ways to determine the tabu tenure of each visited solution. The first is the approach used by Toth & Vigo (2003), which specifies the tabu tenure of each move as a uniformly distributed random variable within a fixed range. The second and third use the approach in which the range of distribution is adjusted flexibly during the evolutionary process such that the upper bound of the distribution is determined as a function of n (lower bound remains constant). Specifically, the second approach uses an exponential function, while the third approach uses a logistic function, to specify the upper bound (i.e., upper bounds are increasing functions of n). The latter two approaches provided significantly better solution qualities and moderately faster CPU times than the first.

Simulated Annealing (SA) Run

We tested whether performing a quick SA run(s) during the evolutionary process would help improve the solution quality. We examined three ways of running SA within our framework. The first is to perform a quick SA run on P_M before the TS is executed. The second is to perform a quick SA run on each P_m (before TS). The third is the same as the second, except that the SA run for P_M is more extensive (yet still a relatively quick run) than other SA runs. The fourth is to perform two SA runs; one on P_1 and one on P_M (before TS). The fifth is to perform a special SA run on each P_m (before TS), which moves (relocates) only "0"s (depots). Results showed that there is little merit to using these approaches for improving the solution quality or the CPU time (observe in Table 1 that none of the top-performing algorithms use SA).

Random Number Generation

We explored the possibility of improving the performance of our framework by finding good random number generators (RNGs). We tested, in addition to the standard Java Random class, another pseudo–random number generator available in Java called the *Mersenne Twister* (Matsumoto & Nishimura, 1998). Results did not show any statistical difference in solution quality between the two RNGs (For further details refer to Table 1, Algorithms No. 23 and 24).

The CVRP Algorithm

The final version of the CVRP algorithm selected for this study, which reflects the best-performing algorithm found during our preliminary experiments (Table 1, Algorithm No. 22), is shown below.

Step 1: (Initialization). Set $m = 1$ and $T = \infty$

Step 2: (Define existing solution). If $m = T + 1$ then stop. Otherwise, define the existing solution either as S_{m-1}, the best solution found for the immediate proceeding problem P_{m-1} (if $m > 1$), or as $\{0, k^*, 0\}$, where $k^* \in V \setminus \{0\}$ is the node closest to the depot (if $m = 1$).

Step 3: (Expand solution). Compute for each unvisited node $k \in V \setminus \{0\}$ the insertion cost $C_k = \min\{d_{ik} + d_{kj} - d_{ij}\}$ for all adjacent nodes i and j of the existing solution. Choose the node with lowest C_k value and insert it between i^* and j^* where i^* and j^* are the two nodes yielding C_k.

Step 4: (Create P_m). Repeat step 3 until the vehicle-capacity constraint is violated in at least one route. The existing solution now includes all the nodes from P_{m-1} and the ones added in step 3 (including the node which triggered the capacity violation). The set of customers and vehicles included in the resulting solution defines P_m. This solution also defines the initial P_m solution.

Step 5: (Execute TS). Using the initial solution obtained in Step 4, run TS to solve P_m (rate of diversification must be controlled such that the smaller the m the higher the diversification frequency). If no feasible solution is found, add one vehicle to the solution (insert "0" at the end of solution string) and re-run TS. Store in memory the best feasible solution found (S_m). If the set of customers in P_m contains all $k \in V \setminus \{0\}$ let $T = m$. Increment m by 1 and return to Step 2.

Specifics of TS

So far, we have been using the term "TS" in a generic way without providing details. There are many types of TS procedures proposed in the literature, and any type can be used in our framework. In our CVRP algorithm, we use the Granular Tabu Search (GTS) developed by Toth & Vigo (2003). The concept of GTS is based on the use of restricted neighborhoods, which do not contain solutions involving long edges. The GTS's granular neighborhoods can be seen as a form of a candidate-list strategy (Glover & Laguna, 1997) in which, given a set of all available moves $N(x)$, only a subset $N'(x)$ is considered for a given solution x (thus saving considerable computing time at each iteration). Specifics of the GTS are beyond the scope of this chapter, and are not discussed. We, however, discuss below the four major adjustments we made to the GTS.

First, we use only two definitions of neighborhoods in our GTS. Although Toth & Vigo (2003) suggest that four definitions be used when selecting a move in each GTS iteration (two exchange, customer insertion, two-customer exchange, and customer swap), this approach, while effective, can be time-consuming. Based on the empirical findings reported in the VRP literature (e.g. Ohlmann & Thomas, 2007; Xiao et al., 2012), we use only two definitions (rules) to shorten the total TS run time; namely the customer insertion and the two exchange (also known as 2-Opt).

Second, we use flexible diversification tactics. Following Toth & Vigo (2003), we trigger a diversification procedure by increasing the *sparsification parameter* β (cut-off value of edge length that defines $N'(x)$) from its standard value (1.25) to a higher value (denoted β^h). Instead of fixing the β^h value (the approach adopted by Toth & Vigo, 2003), however, we adjust β^h flexibly from one diversification to the next by the formula: $\beta^h = 1.25 \times 1.4^{1+u}$, where u is the number of unsuccessful diversifications (no new-best solution is found before reaching the maximum iterations) counted since the last successful diversification. Our experience shows that that this approach gives better solutions.

Third, we use longer tabu tenure. Toth & Vigo (2003) suggest that the tabu tenure t for each performed move be specified by a uniformly distributed integer random variable in the interval $[t_{min}, t_{max}]$, where $t_{min} = 5$ and $t_{max} = 10$. In our GTS, however, we use a larger upper bound for the interval, especially for problems with large n. Specifically, we set $t_{min} = 10$ and adjust t_{max} dynamically from one problem (P_m) to another (P_{m+1}) by using the following functional form:

$$t^m_{max} = \left| (\hat{\alpha} - \alpha_{min}) \frac{1}{1 + e^{a_1 + b_1 m}} + \alpha_{min} \right| \qquad \forall \ m \in \{1, 2, ..., M\} \qquad (1)$$

where t^m_{max} is the t_{max} for P_m, $\alpha_{min} = 20$, $\hat{\alpha} = 10\alpha_{min}$, $a_1 \approx 4.545$, and $b_1 \approx -0.017$. Eqn. (1) indicates that t_{max} is an increasing function of n, and ranges roughly from 20 to 200. Our experience indicates that this strategy, which reduces the risk of "being trapped" at local optima when n is large, allows us to shorten the run time of GTS noticeably without compromising the solution quality drastically.

Fourth, we use a hybrid stopping rule. Toth & Vigo (2003) suggest using a termination criterion based on the number of non-improving iterations. However, in addition to this rule, we also use a run-time based criterion to control the run time (TS stops when one of these two criteria is met). Specifically, we define T_m, the maximum TS run time (seconds) allowed so solve P_m, as:

$$T_m = \begin{cases} e^{a_2 + b_2 m} & m < M \\ \beta & m = M \end{cases} \qquad \forall \ m \in \{1, 2, ..., M\} \qquad (2)$$

where $a_2 \approx -2.933$, $b_2 \approx 0.006$, and $\beta = 3600$. This hybrid termination rule allows us not only to control the overall run time, but also to implement the "SA-like" search strategy discussed earlier (in section Diversification and Intensification) by controlling the TS diversification frequency (i.e., the larger the m the lower the frequency of diversification). Note that, although eqn. (2) above shows a positive relationship between the run time and m, the number (frequency) of diversifications permitted per run will actually diminish with the increase of m. This is because, as m (n) becomes larger, the size of the neighborhood that must be explored by TS in each iteration increases exponentially (i.e., the speed by which the neighborhood size increases with m is faster than that by which T_m increases with m).

PERFORMANCE TESTING OF THE CVRP ALGORITHM

Design

Our goal is to compare the quality and speed of solutions between the following two algorithms: (*i*) one that executes the GTS (as described in the previous section) in a standard way (without changing the problem size during optimization) (GTS-I), and (*ii*) one that executes the (same) GTS but in a manner according to our framework

(GTS-II). GTS-I uses SA to generate the initial solution, and adopts the termination rule of Toth & Vigo (2003) (not the hybrid rule of section Specifics of TS).

Because scenarios with specific properties that we require for experiments were not readily available from the CVRP literature, we generated our own instances. In these instances, the four parameters of our interest (n, variance of the arcs' length, variance of the customers' demand, and vehicle capacity) were varied across three levels (low, medium, and high). Characteristics of these instances are shown in Table 2. The available number of vehicles per instance was determined by the formula: $\lceil q(V\backslash\{0\})/Q \rceil + 2$, where $q(V)$ is the summed demand of all the nodes in the set $V\backslash \{0\}$ (see Toth & Vigo, 2002). Although we performed nearly 2,000 optimization runs, only the results of 90 runs are reported here (10 runs per each of the nine instances shown in Table 2), which are most appropriate to directly compare GTS-I and GTS-II. Results are reported in Tables 3 and 4.

Solution Quality

In 8 out of 9 instances (89%), GTS-II delivered better lower bounds of the solution value (minimum value out of the 10 runs) than GTS-I. This suggests that, in terms of the ability to find the best solution for a given instance, GTS-II does a better job than GTS-I. With respect to the average solution value (average of the 10 runs), we see that, in 5 out of 9 instances (56%), GTS-II outperformed GTS-I; i.e., the former outperformed the latter in the majority of instances. However, GTS-II slightly un-

Table 2. Experimental design

Instance No.	Size	Capacity (No. of vehicles)	Variance (arcs)[a]	Variance (demand)[a]
1	**50**	750 (15)	100%	100%
2	150	**500 (22)**	100%	100%
3	150	750 (15)	**54%**	100%
4	150	750 (15)	100%	**27%**
5	150	750 (15)	100%	100%
6	150	750 (15)	100%	**255%**
7	150	750 (15)	**205%**	100%
8	150	**1000 (12)**	100%	100%
9	**250**	750 (15)	100%	100%

[a]Each value shown in these columns represents the extent to which the variance is smaller or larger than the standard value. For example, 54% means that the variance is set to be 54% of the standard value.

Note: Bold figures represent the upper and lower bounds of the experimental factors used in our computational experiments.

Table 3. Computational results

Instance No.	GTS-I			GTS-II		
	Average sol. value	Minimum sol. value	Average run time	Average sol. value	Minimum sol. value	Average run time
1	2,243.33	2,221.21	1.49	**2,225.22**	**2,210.66**	5.92
2	3,485.85	3,465.93	37.31	3,507.69	3,469.50	38.61
3	2,247.02	2,238.75	98.69	**2,242.49**	**2,235.22**	**45.97**
4	2,407.21	2,387.81	52.69	2,416.15	**2,386.50**	**35.11**
5	2,401.64	2,381.86	65.83	2,417.74	**2,379.90**	**34.49**
6	2,394.18	2,370.50	4.71	2,399.48	**2,370.08**	28.50
7	2,612.77	2,592.54	3.31	**2,601.92**	**2,573.20**	24.42
8	1,949.65	1,932.54	15.08	**1,949.35**	**1,925.45**	21.15
9	2,476.99	2,468.47	68.05	**2,469.72**	**2,457.03**	**57.59**
Grand Average	2,468.74	1,932.54	38.57	2,475.82	**1,925.45**	**32.54**

Note: Bold figures indicate the cases where GTS-II outperformed GTS-1.

Table 4. Improvement made by GTS-II over GTS-I

Instance	Average solution value	Minimum solution value	Average run time
1	**0.81%**	**0.47%**	-298.69%
2	-0.63%	-0.10%	-3.48%
3	**0.20%**	**0.16%**	**53.42%**
4	-0.37%	**0.05%**	**33.38%**
5	-0.67%	**0.08%**	**47.60%**
6	-0.22%	**0.02%**	-505.49%
7	**0.42%**	**0.75%**	-638.50%
8	**0.02%**	**0.37%**	-40.29%
9	**0.29%**	**0.46%**	**15.37%**
Grand Average	-0.29%	**0.37%**	**15.63%**

Note: Bold figures indicate the cases where GTS-II outperformed GTS-I.

derperformed GTS-I in terms of the overall average solution value (mean of average solution value across 9 instances). This implies that, while GTS-II generally outperforms GTS-I in terms of the solution quality, it may suffer from large solution-value variances. This finding was surprising to us, as we had expected GTS-II to produce more consistent solution values than GTS-I, given that GTS-II relies less on luck but more on evidence when searching solutions.

It is worth noting that GTS-II demonstrated the worst performance in instance No. 2 (this is the only instance in which GTS-II outperformed GTS-I in *neither* the minimum *nor* the average solution value). Instance 2 reflects to the case where three of the four parameters (problem size, arc variance, and demand variance) are set at the medium level, while the last parameter, vehicle capacity, is set at the low level. This decrease in vehicle capacity, or the increase in the number of vehicles required to serve customers, may have triggered the decline in GTS-II performance.

Run Time

Our testing showed mixed results. On the one hand, GTS-II underperformed GTS-I in CPU time in the majority (5 out of 9) instances (56%), but on the other hand, GTS-II outperformed GTS-I in terms of the overall average CPU time. Such results suggest that the run time of the two algorithms may be similar. Note, however, that GTS-II seems to attain faster run times than GTS-I when n is large. Tables 3 and 4 show that, in terms of CPU time, GTS-II underperforms GTS-I notably in instance No. 1 ($n = 50$), but outperforms GTS-I notably in instance No. 9 ($n = 250$). Run times of the two algorithms seem indistinguishable in the remaining seven instances (where $n = 150$) (GTS-II underperforms GTS-I in 4 out of 7 instances, but outperforms GTS-I in the overall average run time). This implies that GTS-II may be able to solve larger problems at faster speeds than GTS-I.

It is worth noting that GTS-II demonstrated the worst run-time performance in instances No. 6 and 7 (in terms of the percentage gap relative to GTS-I). Interestingly, these represent the instances in which the arc-length variance and the demand variance, respectively, are set to high levels. This might imply that GTS-II's smooth transition process from P_{m-1} to P_m may be distorted by high parameter variances, which, in turn, may worsen the run-time performance of GTS-II.[3]

CONCLUSION

The framework tested in this study, which emulates the gradual evolution process of certain flu viruses, demonstrated interesting results. When compared with a well-known TS method, the framework tends to find a better lower bound of the solution value in most instances, while using roughly the same amount of computing time. Our framework, therefore, may work nicely in cases where finding the best solution just once is more important than finding good solutions consistently over many optimization runs (e.g., for solving strategic, rather than tactical, business problems). The framework also seems to achieve faster run times than the standard TS method when solving large problems. Future research may wish to extend our study by modifying the framework such that it can produce more consistent solution values and run times over many optimization runs.

REFERENCES

Arakawa, T., Kubota, N., & Fukuda, T. (1996). Virus-evolutionary genetic algorithm with subpopulations: application to trajectory generation of redundant manipulator through energy optimization. *1996 IEEE International Conference on Systems, Man and Cybernetics. Information Intelligence and Systems*, *3*, 1930–1935. doi:10.1109/ICSMC.1996.565413

Christofides, N., & Eilon, S. (1969). An Algorithm for the Vehicle- dispatching Problem. *Operations Research*, *20*(3), 309–318. doi:10.1057/jors.1969.75

Chun, J., Jung, H., & Hahn, S. (1998). A study on comparison of optimization performances between immune algorithm and other heuristic algorithms. *IEEE Transactions on Magnetics*, *34*(5), 2912–2915.

Cortes, P., Onieva, L., Munuzuri, J., & Guadix, J. (2013). A viral system algorithm to optimize the car dispatching in elevator group control systems of tall buildings. *Computers & Industrial Engineering*, *64*(1), 403–411. doi:10.1016/j.cie.2012.11.002

Gendreau, M., & Potvin, J.-Y. (Eds.). (2010). Handbook of Metaheuristics. Boston, MA: Springer US. doi:10.1007/978-1-4419-1665-5

Glover, F., & Laguna, M. (1997). *Tabu Search* (1st ed.). Boston, MA: Kluwer Academic Publishers. doi:10.1007/978-1-4615-6089-0

Ho, S. L., Shiyou Yang, , Guangzheng Ni, , & Wong, H. C. (2001). An improved Tabu search for the global optimizations of electromagnetic devices. *IEEE Transactions on Magnetics*, *37*(5), 3570–3574. doi:10.1109/20.952664

Kanoh, H., & Tsukahara, S. (2010). Solving real-world vehicle routing problems with time windows using virus evolution strategy. *International Journal of Knowledge-Based and Intelligent Engineering Systems*, *14*(3), 115–126. doi:10.3233/KES-2010-0194

Matsumoto, M., & Nishimura, T. (1998). Mersenne twister: A 623-dimensionally equidistributed uniform pseudo-random number generator. *ACM Transactions on Modeling and Computer Simulation*, *8*(1), 3–30. doi:10.1145/272991.272995

Ohlmann, J. W., & Thomas, B. W. (2007). A Compressed-Annealing Heuristic for the Traveling Salesman Problem with Time Windows. *INFORMS Journal on Computing, 19*(1), 80–90. doi:10.1287/ijoc.1050.0145

Prins, C. (2004). A simple and effective evolutionary algorithm for the vehicle routing problem. *Computers & Operations Research, 31*(12), 1985–2002. doi:10.1016/S0305-0548(03)00158-8

Suryadi, D., & Kandi, Y. (2012). A Viral Systems Algorithm for the Traveling Salesman Problem.*Proceedings of the 2012 International Conference on Industrial Engineering and Operations Management*, 1989–1994.

Suzuki, Y., & Cortes, J. D. (2016). A Tabu Search with Gradual Evolution Process. *Computers & Industrial Engineering, 100*, 25–57. doi:10.1016/j.cie.2016.08.004

Toth, P., & Vigo, D. (2002). *The Vehicle Routing Problem*. SIAM. doi:10.1137/1.9780898718515

Toth, P., & Vigo, D. (2003). The Granular Tabu Search and Its Application to the Vehicle-Routing Problem. *INFORMS Journal on Computing, 15*(4), 333–346. doi:10.1287/ijoc.15.4.333.24890

Xiao, Y., Zhao, Q., Kaku, I., & Xu, Y. (2012). Development of a fuel consumption optimization model for the capacitated vehicle routing problem. *Computers & Operations Research, 39*(7), 1419–1431. doi:10.1016/j.cor.2011.08.013

ENDNOTES

[1]   Strictly speaking, the sequence P_1, …, P_m,…, P_M needs not be ascending in problem complexity (i.e., problem size needs not grow with m). The sequence can also be descending in problem complexity (i.e., evolutionary process can start with a more complex problem and use its best solution as the initial solution to solve the next, less complex, problem). This latter approach, however, would generally be difficult to implement because of higher computational requirements.

[2]   Though our approach may look similar to dynamic programming (DP), they are fundamentally different. In DP, the original problem is divided into multiple *non-overlapping* sub-problems (stages), each of which is solved to determine the best solution for a multi-stage process. Our approach, in contrast, does not divide the original problem into stages, but instead creates multiple *overlapping, interconnected* problems (each of which is a reduced form representation of

the original problem) and solves them sequentially to obtain a good candidate initial solution for the original problem.

3   In instance No. 6, for example, where the arc length has a higher variance than other instances, any node insertion to S_{m-1} (in the process of creating initial P_m solution) can have a higher risk of inserting long edges to the solution, which can worsen the quality of initial P_m solution and require long computing time to transform it into a good final P_m solution. Similarly, in instance No. 7, where the demand variance is higher than other instances, any node insertion to S_{m-1} can have a higher risk of severely impacting the total payload of the existing tours, which can make the initial P_m solution infeasible and require long CPU time to transform it into a good final (feasible) solution.

Section 3
Collective Intelligence–Based Computational Techniques

Sometimes a group of insects or animals or birds move together in search of food source or shelter. Collective Intelligence deals with the intelligence of a group emerging as the result of actions and reactions among the individual elements of the swarming group. The individual elements of a group follow simple rules and interact with each other for sharing information among them to achieve the overall goal such as finding food source or shelter. Most of the insect colonies such as ants, bees, termites, wasps, lion pride, fish schools and flock of birds etc., form the basis of this category-based nature-inspired computational technique since self-organization and decentralization are the identifying as well motivating features of these colonies.

Chapter 7
Automatic Generation Control of Hydro–Hydro Interconnected Power System Based on Ant Colony Optimization

Jagatheesan Kaliannan
Mahendra Institute of Engineering and Technology, India

Nilanjan Dey
Techno India College of Technology, India

Anand B
Hindusthan College of Engg. & Tech., India

Amira S. Ashour
Tanta University, Egypt

Valentina E. Balas
Aurel Vlaicu University of Arad, Romania

Nguyen Gia Nhu
Duy Tan University, Vietnam

ABSTRACT

Each hydropower system incorporates with appropriate hydro turbine, and hydro governor unit. In the current work, an Automatic Generation Control (AGC) of two equal hydropower systems with Proportional-Integral-Derivative (PID) controller was investigated. The gain values of the PID controllers were tuned using Ant Colony Optimization (ACO) technique with one percent Step Load Perturbation (1% SLP) in area 1. The Integral Square Error (ISE), Integral Time Square Error (ITSE), Integral Absolute Error (IAE) and Integral Time Absolute Error (ITAE) were chosen as the objective function in order to optimize the controller's gain values. The experimental results reported that the IAE based PID controller improved the system performance compared to other objective functions during sudden load disturbance.

DOI: 10.4018/978-1-5225-2322-2.ch007

INTRODUCTION

Generally, the power system (power plant) converts one form of energy into electrical energy with the help of appropriate techniques. For example, the thermal power plant operates with heat energy, while the hydro power plant operates with kinetic energy in water. Additionally, the solar power plant operates using sun light and the wind power plant operates using kinetic energy in wind. Based on literature, it is found that few studies have been carried out involving AGC investigation of hydro power system with PID controller. The load frequency control of interconnected hydro power system has been investigated by considering fuzzy Proportional-Integral (PI) controller in Ramanand Kashyap et al. 2013. Load frequency Control (LFC) of hydro power system has been studied by implementing fuzzy PID controller in Ramanand Kashyap and Sankeswari 2014. Meena and Kumar 2014 discussed the LFC crisis in four area interconnected hydro power system. Furthermore, the performance of the system was improved by implementing Superconducting Magnetic Energy Storage (SMES) unit. The PI controller was designed for AGC of hydropower system in Prajod and Carolin Mabel 2014; while the LFC of two area interconnected power system was discussed with SMES unit in Rajaguru 2015. Sahu *et al.* 2015 designed a fuzzy based PID controller, which implemented in AGC of multi-area power system. In addition, the authors optimized the controller gain values by using Teaching Learning Based Optimization (TLBO) technique. Shabani *et al.* 2015 implemented a PID controller for LFC of power system. Moreover, the gain values are optimized by using Imperialist Competitive Algorithm (ICA). Ant colony optimization technique based PID controller was implemented in hydro thermal power system (Jagatheesan et al. 2015; Omar et al. 2013). From the preceding literature, it is clearly established that fuzzy logic controller is applied effectively in AGC applications (Gomes et al. 2010; Mohsen Ebrahimian Baydokhty et al. 2016, Madic et al. 2012; Engin Yesil 2014, Bevrani, and Daneshmand 2012; Shweta Tyagi 2014; Yousef 2014; Setiawan, Noor Akhmad 2014). In addition, it is reported that using optimization algorithms has a significant role with the PID controllers.

Related Works to LFC/AGC of Multi-Area Interconnected Power System

Based on the literature survey it is evident that many optimization techniques are developed and implemented for tuning of secondary controller gain values in AGC/LFC of power system. The different optimization techniques for tuning of controller gain values using LFC/AGC of power systems are clearly tabulated in Table 1.

Table 1. Related works to the LFC/AGC of multi- area interconnected power systems

Year	Control strategies	Authors and Years
1978	Parameter-plane technique	Nanda and kaul, 1978
1982	Lyapunov Technique	Tripathy, et al. 1982
1983	Continuous and Discrete mode Optimization	Nanda, et al. 1983
1988	Optimal Control theory	Kothari and Nandha, 1988
1989	Adaptive Controller	Pan and Lian, 1989
1991	Variable Structure Control(VSC)	Das, et al. 1991
2006	Artificial Neural Network (ANN)	Demiroren, et al. (2006); Shayeghi et al. (2006)
2009	Genetic Algorithm (GA)	Chidambaram and Paramasivam (2009)
2009	Particle Swarm Optimization (PSO)	Ebrahim, et al. (2009)
2009	Fuzzy Logic Controller (FLC)	Anand and Ebenezer Jeyakumar (2009)
2010	Classical controller,	Nandha and Mishra (2010)
2011	Genetic Algorithm	Arivoli and Chidambaram (2010)
2011	Bacterial Foraging Optimization Algorithm (BFOA)	Ali and Abd-Elazim (2011)
2011	Craziness Based Particle Swarm Optimization (CRAZYPSO)	Gozde et al. (2011)
2012	Artificial Bee Colony (ABC)	Gozde et al. (2012)
2013	Bacterial Foraging (BF) technique	Lalit Chandra Saikia et al. (2013)
2013	Ant Colony Optimization	Omar et al.(2013)
2013	Ant Weight lifting Algorithm	Samanta et al. (2013)
2014	Stochastic Particle Swarm Optimization (SPSO)	Jagatheesan et al. (2014)
2014	Ant Colony Optimization	Jagatheesan and Anand (2014)
2014	Cuckoo Search (CS)	Dey et al. (2014a)
2014	Cuckoo Search	Dey et al.(2014b)
2014	Firefly Algorithm (FA)	Dey et al. (2014)
2014	Firefly Algorithm	Sahu et al. (2014)
2015	Bat inspired algorithm	Das et al. (2015)
2015	Beta Wavelet Neural Network (BWNN)	Francis and Chidambaram (2015)
2015	Teaching Learning Based Optimization (TLBO)	Sahu et al. (2015)

continued on following page

Table 1. Continued

Year	Control strategies	Authors and Years
2015	Cuckoo Search	Das et al. (2015)
2015	Cuckoo Search	Das et al. (2015)
2015	Firefly Algorithm	Padhan et al. (2015)
2016	Ant Colony Optimization	Jagatheesan et al. (2016)
2016	Particle Swarm Optimization	Jagatheesan et al. (2016)
2016	Fuzzy Logic Controller	Jagatheesan et al. (2016)
2016	Flower Pollination Algorithm (FPA)	Jagatheesan et al. (2016)
2016	Ant Colony Optimization	Jagatheesan et al. (2016)

The present work, the performance analysis of two area interconnected hydro-hydro system with ACO technique optimized PID controller based on different objective function was proposed. Since the ISE, ITSE, ITAE cost function based ACO tuned PID controller does not grant satisfactory control performance, when using 1% step load disturbance in either area of the interconnected system. Thus, an IAE cost function based PID controller was proposed in this work. The PID controller effectively improve the performance of the system (Minimum settling time, peak over and under shoot, lesser damping oscillations) compared to other controller performance during sudden load demand in interconnected power system. Since with help of hydro power plants, the kinetic energy stored in the water is converted into useful mechanical energy. In this investigation, the hydro power plant is considered for the analysis. Consequently, the main contribution of proposed work is as follows:

1. Design two area hydro-hydro power system with PID controller
2. Design the suitable controller gain values based on the PID controller for the investigated power system
3. Optimize the controller gain values by using ACO technique with four different cost functions with 1% SLP in area 1
4. Compare the performance of different cost function based the investigated power system response

The remaining work is organized as follows. Details about the investigated power system and control strategy are provided. Afterward, simulation results of the investigated power system are discussed. Finally, the conclusion is represented.

HYDRO-HYDRO INTERCONNECTED POWER SYSTEM WITH PID CONTROLLER

The transfer function model of the investigated two area hydro-hydro power system is given in Figure 1 (Rajaguru et al. 2015). The investigated power system areas are equal size and equipped with suitable hydro governor, hydro turbine, and generator. The primary control loop in the power generating unit is a speed governor unit. It adjusts the power generation based on the load demand. However, the produced control signal by the speed governor is insufficient to satisfy the sudden load demand. In order to overcome this drawback, the PID controller is introduced as a secondary controller.

Figure 1. Transfer function model of two area hydro-hydro power system model

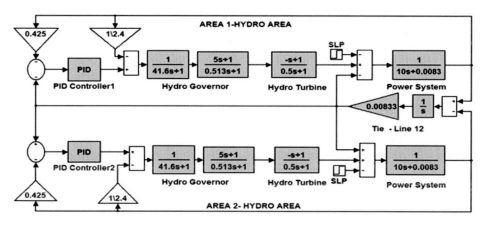

Table 1. Transfer function and nominal parameters of the power system components

Component	Transfer function	Nominal parameters
Hydro governor	$\dfrac{1}{1+sT_1} \cdot \dfrac{1+sT_R}{1+sT_2}$	$\dfrac{1}{1+41.6s} \cdot \dfrac{1+5s}{1+0.513s}$
Hydro turbine	$\dfrac{1-sT_w}{1-0.5sT_w}$	$\dfrac{1-s}{1-0.5s}$
Power system	$\dfrac{K_{p1}}{T_{p1}.s+1} \dfrac{K_{p2}}{T_{p2}.s+1}$	$\dfrac{1}{0.0083+10s}$
Tie-line	$\dfrac{2\Pi T_{12}}{s}$	$\dfrac{0.00833}{s}$

The transfer function of each component in the hydro power system is depicted in Table 1 (Rajaguru et al. 2015).

In Table 1, T_1 and T_2 represents the time constants of hydro governor, T_w shows the water starting time, T_{12} indicates the synchronizing coefficient, Kp_1 and Kp_2 identify the gain constant of generator, and T_{p1} and T_{p2} gives the time constant of a generator. Figure 1 illustrated the two equal hydro power plants, which interconnected through the tie-line. During normal or scheduled value, each power system caters to its own load and maintains nominal system parameters within their prescribed limit and stability. In the case of sudden load demand in any one of the areas in the interconnected power system, it will affect the system stability. Thus, the system response will exhibit more oscillations with large over-/under- shoot with steady state error. In order to overcome this issue, a proper secondary controller is required. In the power system, primary control loop speeds the regulator unit. The PID controller is introduced as a secondary controller in the power system (Sahu et al. 2015; Hamed Shabani et al. 2015; Jagatheesan et al. 2015; Omar et al. 2013). The transfer function of the PID controller is given by:

$$U(S) = K_p E(S) + \frac{K_p}{T_i S} E(S) + K_d E(S) \tag{1}$$

where, K_p is the proportional gain, K_i is the integral gain, K_d is the derivative gain, T_i is the integral time, T_d is the derivative time, S represents the Laplace function, and $E(s)$ identifies the error signal.

ANT COLONY OPTIMIZATION TECHNIQUE

Based on the exploring pheromone chemical information in the ground, the ants find foods from the nest without any visual cues. Randomly, all ants spread around the surroundings to search for food. After a short period of time, there is a difference in the amount of pheromone chemicals stored in the ground based on the food source quality and quantity. The shortest path has sufficiently large chemicals and it is useful for new ants in taking a decision about the shortest path. A new ant will prefer the lower path based on probability, since the decision making point perceives a greater amount of chemical pheromone on the lower path. This turn increases with a positive feedback and a number of new ants choose the lowest and the shortest path quickly. The aforementioned behaviors of real ants inspired researchers to develop ACO algorithm for solving combinatorial optimization problem (Dorigo 1992; Dorigo et al. 1997; Colorni et al. 1991; Jagatheesan et al. 2015; Omar et al. 2013).

The transition probability from town i and j for the k_{th} ant as follows:

$$p_{ij}(t) = \frac{\tau_{ij}(t)^{\alpha} \left(\eta_{ij}\right)^{\beta}}{\sum\limits_{j \in nodes} \tau_{ij}(t)^{\alpha} \left(\eta_{ij}\right)^{\beta}} \tag{2}$$

The pheromone value versus the heuristic information η_{ij} is given by:

$$\eta_{ij} = \frac{1}{d_{ij}} \tag{3}$$

The global updating rule is implemented in the ant system, where all ants start their tours. The pheromone is deposited and updated on all edges based on the following expression:

$$\tau_{ij}(t+1) = (1-\rho)\tau_{ij}(t) + \sum\limits_{\substack{k \in colony\ that \\ used\ edge\ (i,j)}} \frac{Q}{L_k} \tag{4}$$

where P_{ij} is the probability between the town i and j, τ_{ij} is the associated pheromone with the edge joining cities i and j, d_{ij} is the distance between cities i and j, Q is a constant, α, β are constants that find the relative time between pheromone and heuristic values on the decision of the ant, L_k is the length of the tour performed by K_{th} ant, and ρ is the evaporation rate.

In this study, according to experience the initialization parameters, namely the number of ants, pheromone (τ), evaporation rate (ρ), and number of iterations, are selected to give better result. The parameter values are selected as follows: Number of ants=50, pheromone (τ) =0.6, evaporation rate (ρ) =0.95 and number of iterations=100.

Generally, the improved performance of the controller in any power system depends on the proper selection of the controller's gain values. In this work, the controller gain values were optimized by using the ACO technique with four different objective functions. These objective functions are ISE, ITSE, IAE and ITAE objective function [Jagatheesan et al. 2015; Omar et al. 2013; Jagatheesan and Anand 2015]. The expression of ISE, ITSE, IAE and ITAE objective functions are as follows:

$$J = ISE = \int_0^t \left(ACE_i\right)^2 dt \tag{5}$$

$$J = ITSE = \int_0^t t.\left(ACE_i\right)^2 dt \tag{6}$$

$$J = IAE = \int_0^t \left|ACE_i\right| dt \tag{7}$$

$$J = ITAE = \int_0^t t.\left|ACE_i\right| dt \tag{8}$$

Where, J refers to the performance index, t is the simulation time and $e(t)$ is the error signal.

Based on the ACO optimized controller, the optimal gain values are calculated. These optimized gain values are implemented into the investigated power system and compared to the open loop performance of the same power system.

HYDRO-HYDRO INTERCONNECTED POWER SYSTEM WITH PID CONTROLLER

The investigated two area hydro-hydro power system is designed using MATLAB/SIMULINK environment. The open loop performance of the system is obtained by considering one percent Step Load Perturbation (1% SLP) in area 1. For simulation results, the time duration of 300s is used. The PID controller gain values are optimized using ACO technique with different objective function. The optimized based controller gain values based on different cost functions are given in the Table 2.

Table 2. Optimal gain values of PID controller

Cost function	K_{P1}	K_{P2}	K_{I1}	K_{I2}	K_{D1}	K_{D2}
ISE	9.1	7.9	0.2	0.3	9.3	5.1
ITSE	9.5	8.4	0.2	0.1	6.6	3.8
IAE	9.8	9.8	0.2	0.2	8.3	8.5
ITAE	9.5	7.8	0.4	0	9.6	0.5

The performance comparisons of the open loop response and response with the PID controller are demonstrated in Figures 2 to 4. Figure 2 indicates the frequency deviation of the open loop response and the response with PID for the same investigated power system of area 1.

In Figure 2, the dotted line, and the solid bold line represent the open loop response of system and the response of the system with PID controller in the investigated power system; respectively. From the above response, it is established that the optimized controller reduces effectively the damping oscillations with minimal damping oscillations and zero steady state error. Figure 3 illustrates the frequency deviation comparisons in area 2.

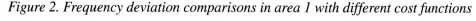

Figure 2. Frequency deviation comparisons in area 1 with different cost functions

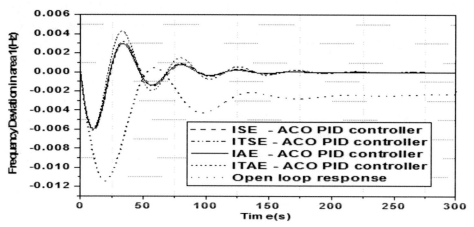

Figure 3. Frequency deviation comparisons in area 2 with different cost functions

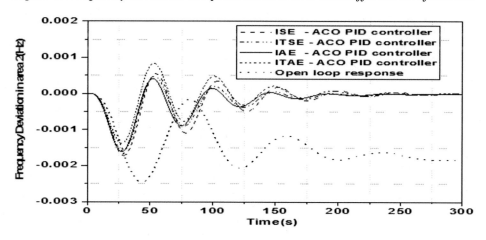

161

Figure 3 depicts that the response with PID controller guarantees better dynamic response. In addition, it improves the performance of the system during sudden loading conditions. Figure 4 represents the response comparison of tie-line power flow deviations comparisons between area 1 and area 2.

Figures 2-4 establish the improvement of the power system dynamic performance during normal or sudden loading conditions by implementing properly tuned secondary PID controller. The performance of the power system is measured in terms of the time domain specifications such as: Settling time, peak over shoot, and under shoot. The numerical values of these metrics are given in the Table 3.

Based on the numerical values in the Table 3, the bar chart comparisons of the peak overshoot, peak undershoot, settling time and steady state comparisons are given in Figures 5-8; respectively.

From the tabulated numerical values in the Table 3 and the bar chart comparisons in Figure 5, it is clearly illustrated that the IAE objective based ACO-PID controller provides minimum overshoot in the response compared to other objective functions based controller and open loop response of the system response. Meanwhile, Figure 6 demonstrates the bar chart comparisons of the peak undershoot with different objective functions PID controller response.

Figure 6 depicts that the open response has more under shoot values without any controller in the system. The undershoot values in the system response is effectively reduced by using the ITAE objective function based ACO-PID controller compared to other objective functions based control response in the interconnected power system.

Figure 4. Tie-line power flow deviations in between area 1 and 2 with different cost functions

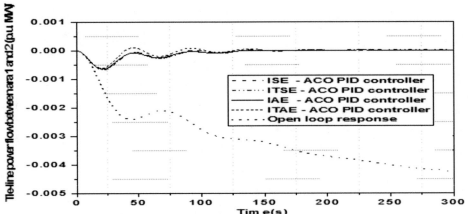

Table 3. Time domain specification parameters (O_{sh}, U_{sh}, T_s and e_{ss}) of investigated power system with different objective functions

Cost function	Parameter / Response	delF1	delF2	delPtie
ISE	O_{sh}	0.0029	0.00054	**0.000015**
	U_{sh}	0.0058	0.0017	**0.0006**
	T_s	**204.1**	278.89	239.09
	e_{ss}	0	0	0
ITSE	O_{sh}	0.0031	0.00047	**0.00001**
	U_{sh}	0.006	0.0015	**0.00066**
	T_s	200.6	274.14	**196.29**
	e_{ss}	0	0	**0**
IAE	O_{sh}	0.0028	0.0004	**0.000004**
	U_{sh}	0.0059	0.0016	**0.00064**
	T_s	**154.52**	226.78	167.61
	e_{ss}	0	0	0
ITAE	O_{sh}	0.0042	0.0008	**0.000095**
	U_{sh}	0.0057	0.0013	**0.00061**
	T_s	**201.8**	251.37	212.02
	e_{ss}	0	0	0
Open loop response	O_{sh}	0.00037	**0**	**0**
	U_{sh}	0.0113	0.0024	**0.0023**
	T_s	**219.96**	274.18	293.64
	e_{ss}	0.0023	**0.0018**	0.0042

Figure 5. Bar chart comparisons of peak overshoots with different objective functions

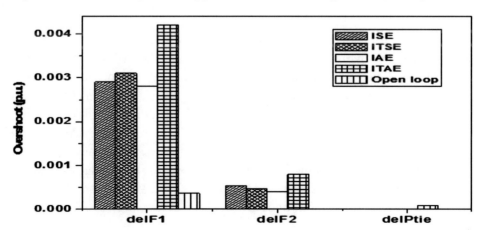

Figure 6. Bar chart comparisons of peak undershoots with different objective functions

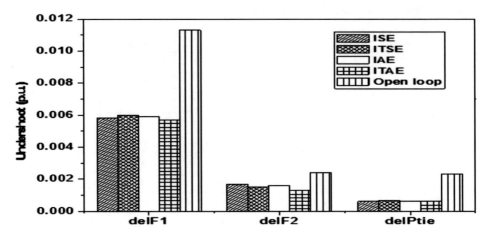

Figure 7. Bar chart comparisons of settling time with different objective functions

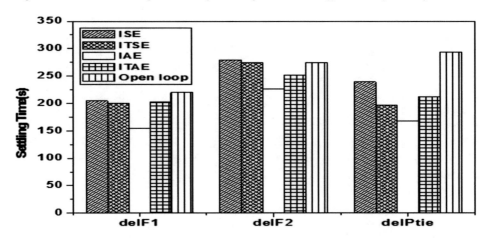

Moreover, the tabulated values in Table 3 along with the bar chart comparisons of the settling time in Figure 7 are clearly illustrated that the IAE objective function based ACO-optimized PID controller provides the fast settle response compared to other objective function in the system response. Figure 8 demonstrates the steady state error comparisons in the system response with open loop and different objective function based ACO-PID controller performance. It is clearly evident that the closed loop response does not yield error values in the system response.

The numerical values in the Table 3 and Figures 5-8 report that the dynamic performance of the system is improved by the IAE objective function based ACO-PID controller response in terms of peak over shoot and settling time. However, the

Figure 8. Bar chart comparisons of steady state error with different objective functions

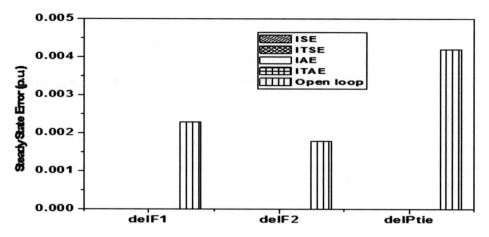

undershot in the response is effectively reduced by the ITAE objective function based ACO-PID controller.

CONCLUSION

In this work, the AGC of two area hydro-hydro power system was investigated with PID controller. The PID controller gain values were optimized by using ACO technique based four different objective functions. The performance of the proposed algorithm based controller was compared with different objective functions based controller performance. In addition, the open loop performance for the same investigated power system was considered. Finally, during sudden loading condition, the simulation result clearly established that the performance of the system was improved by implementing IAE based PID controller compared to other objective functions and open loop response of the system.

REFERENCES

Shabani, Vahidi, & Ebrahimpour. (2015). A robust PID controller based on Imperialist competitive algorithm for load frequency control of power systems. *ISA Transactions*, *52*, 88–95.

Ali, E. S., & Abd-Elazim, S. M. (2011). Bacteria foraging optimization algorithm based load frequency controller for interconnected power system. *Electric Power and Energy Systems*, *33*(3), 633–638. doi:10.1016/j.ijepes.2010.12.022

Arivoli, A., & Chidambaram, I. A. (2011). Design of genetic algorithm (GA) based controller for load-frequency control of power systems interconnected with AC-DC TIE-LINE. *Int J Sci. Engineering Tech, 2*, 280–286.

Baydokhty, M. E., Zare, A., & Balochian, S. (2016). Performance of optimal hierarchical type 2 fuzzy controller for load-frequency system with production rate limitation and governor dead band. *Alexndraia Engineering Journal, 55*(1), 379–397. doi:10.1016/j.aej.2015.12.003

Bevrani, H., & Daneshmand, P. R. (2012). Fuzzy logic-based load-frequency control concerning high penetration of wind turbines. *IEEE Syst. J., 6*(1), 173–180. doi:10.1109/JSYST.2011.2163028

Chidambaram, I. A., & Paramasivam, B. (2009). Genetic algorithm based decentralized controllerfor load-frequency control of interconnected power systems with RFB considering TCPS in the tie-line. International Journal of Electronic Engineering Research, 1, 299-312.

Colorni, Dorigo, & Maniezzo. (1991). *Distributed optimization by at colonies.* Elsevier Publishing.

Dash, Saikia, & Sinha. (2014). Comparison of performances of several Cuckoo search algorithm based 2DOF controllers in AGC of multi-area thermal system. *Electrical Power and Energy Systems, 55*, 429–436.

Dash, Saikia, & Sinha. (2015a). Automatic generation control of multi area thermal system using Bat algorithm optimized PD-PID cascade controller. *Electric Power and Energy Systems, 68*, 364–372.

Dash, Saikia, & Sinha. (2015b). Comparison of performance of several FACTS devices using Cuckoo search algorithm optimized 2DOF controllers in multi-area AGC. *Electric Power and Energy Systems, 65*, 316–324.

Demiroren,A, Zeynelgil, A.Z, & Sengor, N.S. (n.d.). *The application of ANN technique to load frequency control for three-area power systems.* IEEE Porto power tech conference, Porto, Portugal.

Prajod & Mabel. (2014). Design of PI controller using MPRS method for Automatic Generation Control of hydro power system. *International Journal of Theoretical and Applied Research in Mechanical Engineering, 2*(1), 1–7.

Dey, N., Samanta, S., Chakraborty, S., Das, A., Chaudhuri, S. S., & Suri, J. S. (2014). Firefly Algorithm for Optimization of Scaling Factors during Embedding of Manifold Medical Information: An Application in Ophthalmology Imaging. *Journal of Medical Imaging and Health Informatics*, 4(3), 384–394. doi:10.1166/jmihi.2014.1265

Dey, N., Samanta, S., Yang, X. S., Chaudhri, S. S., & Das, A. (2014). Optimization of Scaling Factors in Electrocardiogram Signal Watermarking using Cuckoo Search. *International Journal of Bio-inspired Computation*, 5(5), 315–326. doi:10.1504/IJBIC.2013.057193

Dorigo, M. (1992). *Optimization, Learning and Natural Algorithms* (PhD thesis). Politecnico di Milano.

Dorigo, M., & Gambardella, L. M. (1997). Ant colony system: A cooperative learning approach to the traveling salesman problem. *IEEE Transactions on Evolutionary Computation*, 1(1), 53–66. doi:10.1109/4235.585892

Ebrahim, Mostafa, Gawish, & Bendary. (2009). Design of decentralized load frequency based-PID controller using stochastic Particle swarm optimization technique. *International Conference on Electric Power and Energy Conversion System*, 1-6.

Francis, R., & Chidambaram, I.A. (2015). Optimized PI+ load-frequency controller using BWNN approach for an interconnected reheat power system with RFB and hydrogen electrolyzer units. *Electric Power and Energy Systems, 67*, 381-392.

Gomes, A., Antunes, C. H., & Martins, A. G. (2010). Improving the responsiveness of NSGA-II using an adaptive mutation operator: A case study. *Int. J. of Advanced Intelligence Paradigms*, 2(1), 4–18. doi:10.1504/IJAIP.2010.029437

Gozde, Taplamacioglu. (2011). Automatic generation control application with craziness based particle swarm optimization in a thermal power system. *Electrical Power and Energy Systems, 33*, 8-16.

Gozde, H., & Taplamacioglu, C. (2012). Comparative performance analysis of Artificial Bee Colony algorithm in automatic generation control for interconnected reheat thermal power system. *Electric Power and Energy Systems*, 42(1), 167–178. doi:10.1016/j.ijepes.2012.03.039

Jagatheesan, Anand, Dey, & Ashour. (2016). Ant Colony Optimization algorithm based PID controller for LFC of single area power system with non-linearity and boiler dynamics. World Journal of Modeling and Simulation, 12(1), 3-14.

Jagatheesan, Anand, Dey, & Balas. (2016). *Load Frequency Control of Hydro-Hydro System with Fuzzy Logic Controller Considering Non-Linearity.* World Conference on Soft Computing, Berkeley, CA.

Jagatheesan, Anand, Santhi, Dey, Ashour, & Balas. (2016). Dynamic Performance Analysis of AGC of Multi-Area Power System Considering Proportional-Integral-Derivative Controller with Different Cost Functions. *Proceeding of IEEE International Conference on Electrical, Electronics, and Optimization Techniques.*

Jagatheesan, K. (2015). Performance analysis of double reheat turbine in multi-area AGC system using conventional and ant colony optimization technique. *Journal of Electronic and Electrical Engineering, 15*(1), 1849–1854.

Jagatheesan, K. (2015). Automatic generation control of Thermal-Thermal-Hydro power systems with PID controller using ant colony optimization. *International Journal of Service Science, Management, Engineering, and Technology, 6*(2), 18–34. doi:10.4018/ijssmet.2015040102

Jagatheesan, K. (2016). Particle Swarm Optimization based Parameters Optimization of PID Controller for Load Frequency Control of Multi-area Reheat Thermal Power Systems. *International Journal of Artificial Paradigm.*

Jagatheesan, K., Anand, B., & Ebrahim, M.A. (2014). Stochastic Particle Swarm Optimization for tuning of PID Controller in Load Frequency Control of Single Area Reheat Thermal Power System. *International Journal of Electrical and Power Engineering, 8*(2), 33-40.

Jagatheesan, K., & Anand, B. (2016). Application of Flower Pollination Algorithm in Load Frequency Control of multi-area interconnected power system with non-linearity,". *Neural Computing & Applications*, 1–14.

Jagatheesan, K., & Anand, B. (2014). Automatic Generation Control of Three Area Hydro-Thermal Power Systems considering Electric and Mechanical Governor with conventional and Ant Colony Optimization technique. *Advances in Natural and Applied Science, 8*(20), 25-33.

Jagatheesan, K., Anand, B., Dey, N., & S, A. (2015). Artificial Intelligence in Performance Analysis of Load Frequency Control in Thermal-Wind-Hydro Power Systems. *International Journal of Advanced Computer Science and Applications, 6*(7), 203–212. doi:10.14569/IJACSA.2015.060727

Kashyap & Sankeswari. (2014). A simulation model for LFC using fuzzy PID with interconnected hydro power systems. *International Journal of Current Engineering and Technology*, (3), 183-186.

Kothari, M. L., & Nanda, J. (1988). Application of optimal control strategy to automatic generation control of a hydrothermal system. *IEE Proceedings, 135*(4), 268-274. doi:10.1049/ip-d.1988.0037

Madic, M. (2012). Performance comparison of meta-heuristic algorithms for training artificial neural networks in modeling laser cutting. *Int. J. of Advanced Intelligence Paradigms, 2*(4), 316–335.

Nanda, J., & Kaul, B. L. (1978). Automatic generation control of an interconnected power system. *Proc. IEE, 125*(5), 385-390. doi:10.1049/piee.1978.0094

Nanda, J., Kothari, M. L., & Satsangi, P. S. (1983). Automatic generation control of an interconnected hydrothermal system in continuous and discrete modes considering generation rate constraints. *IEE Proc., 130*(1), 17-27. doi:10.1049/ip-d.1983.0004

Omar, M., Solimn, M., Abdel Ghany, A.M., & Bendary, F. (2013). Optimal tuning of PID controllers for hydrothermal load frequency control using ant colony optimization. International Journal on Electrical Engineering and Informatics, 5(3), 348-356.

Padhan, Sahu, & Panda. (2014). Application of Firefly Algorithm for Load Frequency Control of Multi-area interconnected power system. *Electric Power Components and Systems, 42*(13), 1419-1430.

Pan, C. T., & Liaw, C. M. (1989). An adaptive controller for power system load-frequency control,'. *IEEE Transactions on Power Systems, 4*(1), 122–128. doi:10.1109/59.32469

Rajaguru, V., Sathya, R., & Shanmugam, V. (2015). Load Frequency Control in an Interconnected Hydro–Hydro Power System with Superconducting Magnetic Energy Storage Units. *International Journal of Current Engineering and Technology, 5*(2), 1243–1248.

Ramanand Kashyap, S. S. (2013). Load Frequency Control Using Fuzzy PI Controller Generation of Interconnected Hydro Power System. *International Journal of Emerging Technology and Advanced Engineering, 3*(9), 655–659.

Ruby Meenaand, S. (2014). Load Frequency Stabilization of four area hydro thermal system using Superconducting Magnetic Energy Storage System. *IACSIT International Journal of Engineering and Technology, 6*(3), 1564–1572.

Sahu, Panda, & Padhan. (2015). A hybrid firefly algorithm and pattern search technique for automatic generation control of multi area power systems. *Electric Power and Energy Systems, 64*, 9-23.

Sahu, B. K., Pati, S., Mohanty, P. K., & Panda, S. (2015). Teaching-learning based optimization algorithm based fuzzy-PID controller for automatic generation control of multi-area power system. *Applied Soft Computing*, *27*, 240–249. doi:10.1016/j. asoc.2014.11.027

Saikia, L. C., Sinha, N., & Nanda, J. (2013). Maiden application of bacterial foraging based fuzzy IDD controller in AGC of a multi-area hydrothermal system. *Electric Power and Energy Systems*, *45*(1), 98–106. doi:10.1016/j.ijepes.2012.08.052

Samanta, S., Acharjee, S., Mukherjee, A., Das, D., & Dey, N. (2013). Ant Weight Lifting Algorithm for Image Segmentation. *2013 IEEE International Conference on Computational Intelligence and Computing Research*,1-5. doi:10.1109/IC-CIC.2013.6724160

Setiawan. (2014). Fuzzy Decision Support System for Coronary Artery Disease Diagnosis Based on Rough Set Theory. *International Journal of Rough Sets and Data Analysis, 1*(1), 65-80.

Tripathy, S. C., Hope, G. S., & Malik, O. P. (1982). Optimization of load-frequency control parameters for power systems with reheat steam turbines and governor dead band nonlinearity. *IEE Proc.*, *129*(1), 10-16.

Tyagi, S., & Bharadwaj, K. K. (2014). A Particle Swarm Optimization Approach to Fuzzy Case-based Reasoning in the Framework of Collaborative Filtering. *International Journal of Rough Sets and Data Analysis*, *1*(1), 48–64. doi:10.4018/ijrsda.2014010104

Yesil, E. (2014). Interval type-2 fuzzy PID load frequency controller using big bang-big crunch optimization. *Applied Soft Computing*, *15*, 100–112. doi:10.1016/j. asoc.2013.10.031

Chapter 8

Particle Swarm Optimization for Cost Reduction in Mobile Location Management Using Reporting Cell Planning Approach

Smita Parija
NIT Rourkela, India

Sudhansu Sekhar Singh
KIIT University, India

Swati Swayamsiddha
KIIT University, India

ABSTRACT

Location management is a very critical and intricate problem in wireless mobile communication which involves tracking the movement of the mobile users in the cellular network. Particle Swarm Optimization (PSO) is proposed for the optimal design of the cellular network using reporting cell planning (RCP) strategy. In this state-of-the-art approach, the proposed algorithm reduces the involved total cost such as location update and paging cost for the location management issue. The same technique is proved to be a competitive approach to different existing test network problems showing the efficacy of the proposed method through simulation results.

DOI: 10.4018/978-1-5225-2322-2.ch008

The result obtained is also validated for real network data obtained from BSNL, Odisha. Particle Swarm Optimization is used to find the optimal set of reporting cells in a given cellular network by minimizing the location management cost. This RCP technique applied to this cost minimization problem has given improved result as compared to the results obtained in the previous literature.

INTRODUCTION

In a wireless mobile communication, location management is of prime importance as it is concerned with the tracking of the location of the mobile terminals so that the incoming call or data can be forwarded to the relevant cell within the cellular network. The number of mobile subscribers are rising exponentially and inorder to accommodate them within limited spectrum resources the cell capacity and coverage has to be increased which is achieved by decreased cell size according to the concept of frequency reuse (Mukherjee & De, 2016; Sidhu & Singh, 2007).Thus, the probability of movement of the mobile terminals from one cell to another increases within the network which increases the overhead cost for location management of the mobile subcribers. This paper aims to reduce the overhead cost incurred for tracking the exact location of the mobile users.

The wireless cellular network comprises of hexagonal shaped geographical areas called cells. The base station at the center of each cell services and monitors all the mobile devices within its coverage region. The base station is able to make the communication link between two active mobile terminals (MTs) through the mobile switching centre (MSC). The MSCs are connected to Public Switched Telephone Network (PSTN) as illustrated in Figure 1 which shows a typical cellular network.

In each cell, every mobile terminal (MT) communicates with another terminal through wireless links. The base stations are connected to a radio network controller (RNC) which plays an important role during the routing of a call in that service area. Forwarding a call to a MT is a complex operation. For the call delivery first the network need to locate the exact location of the cell where the MT resides. Thus, the location search of the cell where the MT is currently residing is an important and essential issue of mobile location management. Mobile location management is basically concerned with tracking an active MT within the wireless mobile network. As the MTs are free to move within the network area a certain amount of cost is associated with the network for locating them. The network resources management and development of strategies for reducing this network cost is called mobile location management (Anisetti et al., 2011; J & M, 2010). It mainly involves two fundamental operations i.e. location registration(update) and location search (pag-

Figure 1. Cellular network

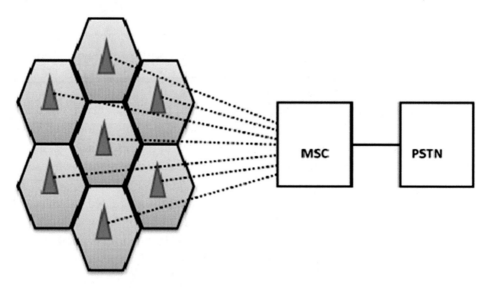

ing). Location update is performed whenever a MT changes it cellular position, by automatically sending a location registration request signal to the MSC. Location update is necessary for keeping the record of the position of the MT within the mobile cellular network. Thus, the mobile location is updated to the current residing cell and after that all the call procedures are carried out by the present residing cell base station until the mobile moves to a new cell. When there is an incoming call to a mobile user, the MSC routes the call to the base station in which the mobile terminal is currently residing.The base station then sends a broadcast signal to all the mobile terminals within its coverage area and routes the call to that mobile terminal which responds to the broadcast signal.Thus, the call is established between the two MTs.This phenomenon is called paging where the signal is broadcast to the MTs within the range of the cellular base station (Al-Surmi, Othman, & Mohd Ali, 2012).

In this paper, BPSO is used to solve the location management issue.The paper is organized as follows: in section II problem formulation is elaborated.Section III explains particle swarm optimization technique for location management issue. Simulation results and analysis is discussed in section IV.Section V presents the conclusion and future scope.

PROBLEM FORMULATION

Reporting cell planning (RCP) is one of the popular approaches for location management issue proposed in(S. M. Almeida-Luz, Vega-Rodríguez, Gómez-Pulido, & Sánchez-Pérez, 2009; Berrocal-plaza, Vega-rodríguez, Sánchez-pérez, & Gómez-pulido, 2012; Vega-rodr & Juan, 2014).In RCP, a subset of cells in the cellular network are assigned as reporting cells and it periodically transmits short messages for identification of its role. Upon entering a new reporting cell only a mobile terminal (MT) performs its location update.Paging is restricted to the last updated reporting cell and to its neighboring non- reporting cells during a call arrival to a mobile user. In other words, this set of reporting cells is considered as a boundary, where the locations of the mobile terminals are updated and the calls are routed (Al-Surmi et al., 2012; Subrata, Zomaya, & Member, 2003). The objective of this work is optimal design of RCP configuration so that the total cost of location update and paging is minimum. It is viewed as a discrete optimization problem because the RCP network configuration represented by the binary values 0s (non-reporting cells) and 1s (reporting cells) are the potential solutions for the optimization problem where the Particle Swarm Optimization (PSO) is used as a global optimization tool. The RCP problem which is a combinatorial optimization problem is an NP-complete problem (Alba, 2008; Berrocal-plaza et al., 2012; Kim, Kim, JI-HWAN BYEON, & Taheri, 2012; Singh & Karnan, 2010).

For example, in Figure 2, reporting cells/centers are 3, 6, 10, 11, 12, 13 and 16 and the others are non-reporting cells shown below in the RCP configuration. Suppose, a MT's location has been last updated in the reporting cell 3, so upon arrival of a call to the mobile, the paging/location search is performed in the current reporting cell and its vicinity non-reporting cells ie. in cell numbered 1, 2, 3, 4, 5, 7, 8 and 9.

The total location management cost of a specific cellular network is formulated as the sum of location updates and paging transactions completed over a period of time.

$$TotalManagement \cos t = \beta X N_{LU} + N_P \tag{1}$$

where, NLU is the number of location updates and NP is the total number of paging performed in the cellular network during time t. β is a constant representing the ratio of location update cost to paging cost, and is usually set as 10, i.e. $\beta = 10$ (Gondim, 1996), because it is recognised that the location update cost is usually much higher than the paging cost. In a given cellular network the total number of location updates and paging performed in a network during a certain period of time t can be calculated as follows:

Figure 2. Reporting cell configuration

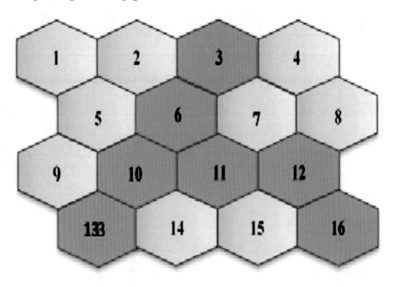

$$N_{LU} = \sum_{i \in S} w_{mi} \qquad (2)$$

$$N_P = \sum_{j=0}^{N} w_{cj} * v(j) \qquad (3)$$

where w_{mi} is the movement weight is associated with cell i and w_{cj} is call arrival weight of cell j. w_{mi} represents the total number (frequency) of MTs entering into a cell. w_{cj} represents the total number of calls arriving to a cell. Total number of cells in the network is N and S is the set of reporting cells and $v(j)$ is the vicinity value of cell j. Vicinity factor of a cell j is defined as the maximum cells where the search operation is performed when an call arrives in j. Movement weights and call arrival weights for each cell in the 4x4 test network and realistic BSNL network is shown in Table 1 and Table 2 respectively.

Hence, the total location management cost (Kim et al., 2012; Parija, Addanki, Sahu, & Singh, 2013) corresponding to a particular RCP configuration is computed as:

$$Total\ Cos\,t = \beta \times \sum_{i \in S} w_{mi} + \sum_{j=0}^{N} w_{cj} \times v(j) \qquad (3)$$

Table 1. Call arrival weights and Movement weights of Test network

Cell	w_{ci}	w_{mi}	Cell	w_{ci}	w_{mi}
1	517	518	9	251	445
2	573	774	10	224	2149
3	155	153	11	841	1658
4	307	1696	12	600	952
5	642	1617	13	25	307
6	951	472	14	540	385
7	526	650	15	695	1346
8	509	269	16	225	572

Source: (Kim et al., 2012)

Table 2: Call arrival weights and Movement weights of Real network(BSNL, Odisha)

Cell	w_{ci}	w_{mi}	Cell	w_{ci}	w_{mi}
1	807	349	9	163	36
2	700	61	10	497	289
3	398	321	11	3567	2045
4	185	21	12	1917	187
5	1197	6	13	289	38
6	980	30	14	236	105
7	533	285	15	451	193
8	1556	324	16	700	480

The cost per call arrival which is the fitness function is obtained as followed (Kim et al., 2012):

$$\text{Cos}t \ per \ call \ arrival = \frac{Total \ \text{Cos}t}{\sum_{j=0}^{N} w_{cj}} \tag{4}$$

BINARY PARTICLE SWARM OPTIMIZATION

Particle Swarm Optimization is a population based iterative algorithm. It starts with a population of solutions (particles) i.e. RC configurations as binary vectors, and at each iteration, the solutions are moved towards better solutions .The movement of particles in each iteration is based on its local best solution i.e. best solution that it has achieved so far (p_best) and global best i.e. overall best solution (g_best). The objective of our optimization problem is to minimize the total cost and thereby determine the optimal reporting cell configuration. The methodology of BPSO for RCP problem is explained in the following steps(Subrata et al., 2003; Taheri & Zomaya, 2008):

Step 1: Initialize a population of solutions (particles): each solution is a reporting cell configuration to the given RCP problem. Reporting cell is assigned '1' and non-reporting cell is assigned '0'.

Therefore in a 4X4 network, each solution is a 16 bit binary string shown in Table 3.

Ex: '0010010001111001'

Step 2: For each particle (P), evaluate Cost using equation (4).
Step 3: For each particle, store p_best and g_best in the iteration. If the current p_best cost is less than the previous p_best, then replace previous p_best with the current p_best. Similarly, if current g_best cost is less than the previous g_best then replace previous g_best with the current g_best.
Step 4: Compute the velocity and change in position of the particle according to the equations below.

$$V_{next} = w * V_{current} + c_1 * r_1 * [pbest_{current} - P_{current}] + c_2 * r_2 * [g\_best_{current} - P_{current}]$$

(6)

Particle position is moved from $P_{current}$ to P_{next}, using equation (7).

$$P_{next} = P_{current} + V_{next}$$

(7)

Table 3. Populations of solution with 16 Binary string

Cell 1	Cell 2	Cell 3	Cell 4	Cell 5	Cell 6	Cell 7	Cell 8
0	0	1	0	0	1	0	0
Cell 9	Cell 10	Cell 11	Cell 12	Cell 13	Cell 14	Cell 15	Cell 16
0	1	1	1	1	0	0	1

Step 5: Repeat the process from Step 2 until termination criterion is met.

Where *w, c1*r1, c2*r2* are weighting factors.
The flow chart for BPSO algorithm is shown in Fig 3.

COMPUTATIONAL RESULT AND ANALYSIS

The simulation results are carried out for reporting cell planning benchmark problems (Subrata et al., 2003; Taheri & Zomaya, 2008) as well as validated for the realistic networks. In this simulation section the different experiments are carried out on Intel Core (TM) 2 Duo CPU 32- bit operating system, 2.20 GHZ, 4G RAM, using Matlab for different network sizes such as 4x4,8x8 and 7x9. The obtained results, the respective analysis and conclusions are presented. Results are obtained for different iterations i.e. 50, 100 and 500 iterations. The number of iterations is set as stop criterion. The population size used for simulation is set to 100. Here, the RCP problem is implemented for different size networks that includes even as well as odd networks. The experiments are performed for symmetric networks 4x4(16 cells)(Kim et al., 2012) and 8x8(64 cells)(Subrata et al., 2003) test networks as well as realistic network including the asymmetric network 7x9 (63 cells) (Taheri & Zomaya, 2008). The simulation result shows the convergence graphs of the overall best/optimum RCP configuration cost for each of the iteration.

Figure 3. Flow chart for BPSO

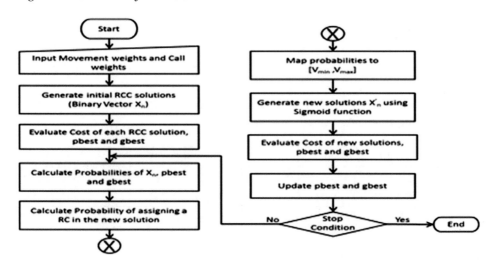

Significance of Fitness Function

In this reporting cell planning problem for measuring the total location management cost of each potential solution which is defined according to Equation 4 the fitness function is used. This signifies that for each potential solution generated, the fitness value is calculated which corresponds to the network configuration comprising of reporting cells and non-reporting cells.

Parameter Definition

The one of the most important step is the initial definition of parameters as it forms the basis of algorithm evolution. The initial population of candidate solution corresponds to the number of particles. Each of the particles is represents a binary solution vector of size N which corresponds to the number of cells in the RCP network. The binary configuration value gives the information about the cell type, either a reporting cell or a non-reporting cell in the RCP network.

The convergence plot of the total location management cost for 4x4 test networks is shown in Figure 4. The 4x4 real network convergence graphs are presented in Figure 5. Then the experimental results for higher network 8x8

test as well realistic network is shown in Figures 6 and 7 respectively. The Figure 8 shows the convergence plot for the odd test network of size 7x9. Similarly the convergence floor for the realistic 7x9 network is presented in Figure 9. From the convergence graphs it is seen that the convergence is fast in the initial iterations and slows down as the iterations increases. The simulation is therefore performed first with lower iteration value of 50 then for increased iteration value of 100 and 500. From the Figure 4, Figure 5, Figure 6, Figure 7, Figure 8 and Figure 9 it is seen that the convergence becomes comparatively smoother and provides the optimized cost value as the iteration progresses. The reason for this is, PSO starts with non-optimal, randomly generated solutions with high cost. As the iterations increases, the cost of particles in the algorithm is close to each other and hence the convergence is slow in improving the results.

The statistical analysis of the network is discussed as follows.

- **4x4 Networks:** For the small size network 4x4 using test data Cost/call obtained is 11.2341. Standard deviation is 0.2004, Mean 11, 2628, Minimum, Median is 11.2341, Max is 14.1703, P_pbest, P_gbest, and Cost_gbest is 0.3125, 0.2187 and 11.2341 respectively. Real data collected from service provider firm is used for validation where Cost/call is 4.2341 and Standard deviation, Mean, Minimum, Median, Maximum, P_pbest, P_gbest, Cost_ gbest are 0.0584, 3.9109, 3.9077, and 4.2341 respectively. The optimized value is also obtained for the expanded network.

Figure 4. Convergence floor of Cost per call arrival of 4 x 4 Test Data Networks for 50,100, and 500 iterations

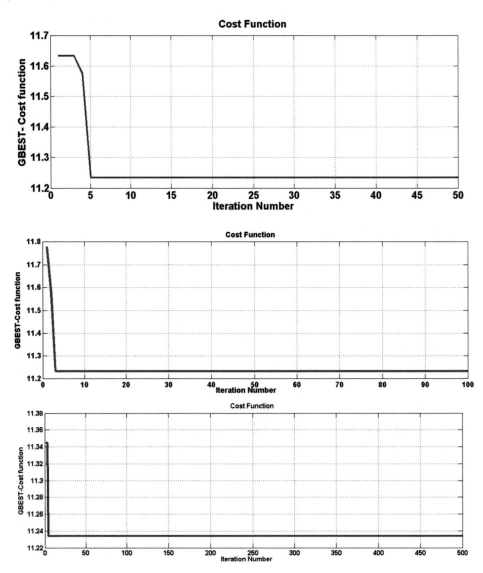

- **8x8 Networks:** The best configuration obtained for the 8x8 network is tested by taking the existing data, Cost/call obtained is 11.2341.Standard deviation is 0.2004, Mean 13. 1338, Minimum, Median is 11.2341, Max is 20.1598, P_pbest, P_gbest, Cost_gbest is 0.3125, 0.2187 and 19.1598 respectively. This simulation is run for 50,100 and 500 iterations, validated for realistic network where the Cost/call is 5.5395.

Figure 5. Convergence floor of Cost per call arrival of 4 x 4 Real Data Networks for 50,100 and 500 iterations

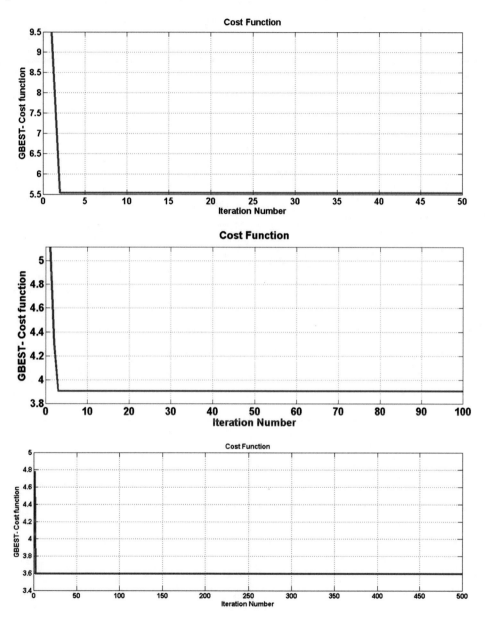

Figure 6. Convergence floor of Cost per call arrival of 8 x 8 Test Data Networks for 50,100, and 500 iterations

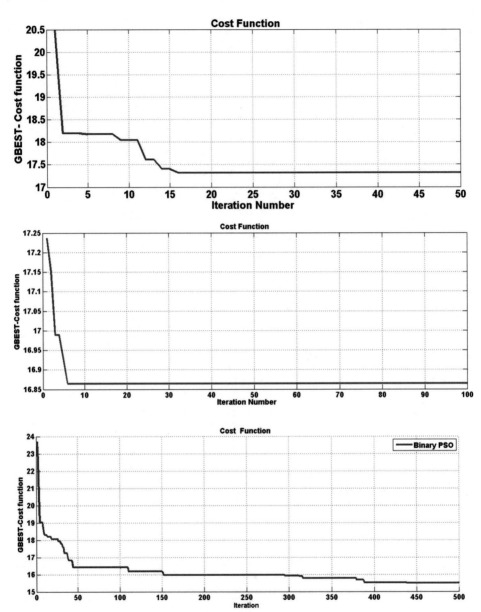

Figure 7. Convergence floor of Cost per call arrival of 8 x 8 Real Data Networks for 50,100, and 500 iterations

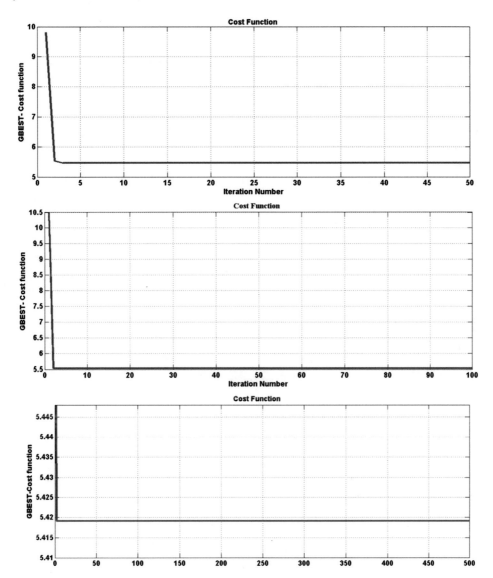

Figure 8. Convergence floor of Cost per call arrival of 7 x 9 Test Data Networks for 50,100 and 500 iterations

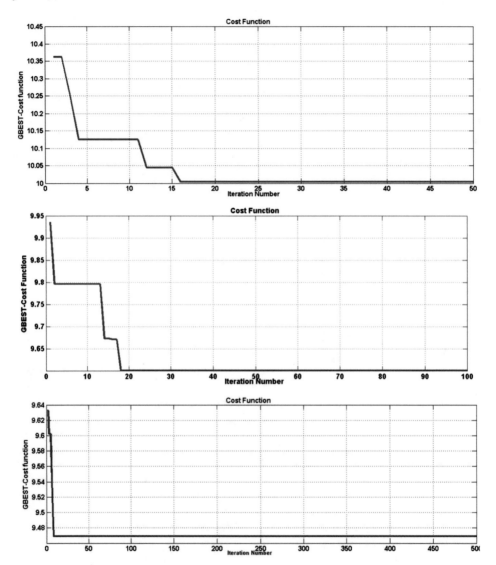

Figure 9. Convergence floor of Cost per call arrival of 7 x 9 Real Data Networks for 50,100 and 500 iterations

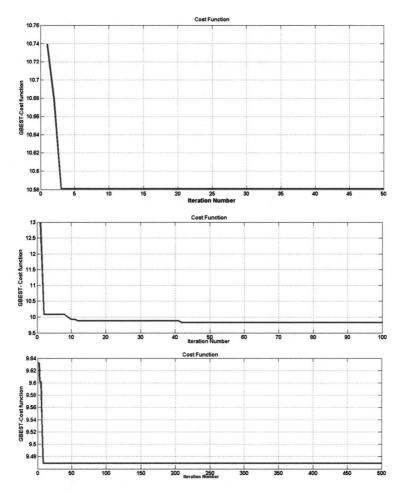

- **7x9 Networks:** The best/optimal solution for 7x9 networks run for 50,100 and 500 iterations, shown in Fig 8 validated for the realistic network where the Cost/call is 10.4873 but for test network Cost/call found to be 10.1777. Standard deviation is 0.1915, Mean 10.4873, Minimum and Median obtained same value i.e 10.1777, Max is 14.3503, P_pbest, P_gbest, Cost_gbest is 0.3125, 0.2187 and 10.4873 respectively for the real network.

Table 4 shows the result of different networks where mean, median, standard deviation and minimum and maximum location management cost is calculated. Table 5 defines the p_best and g_best using PSO that gives the best cost value

Table 4. Stastical Analysis of PSO

Refdatanetwork	Iteration	SD	Mean	Median	Min	Max
4x4	50	0.209	11.3047	11.2341	11.2341	12.3552
4x4	100	0.2987	11.2895	11.2341	11.2341	13.7416
4x4	500	0.1124	**11.2398**	**11.2328**	**11.2328**	**13.7347**
8x8	50	0.3299	17.4675	17.3203	17.3203	19.7239
8x8	100	0.4535	16.8514	16.6768	16.6768	19.6157
8x8	500	0.0999	**16.0138**	**15.4976**	**15.4976**	**19.1598**
7x9	50	0.8065	10.5848	17.4546	17.4546	12.0894
7x9	100	0.1761	9.9931	16.6932	16.6932	11.2491
7x9	500	0.1068	**9.4753**	**9.4690**	**9.4690**	**11.8371**
Realdatanetwork	**Iteration**	**SD**	**Mean**	**Median**	**Min**	**Max**
4x4	50	0.2398	5.6506	5.6506	5.6506	5.9554
4x4	100	0.1613	3.9421	3.9521	3.9421	4.0522
4x4	500	**0.0617**	**3.6197**	**3.5895**	**3.5895**	**4.7725**
8x8	50	0.9042	5.6304	5.5395	5.5395	10.1768
8x8	100	0.3390	5.5395	5.5125	5.5125	8.9486
8x8	500	0.2513	**5.4508**	**5.4113**	**5.4113**	**11.2051**
7x9	50	0.642	10.6757	10.5807	10.5807	15.0086
7x9	100	0.2217	9.8012	9.7621	9.7621	11.5021
7x9	500	0.1721	**9.4912**	**9.4712**	**9.4712**	**10.1432**

Table 5. Defining PSO for best Cost

Ref data network	Iteration	P_pbest	P_gbest	Cost_gbest	Real data network	Iteration	P_pbest	P_gbest	Cost_gbest
4x4	50	0.3125	0.2187	11.2341	4x4	50	0.4688	0.2188	5.6506
4x4	100	0.3125	0.2187	11.2341	4x4	100	0.3125	0.2187	3.9421
4x4	500	0.3125	0.2187	**11.2341**	4x4	500	0.4688	0.2187	**3.5925**
8x8	50	0.3125	0.2187	17.3203	8x8	50	0.3145	0.2201	5.4652
8x8	100	0.3125	0.2187	16.6768	8x8	100	0.4688	0.2188	*5.5884*
8x8	500	0.3125	0.2187	**15.4976**	8x8	500	0.3125	0.2187	**5.4183**
7x9	50	0.3125	0.2188	10.1037	7x9	50	0.3125	0.2187	10.5807
7x9	100	0.3125	0.2188	9.6002	7x9	100	0.3125	0.2187	10.4012
7x9	500	0.3125	0.2187	**9.4690**	7x9	500	0.3125	0.2187	**10.1213**

Table 6. Comparison of cost per call using PSO with respect to earlier studies

Network	PSO Test Network	ACO [17]	TS[18]	MHN [19]	DE[20]	BPSO [21]
6x6	**11.2328**	11.472	11.471	11.471	11.471	11.471
8x8	**15.4976**	14.725	14.725	N/A	13.782	13.782
7x9	**9.4690**	N/A	N/A	34.538	33.819	34.538

which is also validated for the real data network. The test network data is also used in (S. Almeida-Luz, A.Vega-Rodríguez, Gómez-Pulido, & Sánchez-Pérez, 2008; S. M. Almeida-Luz, Vega-Rodríguez, Gómez-Púlido, & Sánchez-Pérez, 2011).The best results are compared with the earlier studies such as modified Hopfield network (MHN), Ant colony optimization (ACO), and Tabu search (TS), Differential Evolution(DE), Binary Particle Swarm Optimisation(BPSO) proposed by the other authors and is presented in Table 6. The data is validated for even and odd network and it shows that the proposed algorithm gives the optimized result. Comparing the results with that of other authors where very high number of iterations are used the proposed algorithm performs well with 500 iterations.

CONCLUSION

Location management strategy using RCP is proposed in this work. The optimization problem is defined in terms of a location management cost function which is minimized using particle swarm optimization algorithm. The optimal set of reporting cells is determined for 16 cell network i.e. 4x4 cellular network which is taken as an example to discuss the problem formulation and solution methodology. The simulation results is then expanded for 4x4, 8x8 and 7x9 and also validated for the same network with the real data which are discussed and analyzed in Table 5 and Table 6.

Future work includes generalization of the optimization problem for any cellular network of size *N*, use of hybrid optimization algorithms and more detailed comparison analysis with other metaheuristic techniques as well as extending to realistic networks. The dynamic mobile location management is to be explored. Since there is an exponential rise in the number of mobile subscribers, and technology upgradation taking from 3G to 4G and beyond, mobile location management is of prime importance and the need of the hour is to implement this operation in a more efficient and optimized way for future generation mobile networks.

ACKNOWLEDGMENT

Authors would like to thank the Director of Bharat Sanchar Nigam Limited (BSNL) for providing the real data and their enormous support in this work. The authors also thank to anonymous reviewers whose feedback improved the quality of this paper.

REFERENCES

Al-Surmi, I., Othman, M., & Mohd Ali, B. (2012). Mobility management for IP-based next generation mobile networks: Review, challenge and perspective. *Journal of Network and Computer Applications*, *35*(1), 295–315. doi:10.1016/j.jnca.2011.09.001

Alba, E. (2008). *New Research in Nature Inspired Algorithms for Mobility Management in GSM Networks*. Academic Press.

Almeida-Luz, S., Vega-Rodríguez, A. M., Gómez-Pulido, J. A., & Sánchez-Pérez, J. M. (2008). Applying Differential Evolution to a Realistic Location Area Problem Using SUMATRA. *2008 The Second International Conference on Advanced Engineering Computing and Applications in Sciences*, 170–175. doi:10.1109/ADVCOMP.2008.19

Almeida-Luz, S. M., Vega-Rodríguez, M. a., Gómez-Pulido, J. a., & Sánchez-Pérez, J. M. (2009). Solving a Realistic Location Area Problem Using SUMATRA Networks with the Scatter Search Algorithm.*2009 Ninth International Conference on Intelligent Systems Design and Applications*, 689–694. doi:10.1109/ISDA.2009.51

Almeida-Luz, S. M., Vega-Rodríguez, M., Gómez-Púlido, J., & Sánchez-Pérez, J. M. (2011). Differential evolution for solving the mobile location management. *Applied Soft Computing*, *11*(1), 410–427. doi:10.1016/j.asoc.2009.11.031

Anisetti, M., Ardagna, C. A., Bellandi, V., Damiani, E., Member, S., & Reale, S. (2011). *Map-Based Location and Tracking in Multipath Outdoor Mobile Networks*. Academic Press.

Berrocal-plaza, V., Vega-rodríguez, M. A., Sánchez-pérez, J. M., & Gómez-pulido, J. A. (2012). *Solving the Location Areas Problem with Strength Pareto Evolutionary Algorithm*. Academic Press.

Gondim, P. R. L. (1996). Genetic Algorithms and The Location Area Partitioning Problem in Cellular Networks.*Proc. of IEEE 46th Vehicular Technology Conference*, 1835–1838. doi:10.1109/VETEC.1996.504075

J, A. P. S., & M, K. (2010). A Dynamic Location Management Scheme for Wirless Networks Using Cascaded Correlation Neural Network. *International Journal of Computer Theory and Engineering, 2*(4), 581–585. doi:10.7763/IJCTE.2010.V2.205

Kim, S.-S., & Kim, G., Byeon, J-H., & Taheri, J. (2012). Particle Swarm Optimization for Location Mobility Management. *International Journal of Innovative Computing, Information, & Control, 8*(12), 8387–8398.

Mukherjee, A., & De, D. (2016). ScienceDirect Location management in mobile network. *Survey (London, England), 19*, 1–14.

Parija, S. R., Addanki, P., Sahu, P. K., & Singh, S. S. (2013). *Cost Reduction in Reporting Cell Planning Configuration Using Soft Computing Algorithm*. Academic Press.

Sidhu, B., & Singh, H. (2007). Location Management in Cellular Networks. *Proceedings of World Academy of Science, Engineering and Technology, 21*, 314–319.

Singh, J. A. P., & Karnan, M. (2010). Intelligent Location Management Using Soft Computing Technique.*2010 Second International Conference on Communication Software and Networks*, 343–346. doi:10.1109/ICCSN.2010.60

Subrata, R., Zomaya, A. Y., & Member, S. (2003). A Comparison of Three Artificial Life Techniques for Reporting Cell Planning in Mobile Computing. *IEEE Transactions on Parallel and Distributed Systems, 14*(2), 142–153. doi:10.1109/TPDS.2003.1178878

Taheri, J., & Zomaya, A. Y. (2008). A modified hopfield network for mobility management. *Wireless Communications and Mobile Computing, 8*, 355–367.

Vega-rodr, M. A., & Juan, M. S. (2014). *Non-dominated Sorting and a Novel Formulation in the Reporting Cells Planning*. Academic Press.

Chapter 9
Intelligent Demand Forecasting and Replenishment System by Using Nature–Inspired Computing

Pragyan Nanda
SOA University, India

Sritam Patnaik
National University of Singapore, Singapore

Srikanta Patnaik
SOA University, India

ABSTRACT

The fashion apparel industry is too diverse, volatile and uncertain due to the fast changing market scenario. Forecasting demands of consumers has become survival necessity for organizations dealing with this field. Many traditional approaches have been proposed for improving the computational time and accuracy of the forecasting system. However, most of the approaches have over-looked the uncertainty existing in the fashion apparel market due to certain unpredictable events such as new trends, new promotions and advertisements, sudden rise and fall in economic conditions and so on. In this chapter, an intelligent multi-agent based demand forecasting and replenishment system has been proposed that adopts features from nature-inspired

DOI: 10.4018/978-1-5225-2322-2.ch009

computing for handling uncertainty of the fashion apparel industry. The proposed system is inspired from the group hunting behaviour of crocodiles such as they form temporary alliances with other crocodiles for their own benefit even after being territorial creatures.

INTRODUCTION

The apparel industry has been going through continuous transitional phases since last few decades. With the increase in the availability of variety in almost all product lines produced by various competitors in the global market segments, the competition among various organisations has been elevated dramatically. In order to survive this global competition, the organizations have adopted faster and flexible product manufacturing systems. But in spite of these adoptions, the organizations are facing many challenges in their attempt to acquire the continuously changing market of apparel industry. Moreover, Apparel industry is inherently diverse and heterogeneous in nature. Some of the factors responsible for the volatile nature of the apparel industry market include (i)globalization of production as well as retailing, (ii) the fast growing instantaneous knowledge about changing trends and brands, (iii) dynamically changing customer requirements leading to segmentation of fashion market (iv) advancement in technology such as automation of several processes across the value chain, (v) information sharing among manufacturers, wholesalers, and retailers and finally (vi) the need for reducing the price of final products to keep pace with the highly competitive market (Marufuzzaman et. al, 2009; Chan and Chan, 2010; Rayman et. al, 2011; Sekozawa et.al, 2011; D'Amico, et al., 2013). Therefore in order to match the rapidly changing environment of the fashion market, the organizations existing in the apparel industry have to be more flexible and responsive.

With the increase in fashion trend consciousness among consumers as a by-product of continuously changing lifestyle and economic conditions, satisfying varying consumer needs has become a survival challenge for most organizations dealing with apparel industry. Instead of producing products in bulk with standardized styles and trends as they used to do previously, organizations now try to refresh their products frequently maintaining uniqueness to survive in the competitive fashion industry. This decision of frequent refreshing of products depends on many factors such as seasons, social events, festivals, trends, locality and many more, so as to predict which kind of fashion products will be in peak demand during which period of the year. In other words, the fragmented market of the apparel industry has now been shifted from product-driven to consumer demand-driven type.

One of the most crucial challenges faced for the smooth operation of apparel industry is to forecast the continuously fluctuating demand of the consumers so as to plan the production of the products. The major characteristics of the products of apparel industry that makes demand forecasting challenging include (i) short duration of selling periods i.e., selling seasons, (ii) balancing the relation between selling seasons and product replenishment, (iii) product life cycle . Although, most of the organisations in apparel industry spend a major portion of their revenue to research various forecasting approaches and tools to predict real-time demands but still mostly fail due to high level of complexity and openness of fashion markets. In today's competitive scenario, demand forecasting plays a significant role in the smooth and efficient execution of production plan, but however, forecasting fails many times due to poor forecasting resulting from the existence of uncertainty and volatility in the consumer demands. This uncertainty in demand forecast occurs due to many co-existing factors such as availability of partial historical data, seasonal trends or any uncertain events and leads to erroneous product planning, manufacturing and distribution. Moreover, inaccuracy in demand forecasts can cost organizations heavily in terms of high inventory with unwanted goods to be sold at a low price or even at loss, stock outs resulting in loss of potential customers due to unavailability of desired products in stock, poor customer service, rush orders due to hike in demand of any particular product and poor utilization of resources. Therefore, to avail the competitive advantage over others, organisations must improve their demand forecasting systems which should be capable of adapting to the highly volatile and uncertain fashion markets.

Multi-Agent Systems (MAS) are capable of capturing the uncertainty and complexity of real-time even though each individual agent is having limited capabilities and resources. A group of agents forming a multi-agent system communicate and collaborate with each other to exchange information and achieve the overall goal of the system. Each individual agent is capable of making dynamic decisions and tries to maximize its personal gain and individual goals which in turn, collectively along with other individual agents, leads to the attainment of the overall system goal. Individual agents can be (i) reactive agents that interact with environment in regular intervals, (ii) proactive agents that are capable of making decisions along with interacting with environment, and finally (iii) social agents that interact with other agents to achieve overall goal [Patnaik, 2007]. Thus, a multi-agent system can be either heterogeneous or homogenous depending on the type of agents employed. An agent can be characterized by the following features (i) its limited capability or incomplete information, (ii) lack of global control over system, (iii) decentralized sharing of information among agents, (iv) asynchronous local computations [Sycara, 1998], [Patnaik, 2007], [Albadvi et.al, 2007], [Bao and Yang, 2008], [Taylor et.al, 2011], [Cao et.al, 2013]. Such a system when adopted to forecast demands of continuously changing market of fashion apparel industry can successfully capture the volatility and uncertainty of the market with a combination of heterogeneous agents.

The chapter is organized as follows. In section II works of various researchers of this area has been discussed. Section-III highlights the factors making demand forecasting complex in the context of the dynamic market of apparel industry, then afterwards we propose an intelligent nature-inspired multi-agent based model for demand forecasting. Section IV discusses the mathematical representation of the local rules of each individual agent. Section V concludes the chapter with future directions.

RELATED WORKS

Since last few decades, demand forecasting has been attracting the attention of many researchers working on apparel industry and a large number of literatures do exist consisting of various proposed approaches to address this problem. However, with the increase of uncertainty in consumer demands as a result of the fragmented markets of apparel industry, availability of variety in products and seasonal trends etc., reducing inaccuracy in demand forecasting still remains a challenge. Many organizations try to forecast demand traditionally through statistical methods such as linear regression, exponential smoothing with/without trend, moving average, weighted moving average, Bayesian analysis, auto regressive integrated moving average (ARIMA) and so on (Brown, 1959; Ghobbar and Chris, 2003; Fumi, Andrea, et al, 2013). All these methods are quite simple, hence, can be implemented easily and give quick results without much over-head. However the efficiency of these traditional methods depends on the reliability of the historical data which is sometimes incomplete or missing in parts because sales are often influenced by many external factors such as colour, size, price, media effect, climatic conditions, change in price, promotions and so on. Again linear regression technique can handle these variables only if the approximation function is strictly restricted for being linear. and leads to inaccuracy in forecasting. In order to overcome the drawbacks of the traditional forecasting methods, a lot of literature has been proposed by the researchers and academicians that explore new soft computing-based techniques for forecasting future demands.

Thomassey et.al (2003) has proposed a classification and data aggregation-based forecasting system that performs forecasts on sales item families and uses classification of items as a metric for evaluating the accuracy of forecasting for new products. Thomassey et.al claims that the aggregated forecasts of product families provide more accurate results as compared to the forecasting of individual items. Their model comprises two parts the first part consisting of an automatic model named as AHFCCX (Automatic Hybrid Forecasting model with Corrective Co-efficient of eXplanatory variable influences). First the automatic model part extracts the influence of explanatory variables such as price, weather, promotions, trends, economical environments calendar data, marketing events etc. from the sales history. Then a sales seasonality-based forecasting model is applied that does not take into account the influence of the explanatory variables. However, the influence of explanatory variables on future seasons are added to the forecasts obtained previously. Since quantifying the influence of explanatory variables such as promotions is quite difficult, Thomassey et.al has employed a Fuzzy Inference System (FIS) to exploit the expert knowledge through trainings. Further, a Takagi-Sugeno FIS based procedure learns automatically from historical data. Finally, genetic algorithm and a gradient-based method are used for parametric adjustment. The second part of the model called IDAC (Items forecasting model based on Distribution of Aggregated forecast and Classification) is based on the classification of sales forecasts into distribution families as generated by the first model AHFCCX from life curves of products. First it partitions the items belonging to same families into classes from sales history and then computes the life curve for the sales data belonging to the same cluster. Further, Thomassey et.al, associates future items with similar clusters and estimates their sales profiles as a part of the second model process. Finally, the model defines the each future item forecasting by distribution of forecasts of respective families based upon the life curves.

Mostard et al, (2011) also has proposed a classification-based forecasting method called "top-flop" method to forecast for a mail order apparel company. They claim that for small group of products, judgement method outperforms advanced methods. In their paper, Mostard et.al has considered the demand forecasting problem of single-period products i.e. forecasting the order to be placed before the season starts. Their proposed 'top-flop' method first divides the stock keeping units (SKU) into equally sized groups and then it finds the 'top' (i.e. the best selling) and 'flop' (i.e. the worst-selling) SKUs in a group. Now since historical data lacks here they require other sources of data for forecasting that has to be obtained from the pre-order by a group of customers specifically selected and also they obtain judgements from experts of the company. Mostard et.al claim that their proposed 'top-flop' method based on advanced demand information out performs other similar type methods.

Artificial neural networks (ANN) have attracted the attention of many researchers due to their capability of dealing with both external as well as internal factors by using non-linear approximation. Frank et al. (2003) have proposed an ANN-based approach for women's apparel retail sales forecasting. They have used the feed forward, back-propagation network consisting of the input vector, output vector and hidden layers, to identify and learn interactive and non-linear relationships to provide accurate forecasts. The error term is given by differencing the actual output from the expected output. Further, Frank et.al compares their model with the statistical model and claim higher accuracy obtained. One major drawback of the ANN model is that due to over-learning the correlation coefficients cannot maintain their goodness-of-fit. Also there is risk of over-fitting with noisy data and outliers can worsen the problem.

Again, since selection of layers in traditional neural networks requires much care, trial-and-error approach is usually adopted. Next evolutionary neural network (ENN) model has been explored as a promising model with a global search approach for sales forecasting. An evolutionary neural network is a hybrid combination of evolutionary computation and neural networks mostly adopted for topology design. The multi-point search approach is capable of searching high-quality local areas quickly even in large and complex search spaces. Au et al. [Au et.al, 2008] proposes an ENN model for searching an ideal network structure for short-term forecasting. They have developed an optimized structure for neural network for the apparel sales forecasting system and compared it with the traditional fully-connected networks and the SARIMA approach for products with weak seasonal trends and low demands. However, since the high computational cost is a major drawback of this approach, Au et al. adopts Bayesian information criteria (BIC) with the pre-search for guiding and it results in faster convergence speed enabling quick decision making in fashion apparel industry.

Although ANN and ENN produce high accuracy in forecasting yet they are time consuming due to gradient-based learning. However, Extreme learning machines (ELM) have evolved as a successful solution to the above problem since it prevents the occurrence of problems due to learning rate, number of epochs, local minima etc. Sun et. al, has proposed a neural network based approach known as Extreme Learning Machine (ELM) for forecasting sales in fashion retailing industry. They identify the relationship between factors influencing demand such as size, colour, price, etc., and the amount of sales. First they extract the sales data of a particular type of fashion clothes from the initial raw data along with the factors influencing the sales. The above mentioned influencing factors form the input for the ELM while the amount of sales forms the output and these sets composed of input/output pair data are divided into three parts namely the training, testing and predicting sets. Sun et.al further normalizes the training and testing data before starting the training process and again applies un-normalization to produce un-normalized units. The ELM computes the sales forecast for the predicting data set, on the basis of the input and output weights generated by the training and testing data. Although when compared to gradient-based conventional learning models, ELM is advantageous and fast but random choice of weights and biases result in varying output in each run and is considered as a major limitation. In order to overcome this problem, Sun et.al, integrates multiple ELMs and reduces the prediction error significantly.

Further Sztandera et.al has developed a multivariate-fuzzy-based model in their paper (Sztandera et.al, 2004), for short-term forecasting. They have considered multiple variables of the product such as size, colour and time etc. for forming the basis of their proposed model along with the calculation of sales values and grouped data for all size-class combination. They further claim that their proposed model is efficient forecasting tool due to its capability to distinguish non-linear relationships existing in input data. Sztandera et.al shows in the comparative analysis that their proposed model out performs traditional statistical models such as the uni-variate model and Winter's three parameter exponential smoothing model (W3PES). Also Hui et.al, applies fuzzy logic system to colour-based demand forecasting system for effective apparel design in fashion industry in their paper (Hui et.al, 2005). Their proposed model forecasts by integrating fuzzy logic learning with colour prediction knowledge. They further evaluate their proposed system in terms of computational efficiency and robustness and claims promising results. Although their proposed model outperforms traditional models, but its application only to single-colour prediction is a major limitation of the system.

The traditional soft computing approaches discussed above have been exploited by many forecasters and seems to have their own advantages and disadvantages. While ANNs are capable of handling the non-linear relationships in sales data, Fuzzy inference systems are capable of quantifying the explanatory variable influences as they are best suited tool for modelling and interpreting human knowledge. However, these approaches have mostly over-looked the existence of uncertainty in consumer demand due to dynamic and segmented market of the fashion apparel industry. Also hybrid combination of more than one soft-computing approach can be explored for learning adaptability in uncertainty. One such approach is integrating multi-agent systems with nature-inspired computing approaches for dealing with uncertainty as multi-agent systems are capable of capturing the dynamics of fashion apparel industry and the features of nature-inspired computing can enable the system to adapt and make decisions in uncertain scenarios. We have proposed a multi-agent based approach to model the volatility of the basic demand forecasting system. Further we integrate the features of nature-inspired computing to this model to handle decision making in uncertain environments. The proposed system has been discussed in the next section.

PROPOSED APPROACH

As observed in the previous sections, inaccuracy in traditional demand forecasting techniques occurs due to the volatile and uncertain nature of consumer demands. Moreover, fashion apparel industry is itself highly volatile and uncertain by nature and this volatility and uncertainty costs organizations in many ways like loss of revenue, large amount of unsold goods due to short life cycle of product trends, loss of potential customers. As we have discussed above many factors such as globalization, increasing outlook of consumers about current trends and brands, change in price, partial historical data and so on, contribute to this uncertainty in consumer demands. Traditional methods fail to capture this uncertainty and volatility of consumer demands. In order to handle this uncertainty and volatility we propose an intelligent multi-agent based demand forecasting model that integrates the features of nature-inspired computing. The multi-agent based system of our proposed method addresses demand forecasting method as a continuous process where the system keeps updating the forecasts at regular intervals. It further keeps track of external variables such as promotions, life cycle of trends, economical and climatic conditions, price reduction by competitors to sustain in market and so on, responsible for inducing uncertainty in customer demands.

Multi-agent systems usually consist of a group of agents that collectively achieve goals by dynamically communicating and collaborating with each other. The individual agents along with being autonomous might be heterogeneous or homogeneous in nature with partial knowledge of the surrounding environment. Because of the above identifying features multi-agent systems are well-suited for capturing the uncertainty lying in the dynamic environment of fashion apparel industry due to missing data in sales history. Further nature finds its own ways of survival in unfavourable conditions and hence has its own ways of dealing with uncertainty. Therefore integrating the features of nature-inspired computing with multi-agent systems, uncertainty and volatility of demand forecasting systems can be handled to a great extent.

The proposed method follows the demand hierarchy existing between the retailers to the supplier of raw materials in the figure below:

Figure 1. Demand hierarchy of demand forecasting and replenishment system

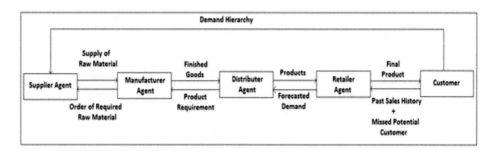

Forecasting consumer demands of future sales, ordering the required amount of products and updating inventory as per requirement is a continuous process that computes the current demand of a product from sales history the forwards product orders to manufacturers via distributers and finally replenishes the requirement. The above Figure 1 presents the demand hierarchy of the demand forecasting and replenishment system. In the proposed approach, each of the phases of the demand forecasting and replenishment system is dealt by an individual agent such as the retailer agent, distributer agent, manufacturer agent and the supplier agent. These agents communicate, share information and collaborate with each other to forecast demands and replenish them collectively.

This co-ordination between the agents in our proposed approach is inspired by the co-ordination among crocodiles during group hunting approach proposed by Nanda et.al (2016). Even though crocodiles are territorial creatures, they collaborate with each other during group hunting by forming temporary alliances. The crocodiles do fail sometimes while hunting individually; therefore they cooperate with each other while hunting as a group and share information among each other learned from previous mistakes where preys would have succeeded in escaping the predators.

Each of the agents of the phases in the above demand hierarchy can be mapped as the crocodiles in group hunting scenario with partial information about the environment/market that can be shared with neighbouring agents to collectively achieve the goal. In the proposed multi-agent based demand forecasting and replenishment system, the collective intelligence of crocodiles can be utilized for handling uncertainty and volatility of market demands as adaptive emerging behaviour of individual agents that interacts with each other to form a communication network. In this communication network information regarding demand or requirement and goods flow in the form of orders and replenishment shipments between the different phases of the proposed model.

The local behaviours of each of the individual agent can be present by behavioural cycles of the individual phase. In the first phase as soon as the customer places an order with the retailer, the retailer agent checks the stock to find out whether the order can be fulfilled immediately or not as shown in Figure 2. If the desired good is available then the order is fulfilled immediately but if it is not readily available the retailer agent records this missed opportunities i.e. the potential customers who leave without purchasing due to unavailability of desired products by raising a stock-out flag. The retailer agent regularly maintains the inventory level by estimating the future amount of products to be desired by future customers by combining the recorded missed opportunities with the current sales history and forwards the demands to the distributer agent for replenishment as shown in Figure 2.

The distributer agent receives the forecasted demand from the retailer and checks whether the demand can be satisfied immediately, if sufficient amount of demand-

Figure 2. Behavioural cycle of the retailer agent of demand forecasting and replenishment system

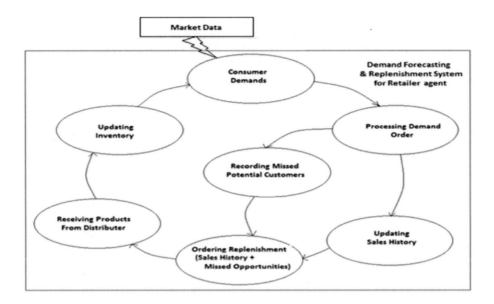

ed product is available then the distributer agent immediately releases the shipment to the retailer to fulfil the requirements and records the stock-out events to place order to the manufacturer. The distributer agent forwards the combination of the unfulfilled demands along with the new demands as order to the manufacturer in a routine manner as shown in Figure 3.

In the proposed demand forecasting and replenishment system, the behavioural cycle of the manufacturer agent has been combined with the behavioural cycle of the supplier agent because of its continual nature as shown in Figure 4. On receiving the forecasted demand from the distributer agent the manufacturer agent tries to replenish it as soon as possible along with recording the unavailable products so as to manufacture them. Finally, the manufacturer agent decides how much product needs to be manufactured and starts manufacturing process at the factory, but it is quite possible that the manufacturing process might be halted due to unavailability of raw materials. Therefore it parallel forwards order to the supplier agent for the required raw materials along with the manufacturing process of other products. The supplier agent supplies the desired raw materials and the manufacturing process is carried on for the halted products as shown in figure 4 below.

Each of the above discussed agents try to attain their individual goal i.e. try to maximize the net gain as well as they try to minimize the overall cost involved at

Figure 3. Behavioural cycle of the distributer agent of demand forecasting and replenishment system

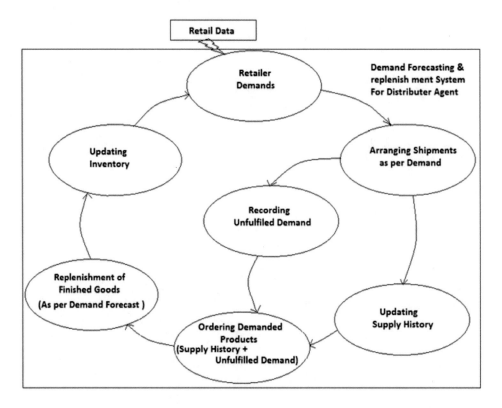

the phase they are responsible for. A monitoring agent has been added to each phase of the demand forecasting and replenishment system to deal with uncertainty. As we have discussed uncertainty in forecasting demand occurs due to many factors such as launching of new products, promotions and advertisements, reduction in price, increase in number of buyers, rise or fall in economy and so on. A threshold value is set for the inventory level in each phase and the monitoring agent keeps track of the inventory level, when the inventory level is lower than the threshold value and demand is at peak, increasing the chances of stock-out the monitoring agent sets the stock-out flag. However, maintaining large amount of inventories can reduce the effect of losing potential customers but it cannot be an exact solution as holding high inventories will induce high storage cost leading to loss of profit.

A potential solution to the above problem of uncertainty can be the addition of a trade-off agent to the system along with the monitoring agent. Whenever the

Figure 4. Behavioural cycle of the manufacturer agent of demand forecasting and replenishment system

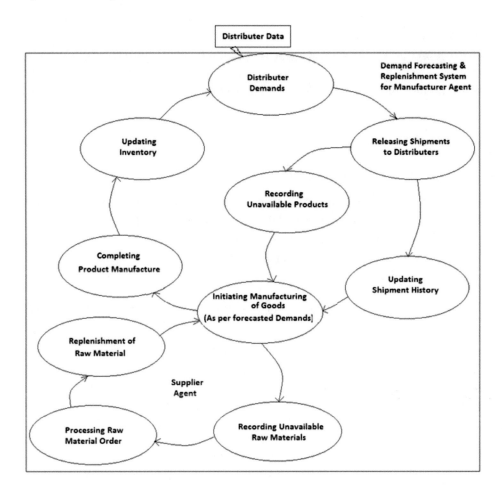

monitoring agent sets the stock-out flag, the trade-off agent can analyse the inventory record of other parallel retailers and distributors in the same phase neighbourhood, previously obtained from the monitoring agent and channelize the products from agents with high inventory to the parallel agent of the same phase with the stock-out flag to balance the quantity of demanded product, so as to prevent the loss of potential customers. This shows the adaptability of the individual agents to uncertain environment by sharing information and collaborating with neighbouring agents to maximize profit, minimize the overall cost and attain equilibrium.

MATHEMATICAL REPRESENTATION

Mathematically, the local rules of each individual agent of the proposed demand forecasting and replenishment system can be represented as the probabilistic binomial combination of the number of actual sales and the number of missed opportunities, since the system has only two outcomes i.e. success in sales and failure in sales. The following equations provide the mathematical representation of the proposed system:

$$probability(k(sales)\ out\ of\ n(customers)) = \binom{n}{k} p^k q^{n-k} \tag{1}$$

where, n is the total number of customers visiting the retailer,k is the total number of actual sales,(n-k) is the number of times a customer returns without purchasing anything i.e. missed opportunities.p is the probability that a customer is converted into an actual sale,q = (1-p), is the probability that a customer is converted into a missed opportunity.

$\binom{n}{k}$ gives k successful sales out of n customers and is computed by equation

(2) given below:

$$\binom{n}{k} = \frac{n!}{k!(n-k)!} \tag{2}$$

Equation (3) below computes the total number of possible future demands as:
Total (future demand) $= \sum Agent_i$ (Probability (Actual sales) + Probability (Missed opportunities)) (3)where i=1,2,.....,n.

CONCLUSION

Demand forecasting and replenishment has become very challenging due to increasing complexity in customer demand and market segments. Although traditional methods are capable of forecasting future demands but still the results consists of inaccuracies that can cost the organization badly. This inaccuracy is induced in the system due to uncertainty in consumer demands occurring as a consequence of many factors such as lack of complete sales history, promotions and advertisements, new product launch, price reductions etc. In order to deal with this uncertainty, a multi-agent based approach integrated with nature-inspired computing has been proposed in this paper. The proposed approach consists of various agents for each of the phases of the demand forecasting and replenishment system. The proposed approach is adaptable and capable of making decisions for profit maximization during uncertain scenario. Further experimental results can approve the application of the proposed technique to the intelligent demand forecasting and replenishment system.

REFERENCES

Albadvi, A., Chaharsooghi, S. K., & Esfahanipour, A. (2007). Decision making in stock trading: An application of PROMETHEE. *European Journal of Operational Research*, *177*(2), 673–683. doi:10.1016/j.ejor.2005.11.022

Au, K.-F., Choi, T.-M., & Yu, Y. (2008). Fashion retail forecasting by evolutionary neural networks. *International Journal of Production Economics*, *114*(2), 615–630. doi:10.1016/j.ijpe.2007.06.013

Bao, D., & Yang, Z. (2008). Intelligent stock trading system by turning point confirming and probabilistic reasoning. *Expert Systems with Applications*, *34*(1), 620–627. doi:10.1016/j.eswa.2006.09.043

Brown, R. G. (1959). *Statistical forecasting for inventory control*. Academic Press.

Cao, Y. (2013). An overview of recent progress in the study of distributed multi-agent coordination. *Industrial Informatics. IEEE Transactions on*, *9*(1), 427–438.

Chan & Chan. (2010). An AHP model for selection of suppliers in the fast changing fashion market. *The International Journal of Advanced Manufacturing Technology*, *51*, 9-12.

D'Amico, Giustiniano, Nenni, & Pirolo. (2013). Product Lifecycle Management as a tool to create value in the fashion system. *International Journal of Engineering Business Management, 5*.

Frank, C., Garg, A., Sztandera, L., & Raheja, A. (2003). Forecasting womens apparel sales using mathematical modeling. *International Journal of Clothing Science and Technology*, *15*(2), 107–125. doi:10.1108/09556220310470097

Fumi, Pepe, Scarabotti, & Schiraldi. (2011). Fourier analysis for demand forecasting in a fashion company. *International Journal of Engineering Business Management, 5*.

Ghobbar, A. A., & Friend, C. H. (2003). Evaluation of forecasting methods for intermittent parts demand in the field of aviation: A predictive model. *Computers & Operations Research*, *30*(14), 2097–2114. doi:10.1016/S0305-0548(02)00125-9

Hui, C. L., Lau, T. W., Ng, S. F., & Chan, C. C. (2005). Learning-based fuzzy colour prediction system for more effective apparel design. *International Journal of Clothing Science and Technology*, *17*(5), 335–348. doi:10.1108/09556220510616192

Marufuzzaman, M., Ahsan, K. B., & Xing, K. (2009). Supplier selection and evaluation method using Analytical Hierarchy Process (AHP): A case study on an apparel manufacturing organisation. *International Journal of Value Chain Management*, *3*(2), 224–240. doi:10.1504/IJVCM.2009.026958

Mostard, J., Teunter, R., & De Koster, R. (2011). Forecasting demand for single-period products: A case study in the apparel industry. *European Journal of Operational Research*, *211*(1), 139–147. doi:10.1016/j.ejor.2010.11.001

Nanda, P., Patnaik, S., & Patnaik, S. (in press). Modeling of Multi Agent Coordination using Crocodile Predatory Strategy. *International Journal of Reasoning-Based Intelligent Systems*.

Patnaik, S. (2007). Robot Cognition and Navigation: An Experiment with Mobile Robots. Springer Science & Business Media.

Rayman, D., Burns, D. J., & Nelson, C. N. (2011). Apparel product quality: Its nature and measurement. *Journal of Global Academy of Marketing*, *21*(1), 66–75. doi:10.1080/12297119.2011.9711012

Sébastien, T., Michel, H., & Jean-Marie, C. (2003). Mean-term textile sales forecasting using families and items classification. *Studies in Informatics and Control*, *12*(1), 41–52.

Sekozawa, T., Mitsuhashi, H., & Ozawa, Y. (2011). One-to-one recommendation system in apparel online shopping. *Electronics and Communications in Japan*, *94*(1), 51–60. doi:10.1002/ecj.10261

Sun, Z. L., Choi, T. M., Au, K. F., & Yu, Y. (2008). Sales forecasting using extreme learning machine with applications in fashion retailing. *Decision Support Systems*, *46*(1), 411–419. doi:10.1016/j.dss.2008.07.009

Sycara, K. P. (1998). Multiagent systems. *AI Magazine*, *19*(2), 79.

Sztandera, L. M., Frank, C., & Vemulapali, B. (2004). Predicting women's apparel sales by soft computing. *Proceedings of the 7th International Conference on Artificial Intelligence and Soft Computing,* 1193–1198. doi:10.1007/978-3-540-24844-6_187

Taylor, M. E. (2011). *Two decades of multi-agent teamwork research: past, present, and future.* Collaborative Agents-Research and Development. Springer Berlin Heidelberg.

Chapter 10
Role Allocation in a Group of Control Objects:
General Purpose Approach

Viacheslav Abrosimov
Smart Solutions, Russia

ABSTRACT

The efficiency of control objects that fulfill economic and military tasks in groups depends on the correct role allocation among them. This paper develops a role allocation algorithm for control objects jointly fulfilling a collective task. Control objects are represented as intelligent agents with some capabilities and needs. The problem is solved by ranking the agents based on their closeness to given roles in terms of their functionality and characteristics. The efficiency of the suggested approach is illustrated by allocating the role of reconnaissance aircraft in the group attack problem with a protected target.

INTRODUCTION

While considering practical problems related to the operation of control objects in a complex conflict environment, researchers pay much attention to the design of appropriate solutions not for single control objects but for their groups. It is well-known that such groups solve tasks with higher reliability and speed, mainly owing to the mutual support of the control objects and their capability for self-organization (e.g., see Rzevski & Skobelev, 2014). The efficiency of a group depends on role al-

DOI: 10.4018/978-1-5225-2322-2.ch010

location within it, whether the group is guided by a leader or has self-organization. Role allocation concerns role assignment, the delegation of authorities to different roles, etc.

As a matter of fact, there exists no clear definition of role in technical systems. Each object occupies a definite position in a group hierarchical structure. This position predetermines the object's status in the group. Role actually describes the functionality that must be implemented by an object while fulfilling a collective task. Role and status are closely associated with each other. Generally, in hierarchical structures a status defines a corresponding role. The self-organizing structures without fixed hierarchies have the opposite picture, i.e., the status of an object is defined after role allocation.

The primary objective of group formation is collective goal setting. As a rule, a collective goal can be decomposed into special tasks. Roles are directly defined by the range of tasks allocated (in hierarchical structures) or undertaken (in self-organizing structures) by a control object. The whole meaning of role consists in the following. Being selected, allocated or accepted for execution by a control object (and further reported to all objects of a group), a role allows this object to predict the behavior of other objects and also the behavior of the whole group; based on roles, other control objects plan their behavior and actions.

Control objects have definite functionality and resources, thereby pretending to the receipt and further execution of roles. There are two fundamentally different ways to occupy a role in a group, namely, (a) assignment (e.g., by Leader) and (b) selection on a competitive basis. The second case is of special interest. In mathematical terms, the relations of control objects during competitive role allocation within a group should be considered using the multiagent approach (Weiss, 2013). Really, the representation of control objects as intelligent agents seems fruitful (Abrosimov, 2015). Intelligent agents may possess properties that are inherent in intelligent control systems, viz., rationality, existing goals and knowledge, and autonomy. In contrast to social agents (whose role functions are mostly connected with the notion of agents interaction for social behavior analysis [Trzebiatowski & Münch,]), here the matter concerns the agents that describe technical systems. For such agents, the well-known belief-desire-intention (BDI) concept is formulated via the notions of capability and need (Rzevski & Skobelev, 2014). Therefore, the capabilities of modern control objects can be expressed as the capabilities of agents, the design features of control systems as the properties or agents and the functional specifics (including constraints) as the needs of agents. This scheme well fits the competition of the agents during role occupation, particularly in the context of self-organization.

In the sequel, we consider the control objects that are representable and formalizable as intelligent agents.

Background

The existing literature dedicated to roles in multiagent systems studies in different forms the connection of roles and goals, rights, obligations and protocols that define the interaction with other roles.

Adamand and Mandiau (2005) considered a hierarchical structure where the layers of agents have communications and negotiations with each other. In this model, agents may have identical roles even if they belong to different layers.

Next, Ward & Henderson-Sellers (2009) constructed a role library as a list with characteristics determining the rules of group behavior and interaction. In such a library, the classes of roles are described in terms of attributes and associations. Among the main characteristics, the cited authors identified the functionality of a given role and its interactability with other roles. Therefore, a role library must establish correspondences between roles and agents that execute them (or not).

The eight principles of role formation were introduced and described by Zhu & Zhou (2008). As emphasize therein, a role may render a service, can be created, modified or deleted, and also has some rights and obligations. A role expresses or restricts the agent's availability in a system, and so on.

Bora, Tiryaki and Dikenelli (2012) proposed the role reallocation among the agents depending on their load. This approach proceeds from the assumption that the agent's load may vary during role execution, possibly causing the overload of some agents or even their failures (non-fulfillment of their tasks) due to insufficient resources.

Xu, Zhang and Patel (2007) has the closest connection to this line of investigations, emphasizing that the majority of the existing multiagent systems design models do not support dynamic role allocation for agents. At the same time, in a series of applications a crucial requirement is that the agents can modify their roles during execution.

The development of Agent Oriented Software Engineering and the use of roles within AOSE have been suggested by Conor and Brian (2009) as an important enabling feature in the future development of robust software systems. This paper seeks to identify and develop the definition of roles within an existing agent-oriented modelling language and discusses the importance of role, the process of role adoption and the advantages of role adaptation.

Chaimowicz, Campos and Kumar (2002) proposes a new methodology for coordinating multi-robot teams in the execution of cooperative tasks. It is based on a dynamic role assignment mechanism, in which the robots assume and exchange roles during cooperation. Using a multi-robot simulator, the methodology is demonstrated in a cooperative transportation task, in which a group of robots must find and cooperatively transport several objects scattered in the environment.

Odell, Parunak and Fleischer (2003) look to social and organizational systems theory as a source of inspiration and examines the notion of role and its implications on how agents might behave in group settings.

Several Agent Oriented Software Engineering (AOSE) methodologies were proposed by Sivakumar and Vivekanandan (2012) build open, heterogeneous and complex internet based systems. The main objective of the paper is to extend the scope and support of role towards testing, thereby the vacancy for software testing perception in the AOSE series will be filled up. The paper presents an overview of role based testing based on the V-Model in order to add the next new component as of Agent-Oriented Software testing in the agent oriented development life.

Selçuk, and Erdoğan (2005) compares the enhanced role model JAWIRO (Java with Roles) with another role model and a design pattern for implementing roles. These three approaches are compared on the basis of their abilities and performances. It is shown that role models are valuable tools for modeling dynamic real world entities as they provide many useful abilities without a significant performance overhead. The dynamic nature of agents represents a good domain for using roles for describing both their behaviors and their

Note an excellent survey prepared by Campbell and Wu (2011) covered 177 publications. In particular, the authors analyzed numerous role-related issues for agents in robotics, sociology and other fields, namely, the coordination and inter-action of roles; the hierarchy and learning of roles; role modeling; role exchange; switching between roles; and others. However and unfortunately, there are a few research works that describe concrete role allocation mechanisms.

Now, we summarize the results on role allocation, stating them in terms of control objects.

1. The same role can be executed by different control objects.
2. The same control object may execute several roles.
3. A role can be assigned to a control object, withdrawn from it or even replaced for another role.
4. Just like agents, control objects interact on the basis of their roles.
5. A control object that is assigned to a role (and executes it) acquires the rights and obligations of this role.
6. In the course of role allocation, it is necessary to check that the candidates have sufficient resources for executing a role or a set of roles.
7. Therefore, the issues of role allocation in a dynamic group of agents operating online still remain topical.

THE GENERAL APPROACH TO THE ROLE'S ALLOCATION

Functions of Roles and Their Attributes

A role in a group of objects is associated with a collective goal. Really, a collective goal that is set for a group must correspond to an aggregate of roles required for goal achievement. The notion of role has a close connection with the notions of rights and obligations. The rights of a role are defined by its status in a group hierarchy. A role can be dominating or dominated. The obligations of a role are expressed in the form of its functionality, i.e., the commitment to fulfill definite tasks. For control objects, we will comprehend a role task as an aggregate of actions yielding a given result. For instance, the role of reconnaissance aircraft in territory monitoring is to implement specific tasks of searching, detection, identification, information transfer and others.

Each role task has certain attributes. The attributes of a role task can be considered as a set of requirements for the resources needed to solve this task. For instance, an unmanned aerial vehicle (drone) assigned to the role of reconnaissance aircraft in a group must have several attributes of the search task such as flight range, flight velocity, flight time, etc. Therefore, we may always fix a sequence of the form "Role - Role task - Role task attribute."

Control objects have the following typical roles:

- **Leader:** Responsible for the tasks of role allocation among group members, instructions generation for group members, monitoring of tasks fulfillment, threat assessment for a collective goal, and communication with a control center;
- **Observer:** Responsible for the tasks of searching, detection, identification, and information transfer for an object or territory under observation;
- **Executor:** Responsible for the tasks of execution;
- **Assistant:** Responsible for the tasks of informational or resource support for the executors of other roles;
- **Communicator:** Responsible for the tasks of communication among all group members.

For the class of problems under consideration, a typical role can be formalized as a sequence

Role:

$$\{Z, Z^n, A^n\}, \tag{1}$$

where

Z gives the number of tasks in Role;

Z^n denotes task n in Role ($n \in Z$);

$A^n : \left\{ A_1^n, A_2^n \ldots A_f^n \ldots A_F^n \right\}$ is the vector of attributes A_f^n for task Z^n in Role.

The attributes substantially depend on the essence of tasks. As a rule, it is difficult to give the precise values of attributes. According to the existing experience, a very efficient approach is to represent the attributes in the form of fuzzy numbers with membership functions $\mu_A\left(0^f\right)$ or in the form of linguistic variables. In the latter case, linguistic variables can be transformed into fuzzy numbers using fuzzification (Piegat, 2001).

For simpler interpretation, it seems reasonable to adopt L-R fuzzy numbers [5], defining them by most preferable (expected) values (modes in the terminology of L-R fuzzy numbers) and functions that describe the variations of these values in the mode neighborhood. Then each attribute A_f^n of task Z^n in Role can be expressed as the triplet

$$A_f^n = (m_f, \alpha_f, \beta_f),\tag{2}$$

where m_f denotes the core of the fuzzy number, while α_f and β_f are the fuzzy coefficients characterizing its left and right borders. With this representation, the membership function of attribute A_f^n takes the form

$$\mu_f(a) = L^f[(m_f - a) / \alpha_f] \,\forall x \leq m_f, \alpha_f > 0,$$

$$\mu_f(a) = R^f[([a - m_f) / \beta_f] \,\forall x \leq m_f, \beta_f > 0.\tag{3}$$

On Agent's Readiness to Occupy and Execute Roles

Let a collective goal be defined for a group of K agents. This goal is decomposed into tasks and each task corresponds to Role.

We will treat control objects as intelligent agents. On the one hand, an agent assigned to Role must have functionality (1) required for it. On the other hand, for each function task Z^n in Role, the agent's characteristics (resources) must agree with (not be worse than) the attributes of task (2)-(3) required for role execution.

Therefore, by analogy with the attributes of tasks, it is possible to fix a sequence of the form "Control object as agent – Agent's function – Characteristic of this function."

Introduce a special logical variable to define the compliance of the functionality D realized by an agent (i.e., a set of functions) with all role tasks Z^n. Let $\Omega = 1$ *if* d-function required for a role task is among the functions implemented by k-agent. Denote this function by D^d. This means that the agents' functionality D includes the function D^d coinciding with the role task $Z^n (D^d \Leftrightarrow Z^n)$. Otherwise, let $\Omega = 0$.

Assume that each k-agent from the set K has a functionality D, i.e., a set of functions defining its implementation capabilities for all role tasks Z^n. By-turn, each d-function of k-agent (designated by D_k^b) can be described by a vector of certain characteristics. And these characteristics can be expressed as fuzzy variables. For instance, consider a control object (drone) that is assigned to the role of reconnaissance aircraft; for executing the search task, this control object must have appropriate motion capabilities in a conflict environment (velocity, altitude, flight time, small reflectivity, cameras, infrared imagers, etc.). Clearly, s-characteristic of d-function must agree in meaning with the attribute of role task $f(s \sim f)$.

Then, by analogy with (1), the capabilities of a control object as an agent can be written in the form

Agent: $\{D, D^d, \ C^d\}$, \hfill (4)

where

D gives the functionality (the number of functions) of the agent pretending for Role;

D^d denotes d-function implemented by this agent ($d \in D$);

$C^d : \{C_1^d, C_2^d....C_s^d\}$ is the vector composed of all s-characteristics for d-function implemented by this agent.

In this case, just like (2) and (3), for g-agent we may represent the s-characteristic of d-function as

$$C_s^d = (m_s, \gamma_s, \delta_s),$$

$$\mu_g^s(a) = L^s[(m_s - a) / \gamma_s] \ \forall c \leq m_s, \gamma_s > 0, \hfill (5)$$

$$\mu_g^s(a) = R^s[([a - m_s) / \delta_s] \; \forall c \geq m_s, \delta_s > 0.$$

An important aspect of role allocation is to compare the agents with each other in terms of their readiness to occupy and execute a role. Control objects as agents can be compared only by their characteristics. A possible way to associate the fuzzy characteristics of an agent with the fuzzy attributes of tasks involves the intersection analysis of the membership function ranges for f-attribute and s-characteristic. However, note that theory of fuzzy sets often defines the membership functions of such intersections "strictly," i.e., using maximin or algebraic operations. Here the result substantially depends on the choice of operation; moreover, due to the absence of unambiguous theoretical results, it is necessary to substantiate the usage of certain operations for new classes of problems.

The aforesaid causes inconvenience in real applications, and sometimes it seems even impossible to substantiate operations. Therefore, a more practical approach is to specify the attributes and characteristics (just like in representations (2)-(5)) in the form of L-R fuzzy numbers. Then the degree of compliance in terms of f-attribute can be easily estimated using operations over L-R fuzzy numbers, i.e., by their subtraction

$$H_g^f = A_f^n - C_s^d = \{m_h, q_h^-, q_h^+\} = \{m_f - m_s, \alpha_f + \delta_s, \beta_f + \gamma_s\} \tag{6}$$

with the membership functions

$$\mu_k^f(a) = \min(L^f, L^s)[m_a - c) / q_h^-] \; \forall c \leq m_a, q_h^- > 0,$$

$$\mu_k^f(a) = \min(R^f, R^s)[c - m_a) / q_h^+] \; \forall c \geq m_a, q_h^+ > 0. \tag{7}$$

Finally, introduce the generalized estimate of the agent's readiness to occupy and execute Role with respect to the function Z^n and f-attribute in the form

$$\pi^f = \Omega * \mu_k^f(a) \leq 1. \tag{8}$$

Clearly, the agents with higher estimates π^f have better chances to occupy a role. Additional constraints can be imposed depending on a specific situation, e.g., all agents satisfying $\pi^f \leq \pi^{f_*}$ are eliminated from the list of candidates (the parameter is π^f nullified for them).

Within the framework of decision theory, the numerical value of the estimate π^f can be treated as a utility criterion related to role task fulfillment in terms of each f-attribute. And the generalization over all Z attributes gives a complex estimate Rd for the task Z^n. By generalizing over all Z functions and all characteristics, we may introduce the notion of the "readiness vector" of k-agent to occupy Role, i.e.,

$$\text{Rd} = \left\{ \pi^1, \pi^2, \ldots, \pi^n \right\}. \tag{9}$$

If at least one element of the readiness vector (9) is zero, then either the agent does not have the required functionality (e.g., the functions of object search and detection are implemented, but the function of object identification is not available), or the agent's capabilities and/or resources are insufficient for role execution. Using this readiness vector, one can choose a subset $G \supset K$ of the set K where all g-agents have the required functionality and sufficient resources to occupy Role.

The experience from applications shows that, for each f-attribute, it is reasonable to consider conditional weights ξ_f describing its significance for role execution. In addition, during role allocation one should take into account some properties of an agent as its advantages over the others. For instance, such properties include:

- The practical experience of g-agent in the same (or similar) role during other projects (the experience level θ_g);
- The skill of g-agent in a required function acquired by learning (e.g., the "sacrifice" function, described by the agent's readiness to perform self-sacrifice (Abrosimov, 2016);
- The significance of g-agent for the whole group (the agent's value, the capability for replacing other agents in other roles, etc.).

Ranking of Agents by the Degree of Adequacy to Role

In the previous section, we have constructed a set $G \supset K$ that includes the agents pretending for Role. The problem is to find a g-agent in G that is most adequate to the requirements imposed by Role. Hence, it is necessary to develop an algorithm showing the preference of certain agents over the others in the sense of role allocation.

Real role allocation problems within groups involve nonstrict preference relations. Furthermore, due to the substantial fuzziness of the role function attributes, it seems natural to choose the class of fuzzy preference relations among the nonstrict ones (Piegat, 2001).If PF^s gives a fuzzy preference relation on the agents set G, then for any pair of agents $(g^x, g^y) \in PF^s$ the domination degree of g^x-agent over

g^x-agent $(g^x \succ g^y)$ in terms of f-characteristic is described by a membership function $\mu(g^x, g^y)$. Two agents can be compared using the formula

$$\mu\ (g^x, g^y) = \{\mu_f(g^x, g^y) - \mu_f(g^y, g^x)\}, \text{ if } \mu_f(g^x, g^y) \succeq \mu_f(g^y, g^x),$$

$$0, if\ \mu_f(g^x, g^y) \prec \mu_f(g^y, g^x). \tag{10}$$

However, for the agents associated with control objects, this comparison in terms of characteristics is not convenient. Instead of comparing such agents with each other, one should rather seek for preferences based on the degree of adequacy to the requirements of a role task. In this case, with the attributes and characteristics represented in the form of L-R fuzzy numbers, the dominating agent is the one satisfying the following conditions (also called criteria):

1. The modes of the agent's function characteristics are as close to the modes of the role task attributes as possible;
2. The values of the membership functions for the L-R fuzzy numbers describing the agent's function characteristics at the critical points (left border, mode (core), right border) exceed the corresponding values for the other agents.

The closeness between the modes of characteristics and attributes is defined by

$$\Delta m_{gs} = \left| m_{gs} - m_f \right| \ , \forall\, g \in G \tag{11}$$

The agent's rank in terms of the first criterion (mode closeness) is assigned as follows:

$$P^1(g^1) = 1, if \Delta m_{g1} = \min_{g \in G}(\Delta m_{gs}),$$

$$P^1(g^2) = 2, if \Delta m_{g2} = \min_{g \in G \ except \ g^1}(\Delta m_{gs}), \tag{12}$$

$$P^1(g^k) = k, if \Delta m_{gk} = \min_{g \in G \ except \ g^1...g^{(k-1)}}(\Delta m_{gs}).$$

For any $g \in G$, the values of the membership functions of the L-R fuzzy numbers describing the s-characteristic of d-function at the critical points (left border, mode (core), right border) can be obtained from the equations

$$\mu_g^{\alpha s} : \quad \mu_g^s(left) = L_g^s(m_f - \alpha_f) \text{ or } R_g^s(m_f - \alpha_f);$$

$$\mu_g^{ms} : \quad \mu_g^s(m_f) = L_g^s(m_f) \text{ or } R_g^s(m_f) \tag{13}$$

$$\mu_g^{\beta s} : \mu_g^s(right) = L_g^s(m_f + \beta_f) \text{ or } R_g^s(m_f + \beta_f).$$

The agent's rank in terms of the second criterion (membership function majorant) is the sum of the ranks over the three components of (13), namely,

$$P^2(g^{1q}) = 1 \quad for \quad \mu_{g1}^{qs} = \max_{g \in G} \mu_g^{qs} \quad q = \alpha, m, \beta,$$

$$P^2(g^{2q}) = 2 \quad for \quad \mu_{g2}^{qs} = \max_{g \in G \; except \; g^1} \mu_g^{qs}, \quad q = \alpha, m, \beta, \tag{14}$$

$$P^2(g^{kq}) = k \quad for \; \mu_{gk}^{qs} = \max_{g \in G \; except \; g^1 \ldots g^{(k-1)}} \mu_g^{qs}, \quad q = \alpha, m, \beta,$$

The total rank in terms of the first and second criteria actually yields the estimated priority of k-agent by the closeness of the mode and membership functions of *s*-characteristic for *d*-function at the critical points to the corresponding requirements of *f*-attribute, also considering its significance ξ_f for collective task fulfillment. The dominating agent is defined from the condition

$$P^{\Sigma}(g^{ds}) = \min_G \{\xi_f * [P^1(g^k) + \Sigma_{(q=\alpha,m,\beta)} P^2(g^{kq})]\} \tag{15}$$

In the final analysis, by summing up the ranks over all Z functions, we find the dominating agent in terms of all *d*-functions of the agents. Whenever necessary (depending on collective task specifics), the ranking procedure may also take into account the agent's properties; to this effect, just introduce the correction coefficients (e.g., the agent's skill θ_g):

$$g^d : Pr(g^d) = min_G \{\Sigma_{(1,2,\ldots F)}[\theta_g * P(g^{ds})]\} \tag{16}$$

And g^d-agent becomes the best candidate for occupying Role.

Further ranking (second best candidate and so on) runs by analogy with (11)-(16).

Role Allocation Algorithm

In view of the above considerations, we propose the following role allocation algorithm for the agents.

1. Role requirements specification. At this step, it is necessary to define Role as aggregate (1) of the required role tasks Z^n and their f-attributes in the form of the L-R fuzzy numbers (2)-(3).
2. Identification of the group of agents having the required functionality for Role.

For all k-agents from the set K that have the functionality D^k, it is necessary to define the role functionality attributes:

$$\Omega = 1, \quad if \ D^k \supset Z,$$

$$\Omega = 0, \quad if \ D^k \supset Z \ \ \forall k \in K. \tag{17}$$

The group $B \supset K$ that includes the agents with $\Omega = 0$ at least for one function F is eliminated from further consideration.

3. Identification of the group of agents having the required characteristics for Role.
4. For all k-agents from the set K except $k \in B$, it is necessary to define the degree of compliance between their characteristics and all f-attributes of the role task Z^n using formulas (6) and (7).
5. Readiness vector construction.

For all k-agents from the set K except $k \in B$, it is necessary to construct the readiness vector for Role using formulas (8) and (9).

6. Identification of the "candidates for role."

Among the agents from the set K, it is necessary to choose a subset $G \supset K$ whose readiness vector contains no zeros. Therefore, each g-agent from the subset $G \supset K$ possesses (a) the required aggregate of s-characteristics for role execution and (b) the required resources for role execution.

7. Definition of the agents' preferences with respect to f-attribute using the ranks $P^1\left(g^k\right)$ and $P^2\left(g^{kq}\right)$ calculated by formulas (11)-(14).

8. Identification of the dominating agent as the best "candidate" for role over all characteristics of d-function taking into account the significance of the attributes using convolution (15).

9. Identification of the best candidate for Role taking into account all functions and properties of the agents using convolution (16).

Reconnaissance Airsraft Allocation in the "Diffuse Bomb" Problem

The so-called "diffuse bomb" problem (i.e., the group penetration through a defense system (Korepanov & Novikov, 2013) involves several roles such as leader, reconnaissance aircraft, communicator, combat aircraft, and others. The role of reconnaissance aircraft is very important. Recently, this role is often assigned to unmanned aerial vehicles (drones). A reconnaissance aircraft performs territory monitoring, the detection and identification of potential targets, online informing of other control objects about the current situation, etc. The key attributes for this role include flight range, flight velocity, flight time, camera resolution, and some others.

Let the attribute vector for the search task of the reconnaissance aircraft role be $A:$ {flight range, flight velocity, flight time}. The parameters of the L-R fuzzy numbers and their numerical values are illustrated by Table 1.

Assume that 5 drones pretend to the role of reconnaissance aircraft, all possessing the three required characteristics (flight range, flight velocity, and flight time) with the experience level θ_g and the associated parameters in the form of R-L fuzzy numbers (see Table 2).

Even without calculations using formulas (8)-(9), Table 2 shows that Drone 5 has a zero component in the readiness vector: this drone does not satisfy the flight time requirements (the ranges of the membership functions of the role task and

Table 1. Attributes and their parameters for the search task of the reconnaissance aircraft role

Attributes	Flight Range, km			Flight Velocity, km/h			Flight Time, h		
Parameters of L-R number	m_d	α_d	β_d	m_v	α_v	β_v	m_t	α_t	β_t
Numerical value	100	20	30	40	10	20	6	1	3

Table 2. Attributes and characteristics of the search function of the candidates for the reconnaissance aircraft role

Candidates for the Reconnaissance Aircraft Role	Experience Level of Agents θ_g	Flight Range, km			Flight Velocity, km/h			Flight Time, h		
		m_d	α_d	β_d	m_v	α_v	β_v	m_t	α_t	β_t
		Attributes of the search function of Role								
		100	20	30	40	10	20	6	1	3
		Characteristics of the search function of agents								
Drone 1	2	95	25	15	30	10	10	5	1	2
Drone 2	1	70	10	50	35	15	35	4	1	6
Drone 3	2	90	30	50	50	20	10	7	3	4
Drone 4	3	120	30	20	30	10	30	5	2	3
Drone 5	1	90	10	20	20	20	40	3	1	1

(5)-(7) and the agent's characteristics (2)-(3) have empty intersection). Therefore, Drone 5 is eliminated from further consideration.

Now, we define the closeness of the modes of the attributes and characteristics, as well as the values of the membership function at the three critical points for the corresponding role attributes (by formulas (3), (5)).

The corresponding ranks are presented in Tables 4 and 5.

Therefore, the agents have the following priority of being allocated to the role of reconnaissance aircraft: Drone 2, Drone 3, Drone 4, Drone 1 (without their experience levels) and Drone 2, Drone 3, Drone 1, Drone 4 (with their experience levels).

Now, study how the distribution of ranks changes as we assign priorities to different attributes of the role function. For instance, suppose that the defense system is organized so that the agent's velocity in the defense zone has higher priority. Introduce the priority characteristics, namely, the conditional weights ξ_f of the functions that define their significance for role execution. Choose

$\xi_f : \left\{ \xi_d = 0.2, \ \xi_v = 0.6, \ \xi_t = 0.2 \right\}$. Then we obtain the new distribution of ranks, as illustrated by Table 6.

Let us analyze the results.

Four drones have competed for the role of reconnaissance aircraft, each possessing the required characteristics that coincide with the attributes of the search

Table 3. Comparative assessment of the agents' characteristics and attributes of the search task

Agents	The "core" difference of fuzzy numbers $m_f - m_s$	The values of membership function at three critical points		
		Core $\mu_g^s\left(m_f\right)$	Left bound $\mu_g^s\left(m_f - \alpha_f\right)$	Right bound $\mu_g^s\left(m_f + \beta_f\right)$
Flight range attributes		**100**	**80**	**130**
Drone 1	5	0.7	0	0
Drone 2	30	0.4	0.8	0
Drone 3	10	0.8	0.67	0.2
Drone 4	20	0.5	0	0.5
Flight velocity attributes		**40**	**10**	**20**
Drone 1	10	0	1	0
Drone 2	5	0.85	0.66	0.57
Drone 3	10	0.5	0	1
Drone 4	20	0.5	0.7	0.22
Flight time attributes		**6**	**1**	**3**
Drone 1	1	0.5	0.67	0.18
Drone 2	2	0.66	0.74	0
Drone 3	1	0.66	0.5	0.47
Drone 4	1	0.8	0.85	0.2

function, namely, flight range, flight velocity, and flight time. Drone 1 has the best efficiency (closeness to an appropriate attribute) in terms of flight range and a rather good efficiency in terms of flight time, yet demonstrating lower efficiency than the opponents in terms of flight velocity. In addition, Drone 1 yields to Drone 2 in the experience level. However, even based on the flight range comparison, Drone 1 receives no absolute priority (merely rank 2) due to a very narrow range of the membership function. Drones 2 and 3 become equivalent by taking into account the higher priority of the velocity attribute for the search task (three times higher than the other attributes), which is dictated by the defense system specifics. But in this case the key factor is the experience level; and the highest priority for occupying

Table 4. The distribution of ranks

Agent	$m_f - m_s$	Ranks			Rank by characteristic	Final rank for role execution
		m_d	α_d	β_d		
Flight range						
Drone 1	1	2	3	3	9	2
Drone 2	3	4	1	3	11	3
Drone 3	2	1	2	2	7	1
Drone 4	4	3	3	1	11	3
Flight velocity						
Drone 1	2	3	1	4	10	3
Drone 2	1	1	3	2	7	1
Drone 3	2	2	4	1	9	2
Drone 4	3	2	2	3	10	3
Flight time						
Dron 1	1	3	3	4	11	4
Dron 2	2	2	2	3	9	3
Dron 3	1	2	4	1	8	2
Dron 4	1	1	1	2	5	1

Table 5. The distribution of ranks with experience levels

Agent	Flight range	Flight velocity	Flight time	Rank by all characteristics	Rank without experience level	θ_g	Rank with θ_g	Final rank for role execution with experience level
			Initial ranks					
Drone 1	2	3	4	9	3	2	18	3
Drone 2	3	1	3	7	2	1	7	1
Drone 3	1	2	2	5	1	2	10	2
Drone 4	3	3	1	7	2	3	21	4

Table 6. The new distribution of ranks with the priorities of different attributes of the role function and experience levels of agents

Agent	Flight range $\xi_d = 0.2,$	Flight velocity $\xi_v = 0.6$	Flight time $\xi_t = 0.2$	Rank with attribute priority	Ranks without experience levels	θ_g	Ranks with experience levels	Final rank for role execution
Drone 1	0.4	1.8	0.8	2	3	2	4	3
Drone 2	0.6	0.6	0.6	1.8	1	1	1.8	1
Drone 3	0.2	1.2	0.4	1.8	1	2	3.6	2
Drone 4	0.6	1.8	0.2	2.6	4	3	7.8.	4

the role of reconnaissance aircraft is assigned to Drone 2. Rank 2 is given to Drone 3, possessing relatively good characteristics in terms of all the three attributes. And further ranking seems of little importance.

CONCLUSION

The human society has developed numerous role allocation algorithms within collectives. The vocational fitness of a future candidate is checked using his resume, with thorough consideration of his education, accumulated experience and recommendations. A candidate undergoes tests and probationary appointment. The things are somewhat more complicated with technical systems, particularly, control objects. They are initially designed to solve definite tasks (e.g., fighters or bombers in aviation); also there exist multi-purpose control objects.

This paper has proposed a role allocation algorithm for control objects that jointly fulfill a collective task within a group. The control objects are represented by agents. Each agent has a definite functionality. The group task analysis separates out tasks that are further associated with roles. The roles are related to the functions required for their execution, and the attributes of such functions are expressed by L-R fuzzy numbers. The capabilities of the agents and their characteristics are described in a similar way. Therefore, we establish a correspondence between the capabilities (functionality) of the agents and the functions required for role execution, as well as a correspondence between the attributes of the role functions and the characteristics of the agents' functionality. The former must comply with the latter.

The role allocation algorithm is based on a formalization of the number and type of the functions required for role execution, as well as on a formal description of their attributes. The general criterion consists in the best satisfaction of the role requirements. The first step of the algorithm eliminates all agents without the functionality and characteristics (resources) required for role execution. At the forthcoming steps, definite rules are used to construct the preference table where the agents are assigned appropriate ranks (first, in terms of separate attributes and then in terms of their aggregate) that reflect the domination degree of the agents. The ranks are generalized over all role functions by the convolution transformation. The ranking procedure takes into account the agent's experience level in a similar role within another project, the skill level for a necessary function, and the agent's value for the whole group (fleet).

The resulting rank sequence makes it possible to choose the most adequate (best) agent for role execution or replace it with the second best agent (and so on) if necessary, e.g., in case of destruction.

REFERENCES

Abrosimov, V. (2015). Group Control Strategy for a Fleet of Intelligent Vehicles-Agent Performing Monitoring, *Proceedings of 9th KES International Conference "Agent and Multi-Agent Systems: Technologies and Applications"(KES-AMSTA 2015)*. doi:10.1007/978-3-319-19728-9_11

Abrosimov, V. (2016). The Property of Agents Sacrifice: Definition, Measure, Effect and Applications. *International Journal of Reasoning-based Intelligent Systems*, 8(1/2), 76–83. doi:10.1504/IJRIS.2016.080069

Adamand, E., & Mandiau, R. (2005). Roles and Hierarchy in Multi-agent Organizations, Multi-Agent Systems and Applications. *Proceedings of 4th International Central and European Conf. on Multiagent Systems (CEEMAS 2005)*.

Bora, S., Tiryaki, A. M., & Dikenelli, O. (2012). Load Sharing Based on Moving Roles in Multiagent Systems, *Turk J. Elec. Eng. & Comp. Sci*, 20(2), 219–229.

Campbell, A., & Wu, A. S. (2011). Multi-agent Role Allocation: Issues, Approaches, and Multiple Perspectives. *Autonomous Agents and Multi-Agent Systems*, 22(2), 317–355. doi:10.1007/s10458-010-9127-4

Conor, B. W., & Brian, H. S. (2009). Utilizing Dynamic Roles for Agents. *Journal of Object Technology*, 8(5), 177–198. doi:10.5381/jot.2009.8.5.a5

Korepanov, V. O., & Novikov, D. A. (2013). The diffuse Bomb Problem. *Automation and Remote Control*, 74(5), 5, 863–874. doi:10.1134/S000511791305010X

Lindemann-von Trzebiatowski, G., & Münch, I. (n.d.). *The Role Concept for Agents in Multi Agent Systems*. Retrieved from http://www.informatik.uni-hamburg.de/TGI/forschung/projekte/sozionik/journal/3/masho-3.pdf

Odell, J., Parunak, V. D., & Fleischer, M. (2003). The Role of Roles. *Journal of Object Technology*, 2(1), 39–51. doi:10.5381/jot.2003.2.1.c5

Piegat, A. (2001). *Fuzzy Modelling and Control*. Berlin: Physica-Verlag Heidelberg. doi:10.1007/978-3-7908-1824-6

Rzevski, G., & Skobelev, P. (2014). Managing Complexity. WIT Press.

Selçuk, Y. M., & Erdoğan, N. (2005). A Role Model for Description of Agent Behavior and Coordination. *Proceedings of the 6th international conference on Engineering Societies in the Agents World (ESAW'05)*.

Sivakumar, N., & Vivekanandan, K. (2012). Agent Oriented Software Testing – Role Oriented Approach, International. *Journal of Advanced Computer Science and Applications*, 3(12), 156–163.

Ward, C. B., & Henderson-Sellers, B. (2009). Utilizing Dynamic Roles for Agents. *Journal of Object Technology*, 8(5), 177–198. doi:10.5381/jot.2009.8.5.a5

Weiss, G. (Ed.). (2013). *Multiagent Systems*. MIT Press.

Xu, H., Zhang, X., & Patel, R. J. (2007). Developing Role-Based Open Multi-Agent Software Systems. *International Journal of Computational Intelligence Theory and Practice*, 2(1), 39–56.

Zhu, H. ,., & Zhou, M. C. (2008). Role-Based Multi-Agent Systems. In *Personalized Information Retrieval and Access: Concepts, Methods, and Practices* (pp. 254–286). IGI Global. doi:10.4018/978-1-59904-510-8.ch012

Compilation of References

Abhishek, K., Datta, S., & Mahapatra, S. S. (2015). Multi-objective optimization in drilling of CFRP (polyester) composites: Application of a fuzzy embedded harmony search (HS) algorithm. *Measurement*, *77*, 222–239. doi:10.1016/j.measurement.2015.09.015

Abrosimov, V. (2015). Group Control Strategy for a Fleet of Intelligent Vehicles- Agent Performing Monitoring, *Proceedings of 9th KES International Conference "Agent and Multi-Agent Systems: Technologies and Applications"(KES-AMSTA 2015)*. doi:10.1007/978-3-319-19728-9_11

Abrosimov, V. (2016). The Property of Agents Sacrifice: Definition, Measure, Effect and Applications. *International Journal of Reasoning-based Intelligent Systems*, *8*(1/2), 76–83. doi:10.1504/IJRIS.2016.080069

Adamand, E., & Mandiau, R. (2005). Roles and Hierarchy in Multi-agent Organizations, Multi-Agent Systems and Applications. *Proceedings of 4th International Central and European Conf. on Multiagent Systems (CEEMAS 2005)*.

Adenso-Díaz, B., Lozano, S., Racero, J., & Guerrero, F. (2001). Machine cell formation in generalized group technology. *Computers & Industrial Engineering*, *41*(2), 227–240. doi:10.1016/S0360-8352(01)00056-0

Akin, A., & Saka, M. P. (2015). Harmony search algorithm based optimum detailed design of reinforced concrete plane frames subject to ACI 31805 provisions. *Computers & Structures*, *147*, 79–95. doi:10.1016/j.compstruc.2014.10.003

Alba, E. (2008). *New Research in Nature Inspired Algorithms for Mobility Management in GSM Networks*. Academic Press.

Albadvi, A., Chaharsooghi, S. K., & Esfahanipour, A. (2007). Decision making in stock trading: An application of PROMETHEE. *European Journal of Operational Research*, *177*(2), 673–683. doi:10.1016/j.ejor.2005.11.022

Albeanu, G., Madsen, H., & Popentiu-Vladicescu, F. (2016). Learning from Nature: Nature Inspired Algorithms. *The 12th International Scientific Conference eLearning and Software for Education*. doi:10.12753/2066-026X-16-158

Al-Betar, M. A., Awadallah, M. A., Khader, A. T., & Abdalkareem, Z. A. (2015). Island-based harmony search for optimization problems. *Expert Systems with Applications*, *42*(4), 2026–2035. doi:10.1016/j.eswa.2014.10.008

Al-Betar, M. A., Doush, I. A., Khader, A. T., & Awadallah, M. A. (2012). Novel selection schemes for harmony search. *Applied Mathematics and Computation*, *218*(10), 6095–6117. doi:10.1016/j.amc.2011.11.095

Al-Betar, M. A., Khader, A. T., Geem, Z. W., Doush, I. A., & Awadallah, M. A. (2013). An analysis of selection methods in memory consideration for harmony search. *Applied Mathematics and Computation*, *219*(22), 10753–10767. doi:10.1016/j.amc.2013.04.053

Ali, E. S., & Abd-Elazim, S. M. (2011). Bacteria foraging optimization algorithm based load frequency controller for interconnected power system. *Electric Power and Energy Systems*, *33*(3), 633–638. doi:10.1016/j.ijepes.2010.12.022

Almeida-Luz, S., Vega-Rodríguez, A. M., Gómez-Pulido, J. A., & Sánchez-Pérez, J. M. (2008). Applying Differential Evolution to a Realistic Location Area Problem Using SUMATRA. *2008 The Second International Conference on Advanced Engineering Computing and Applications in Sciences*, 170–175. doi:10.1109/ADVCOMP.2008.19

Almeida-Luz, S. M., Vega-Rodríguez, M. a., Gómez-Pulido, J. a., & Sánchez-Pérez, J. M. (2009). Solving a Realistic Location Area Problem Using SUMATRA Networks with the Scatter Search Algorithm. *2009 Ninth International Conference on Intelligent Systems Design and Applications*, 689–694. doi:10.1109/ISDA.2009.51

Almeida-Luz, S. M., Vega-Rodríguez, M., Gómez-Púlido, J., & Sánchez-Pérez, J. M. (2011). Differential evolution for solving the mobile location management. *Applied Soft Computing*, *11*(1), 410–427. doi:10.1016/j.asoc.2009.11.031

Al-Surmi, I., Othman, M., & Mohd Ali, B. (2012). Mobility management for IP-based next generation mobile networks: Review, challenge and perspective. *Journal of Network and Computer Applications*, *35*(1), 295–315. doi:10.1016/j.jnca.2011.09.001

Amini, F., & Ghaderi, P. (2013). Hybridization of Harmony Search and Ant Colony Optimization for optimal locating of structural dampers. *Applied Soft Computing*, *13*(5), 2272–2280. doi:10.1016/j.asoc.2013.02.001

Anisetti, M., Ardagna, C. A., Bellandi, V., Damiani, E., Member, S., & Reale, S. (2011). *Map-Based Location and Tracking in Multipath Outdoor Mobile Networks*. Academic Press.

Arakawa, T., Kubota, N., & Fukuda, T. (1996). Virus-evolutionary genetic algorithm with subpopulations: application to trajectory generation of redundant manipulator through energy optimization. *1996 IEEE International Conference on Systems, Man and Cybernetics. Information Intelligence and Systems*, *3*, 1930–1935. doi:10.1109/ICSMC.1996.565413

Compilation of References

Arivoli, A., & Chidambaram, I. A. (2011). Design of genetic algorithm (GA) based controller for load-frequency control of power systems interconnected with AC-DC TIE-LINE. *Int J Sci. Engineering Tech, 2*, 280–286.

Arul, R., Ravi, G., & Velusami, S. (2013). Solving optimal power flow problems using chaotic self adaptive differential harmony search algorithm. *Electric Power Components and Systems, 41*(8), 782–805. doi:10.1080/15325008.2013.769033

Arul, R., Ravi, G., & Velusami, S. (2013a). Chaotic self-adaptive differential harmony search algorithm based dynamic economic dispatch. *International Journal of Electrical Power & Energy Systems, 50*, 85–96. doi:10.1016/j.ijepes.2013.02.017

Arul, R., Ravi, G., & Velusami, S. (2013b). Non-convex economic dispatch with heuristic load patterns, valve point loading effect, prohibited operating zones, ramp-rate limits and spinning reserve constraints using harmony search algorithm. *Electrical Engineering, 95*(1), 53–61. doi:10.1007/s00202-012-0241-y

Arul, R., Ravi, G., & Velusami, S. (2014). An improved harmony search algorithm to solve economic load dispatch problems with generator constraints. *Electrical Engineering, 96*(1), 55–63. doi:10.1007/s00202-012-0276-0

Ashrafi, S. M., & Dariane, A. B. (2013). Performance evaluation of an improved harmony search algorithm for numerical optimization: Melody Search (MS). *Engineering Applications of Artificial Intelligence, 26*(4), 1301–1321. doi:10.1016/j.engappai.2012.08.005

Askarzadeh, A. (2013a). Developing a discrete harmony search algorithm for size optimization of wind–photovoltaic hybrid energy system. *Solar Energy, 98*(Part C), 190–195. doi:10.1016/j.solener.2013.10.008

Askarzadeh, A. (2013b). A discrete chaotic harmony search-based simulated annealing algorithm for optimum design of PV/wind hybrid system. *Solar Energy, 97*, 93–101. doi:10.1016/j.solener.2013.08.014

Askarzadeh, A., & Rezazadeh, A. (2011). A grouping-based global harmony search algorithm for modeling of proton exchange membrane fuel cell. *International Journal of Hydrogen Energy, 36*(8), 5047–5053. doi:10.1016/j.ijhydene.2011.01.070

Askarzadeh, A., & Rezazadeh, A. (2012). Parameter identification for solar cell models using harmony search-based algorithms. *Solar Energy, 86*(11), 3241–3249. doi:10.1016/j.solener.2012.08.018

Askarzadeh, A., & Zebarjadi, M. (2014). Wind power modeling using harmony search with a novel parameter setting approach. *Journal of Wind Engineering and Industrial Aerodynamics, 135*, 70–75. doi:10.1016/j.jweia.2014.10.012

Askin, R. G., & Chiu, K. S. (1990). A graph partitioning procedure for machine assignment and cell formation in group technology. *International Journal of Production Research, 28*(8), 1555–1572. doi:10.1080/00207549008942812

Atanassov, K. T. (1986). Intuitionistic Fuzzy Sets. *Fuzzy Sets and Systems*, *20*(1), 87–96. doi:10.1016/S0165-0114(86)80034-3

Atrabi, H. B., Kourosh, Q., Rheinheimer, D. E., & Sharifi, E. (2015). Application of harmony search algorithm to reservoir operation optimization. *Water Resources Management*, *29*(15), 5729–5748. doi:10.1007/s11269-015-1143-3

Au, K.-F., Choi, T.-M., & Yu, Y. (2008). Fashion retail forecasting by evolutionary neural networks. *International Journal of Production Economics*, *114*(2), 615–630. doi:10.1016/j.ijpe.2007.06.013

Avriel, M. (2008). *Nonlinear Programming: Analysis and Methods*. Dover Publishing.

Baek, C. W., Jun, H. D., & Kim, J. H. (2010). Development of a PDA model for water distribution systems using harmony search algorithm. *KSCE Journal of Civil Engineering*, *14*(4), 613–625. doi:10.1007/s12205-010-0613-7

Balanis, C. A. (2005). *Antenna theory: Analysis and design*. Academic Press.

Banerjee, I., & Das, P. (2012). Group technology based adaptive cell formation using predator-prey genetic algorithm. *Applied Soft Computing*, *12*(1), 559–572. doi:10.1016/j.asoc.2011.07.021

Bao, D., & Yang, Z. (2008). Intelligent stock trading system by turning point confirming and probabilistic reasoning. *Expert Systems with Applications*, *34*(1), 620–627. doi:10.1016/j.eswa.2006.09.043

Batsyn, M., Bychkov, I., Goldengorin, B., Pardalos, P., & Sukhov, P. (2013). Pattern-based heuristic for the cell formation problem in group technology. In M. V. Batsyn, V. A. Kalyagin, & P. M. Pardalos (Eds.), *Models, algorithms, and technologies for network analysis* (pp. 11–50). New York, NY: Springer. doi:10.1007/978-1-4614-5574-5_2

Baydokhty, M. E., Zare, A., & Balochian, S. (2016). Performance of optimal hierarchical type 2 fuzzy controller for load-frequency system with production rate limitation and governor dead band. *Alexndraia Engineering Journal*, *55*(1), 379–397. doi:10.1016/j.aej.2015.12.003

Bekdas, G. (2015). Harmony search algorithm approach for optimum design of post-tensioned axially symmetric cylindrical reinforced concrete walls. *Journal of Optim Theory Application*, *164*(1), 342–358. doi:10.1007/s10957-014-0562-2

Berrocal-plaza, V., Vega-rodríguez, M. A., Sánchez-pérez, J. M., & Gómez-pulido, J. A. (2012). *Solving the Location Areas Problem with Strength Pareto Evolutionary Algorithm*. Academic Press.

Bertsekas. (2000). Dynamic Programming and Optimal Control. Athena Scientific.

Bevrani, H., & Daneshmand, P. R. (2012). Fuzzy logic-based load-frequency control concerning high penetration of wind turbines. *IEEE Syst. J.*, *6*(1), 173–180. doi:10.1109/JSYST.2011.2163028

Birbil, S. I., & Fang, S. C. (2003). An electromagnetism-like mechanism for global optimization. *Journal of Global Optimization*, *25*(3), 263–282. doi:10.1023/A:1022452626305

Compilation of References

Boctor, F. F. (1991). A linear formulation of the machine-part cell formation problem. *International Journal of Production Research*, 29(2), 343–356. doi:10.1080/00207549108930075

Bora, S., Tiryaki, A. M., & Dikenelli, O. (2012). Load Sharing Based on Moving Roles in Multiagent Systems, *Turk J. Elec. Eng. & Comp. Sci*, 20(2), 219–229.

Broere, F., Apasov, S. G., Sitkovsky, M. V., & van Eden, W. (2011). T cell subsets and T cell-mediated immunity. In F. P. Nijkamp & M. J. Parnham (Eds.), *Principles of Immunopharmacology* (pp. 15–27). Springer. doi:10.1007/978-3-0346-0136-8_2

Brown, R. G. (1959). *Statistical forecasting for inventory control*. Academic Press.

Brownlee, J. (2005). *Immunos-81. The Misunderstood Artificial Immune System*. Technical Report No. 3-01. Swinburne University of Technology.

Brownlee, J. (2011). *Clever Algorithms: Nature-Inspired Programming Recipes*. Retrieved from http://www.cleveralgorithms.com/

Brusco, M. J. (2015). An iterated local search heuristic for cell formation. *Computers & Industrial Engineering*, 90, 292–304. doi:10.1016/j.cie.2015.09.010

Brusic, V., & Petrovsky, N. (2003). Immunoinformatics - the new kid in town. In *Symposium on Immunoinformatics: Bioinformatic strategies for better understanding of immune function*. Wiley and Sons.

Burnet, F. M. (1957). A modification of Jerne's theory of antibody production using the concept of clonal selection. *Australian Journal of Science*, 20, 67–69.

Burnet, F. M. (1959). *The clonal selection theory of acquired immunity*. Vanderbilt University Press. doi:10.5962/bhl.title.8281

Campbell, A., & Wu, A. S. (2011). Multi-agent Role Allocation: Issues, Approaches, and Multiple Perspectives. *Autonomous Agents and Multi-Agent Systems*, 22(2), 317–355. doi:10.1007/s10458-010-9127-4

Cao, Y. (2013). An overview of recent progress in the study of distributed multi-agent coordination. *Industrial Informatics. IEEE Transactions on*, 9(1), 427–438.

Carbas, S., & Saka, M. P. (2012). Optimum topology design of various geometrically nonlinear latticed domes using improved harmony search method. *Struct Multidisc Optim*, 45(3), 377–399. doi:10.1007/s00158-011-0675-2

Castelli, M., Silva, S., Manzoni, L., & Vanneschi, L. (2014). Geometric Selective Harmony Search. *Information Sciences*, 279, 468–482. doi:10.1016/j.ins.2014.04.001

Ceylan, H., & Ceylan, H. (2012). A Hybrid Harmony Search and TRANSYT hill climbing algorithm for signalized stochastic equilibrium transportation networks. *Transportation Research Part C, Emerging Technologies*, 25, 152–167. doi:10.1016/j.trc.2012.05.007

Chaisson & McMillan. (n.d.). Astronomy Today: Stars and Galaxies. *Benjamin-Cummings*.

Chakraborty, P., Roy, G. G., Das, S., Jain, D., & Abraham, A. (2009). An improved harmony search algorithm with differential mutation operator. *Fundamenta Informaticae, 95*, 1–26.

Chan & Chan. (2010). An AHP model for selection of suppliers in the fast changing fashion market. *The International Journal of Advanced Manufacturing Technology, 51*, 9-12.

Chang, C. C., Wu, T. H., & Wu, C. W. (2013). An efficient approach to determine cell formation, cell layout and intracellular machine sequence in cellular manufacturing systems. *Computers & Industrial Engineering, 66*(2), 438–450. doi:10.1016/j.cie.2013.07.009

Chang, P. C., Chen, S. H., & Fan, C. Y. (2009). A hybrid electromagnetism-like algorithm for single machine scheduling problem. *Expert Systems with Applications, 36*(2, Part 1), 1259–1267. doi:10.1016/j.eswa.2007.11.050

Chattopadhyay, M., Sengupta, S., Ghosh, T., Dan, P. K., & Mazumdar, S. (2013). Neuro-genetic impact on cell formation methods of cellular manufacturing system design: A quantitative review and analysis. *Computers & Industrial Engineering, 64*(1), 256–272. doi:10.1016/j.cie.2012.09.016

Chen, J., Pan, Q., & Li, J. (2012). Harmony search algorithm with dynamic control parameters. *Applied Mathematics and Computation, 219*(2), 592–604. doi:10.1016/j.amc.2012.06.048

Chen, L. C., Jan, M. R., Lee, Y. T., & Chen, H. C. (2011). A Particle Swarm Optimization with Improved Inertia Weight Algorithm Solution of Economic Dispatch With Valve Point Loading. *Journal of Marine Science and Technology, 19*(1), 43–51.

Chidambaram, I. A., & Paramasivam, B. (2009). Genetic algorithm based decentralized controllerfor load-frequency control of interconnected power systems with RFB considering TCPS in the tie-line. International Journal of Electronic Engineering Research, 1, 299-312.

Christofides, N., & Eilon, S. (1969). An Algorithm for the Vehicle- dispatching Problem. *Operations Research, 20*(3), 309–318. doi:10.1057/jors.1969.75

Chung, S. H., Wu, T. H., & Chang, C. C. (2011). An efficient tabu search algorithm to the cell formation problem with alternative routings and machine reliability considerations. *Computers & Industrial Engineering, 60*(1), 7–15. doi:10.1016/j.cie.2010.08.016

Chung, Y. C., & Haupt, R. L. (1999, July). Adaptive nulling with spherical arrays using a genetic algorithm.*Antennas and Propagation Society International Symposium*, 2000-2003. doi:10.1109/APS.1999.788352

Chun, J., Jung, H., & Hahn, S. (1998). A study on comparison of optimization performances between immune algorithm and other heuristic algorithms. *IEEE Transactions on Magnetics, 34*(5), 2912–2915.

Civicioglu, P., & Besdok, E. (2011). A conceptual comparison of the Cuckoo-search, particle swarm optimization, differential evolution and artificial bee colony algorithms. *Artificial Intelligence Review, 39*(4), 315–346. doi:10.1007/s10462-011-9276-0

Colorni, Dorigo, & Maniezzo. (1991). *Distributed optimization by at colonies*. Elsevier Publishing.

Compilation of References

Colorni, , Dorigo, & Maniezzo. (1992). An Investigation of some Properties of an Ant Algorithm. *Proc. of the Parallel Problem Solving from Nature Conference*, 509 – 520.

Conor, B. W., & Brian, H. S. (2009). Utilizing Dynamic Roles for Agents. *Journal of Object Technology*, *8*(5), 177–198. doi:10.5381/jot.2009.8.5.a5

Contreras, J., Amaya, I., & Correa, R. (2014). An improved variant of the conventional Harmony Search algorithm. *Applied Mathematics and Computation*, *227*, 821–830. doi:10.1016/j.amc.2013.11.050

Cortes, P., Onieva, L., Munuzuri, J., & Guadix, J. (2013). A viral system algorithm to optimize the car dispatching in elevator group control systems of tall buildings. *Computers & Industrial Engineering*, *64*(1), 403–411. doi:10.1016/j.cie.2012.11.002

CST-Microwave Studio. (2013). User's Manual. Author.

Cuevas, E. (2013). Block-matching algorithm based on harmony search optimization for motion estimation. *Applied Intelligence*, *39*(1), 165–183. doi:10.1007/s10489-012-0403-7

Dai, X., Yuan, X., Wu, L. (in press). A novel harmony search algorithm with gaussian mutation for multi-objective optimization. *Soft Comput*.

D'Amico, Giustiniano, Nenni, & Pirolo. (2013). Product Lifecycle Management as a tool to create value in the fashion system. *International Journal of Engineering Business Management, 5*.

Danet, N. (2012). Some remarks on the Pompeiu-Hausdorff distance between order intervals. *ROMAI J.*, *8*(2), 51–60.

Dasgupta, D. (2010). *Artificial Immune Systems: A Bibliography*. Computer Science Department, University of Memphis. Retrieved from http://ais.cs.memphis.edu/files/papers/AIS-bibliography-March2010.pdf

Dasgupta, D. (Ed.). (1999). *Artificial Immune Systems and Their Applications*. Springer-Verlag. doi:10.1007/978-3-642-59901-9

Dasgupta, D., & Michalewicz, Z. (2013). *Evolutionary algorithms in engineering applications*. Berlin, Germany: Springer-Verlag Berlin Heidelberg.

Dasgupta, D., & Nino, L. F. (2009). *Immunological Computation, Theory and Applications*. CRC Press.

Dasgupta, D., Yu, S., & Nino, F. (2011). Recent Advances in Artificial Immune Systems: Models and Applications. *Applied Soft Computing*, *11*(2), 1574–1587. doi:10.1016/j.asoc.2010.08.024

Dash, R., Dash, P. K., & Bisoi, R. (2014). A self adaptive differential harmony search based optimized extreme learning machine for financial time series prediction. *Swarm and Evolutionary Computation*, *19*, 25–42. doi:10.1016/j.swevo.2014.07.003

Dash, R., Dash, P. K., & Bisoi, R. (2015). A differential harmony search based hybrid interval type2 fuzzy EGARCH model for stock market volatility prediction. *International Journal of Approximate Reasoning, 59*, 81–104. doi:10.1016/j.ijar.2015.02.001

Dash, Saikia, & Sinha. (2014). Comparison of performances of several Cuckoo search algorithm based 2DOF controllers in AGC of multi-area thermal system. *Electrical Power and Energy Systems, 55*, 429–436.

Dash, Saikia, & Sinha. (2015a). Automatic generation control of multi area thermal system using Bat algorithm optimized PD-PID cascade controller. *Electric Power and Energy Systems, 68*, 364–372.

Dash, Saikia, & Sinha. (2015b). Comparison of performance of several FACTS devices using Cuckoo search algorithm optimized 2DOF controllers in multi-area AGC. *Electric Power and Energy Systems, 65*, 316–324.

de Castro, L. N., & Von Zuben, F. (2001). aiNET: An Artificial Immune Network for Data Analysis. In Data Mining: A Heuristic Approach. Idea Group Publishing.

de Castro, L.N., & Timmis, J. (2002). *Artificial Immune System: A New Computational Approach.* Springer-Verlag.

de Castro, L. N., & Timmis, J. (2002). An artificial immune network for multimodal function optimization.*Proceedings of IEEE Congress on Evolutionary Computation*, 699-704. doi:10.1109/CEC.2002.1007011

de Castro, L. N., & Von Zuben, F. J. (2000). The clonal selection algorithm with engineering applications.*Proceedings of GECCO*, 36–39.

De, B. P., Kar, R., Mandal, D., & Ghoshal, S. P. (2016). Optimal design of high speed symmetric switching CMOS inverter using hybrid harmony search with differential evolution. *Soft Computing, 20*(9), 3699–3717. doi:10.1007/s00500-015-1731-4

Degertekin, S. O. (2012). Improved harmony search algorithms for sizing optimization of truss structures. *Computers & Structures, 92–93*, 229–241. doi:10.1016/j.compstruc.2011.10.022

Degertekin, S. O., & Hayalioglu, M. S. (2010). Harmony search algorithm for minimum cost design of steel frames with semi-rigid connections and column bases. *Struct Multidisc Optim, 42*(5), 755–768. doi:10.1007/s00158-010-0533-7

Demiroren,A, Zeynelgil, A.Z, & Sengor, N.S. (n.d.). *The application of ANN technique to load frequency control for three-area power systems.* IEEE Porto power tech conference, Porto, Portugal.

Dey, N., Samanta, S., Chakraborty, S., Das, A., Chaudhuri, S. S., & Suri, J. S. (2014). Firefly Algorithm for Optimization of Scaling Factors during Embedding of Manifold Medical Information: An Application in Ophthalmology Imaging. *Journal of Medical Imaging and Health Informatics, 4*(3), 384–394. doi:10.1166/jmihi.2014.1265

Compilation of References

Dey, N., Samanta, S., Yang, X. S., Chaudhri, S. S., & Das, A. (2014). Optimization of Scaling Factors in Electrocardiogram Signal Watermarking using Cuckoo Search. *International Journal of Bio-inspired Computation*, *5*(5), 315–326. doi:10.1504/IJBIC.2013.057193

Dorigo, M. (1992). *Optimization, Learning and Natural Algorithms* (PhD thesis). Politecnico di Milano.

Dorigo, M., & Gambardella, L. M. (1997). Ant colony system: A cooperative learning approach to the traveling salesman problem. *IEEE Transactions on Evolutionary Computation*, *1*(1), 53–66. doi:10.1109/4235.585892

Dorigo, M., Maniezzo, V., & Colorni, A. (1996). Ant System: Optimization by a colony of cooperating agents. *IEEE Trans. on Systems, Man, and Cybernetics – Part B.*, *26*(1), 29–41. doi:10.1109/3477.484436 PMID:18263004

Duran, O., Rodriguez, N., & Consalter, L. (2010). Collaborative particle swarm optimization with a data mining technique for manufacturing cell design. *Expert Systems with Applications*, *37*(2), 1563–1567. doi:10.1016/j.eswa.2009.06.061

Ebrahim, Mostafa, Gawish, & Bendary. (2009). Design of decentralized load frequency based-PID controller using stochastic Particle swarm optimization technique. *International Conference on Electric Power and Energy Conversion System*, 1-6.

Elbenani, B., & Ferland, J. A. (2012). An exact method for solving the manufacturing cell formation problem. *International Journal of Production Research*, *50*(15), 4038–4045. doi:10.10 80/00207543.2011.588622

Elbenani, B., Ferland, J. A., & Bellemare, J. (2012). Genetic algorithm and large neighbourhood search to solve the cell formation problem. *Expert Systems with Applications*, *39*(3), 2408–2414. doi:10.1016/j.eswa.2011.08.089

Enayatifar, R., Yousefi, M., Abdullah, A. H., & Darus, A. N. (2013). A novel harmony search algorithm based on learning automata. *Communications in Nonlinear Science and Numerical Simulation*, *18*(12), 3481–3497. doi:10.1016/j.cnsns.2013.04.028

Erwin Diewert, W. (2008). Cost functions. In *The New Palgrave Dictionary of Economics*. Palgrave McMillan.

Esponda, F., Forrest, S., & Helman, P. (2004). *Enhancing Privacy through Negative Representations of Data*. UNM Computer Science Technical Report TR-CS-2004-18.

Ezhilarasi, G. A., & Swarup, K. S. (2012a). Network decomposition using Kernighan–Lin strategy aided harmony search algorithm. *Swarm and Evolutionary Computation*, *7*, 1–6. doi:10.1016/j.swevo.2012.07.002

Ezhilarasi, G. A., & Swarup, K. S. (2012b). Network partitioning using harmony search and equivalencing for distributed computing. *Journal of Parallel and Distributed Computing*, *72*(8), 936–943. doi:10.1016/j.jpdc.2012.04.006

Fahmy, S. A. (2015). Mixed integer linear programming model for integrating cell formation, group layout and group scheduling. In *Proceedings of IEEE international conference on industrial technology (ICIT'15)*. Seville, Spain: IEEE. doi:10.1109/ICIT.2015.7125452

Fathian, M., Jouzdani, J., Heydari, M., & Makui, A. (2016). Location and transportation planning in supply chains under uncertainty and congestion by using an improved electromagnetism-like algorithm. *Journal of Intelligent Manufacturing*, 1–18.

Fattahi, H., Gholami, A., Amiribakhtiar, M. S., & Moradi, S. (2015). Estimation of asphaltene precipitation from titration data: A hybrid support vector regression with harmony search. *Neural Computing & Applications*, *26*(4), 789–798. doi:10.1007/s00521-014-1766-y

Fogel, Owens, & Walsh. (1996). *Artificial Intelligence through Simulated Evolution*. John Wiley.

Fondevila, J., Brégains, J. C., Ares, F., & Moreno, E. (2004). Optimizing uniformly excited linear arrays through time modulation. *IEEE Antennas and Wireless Propagation Letters*, *3*(1), 298–301. doi:10.1109/LAWP.2004.838833

Forrest, S., Perelson, A. S., Allen, L., & Cherukuri, R. (1994). Self-nonself discrimination in a computer.*Proceedings of the IEEE Computer Society Symposium on Research in Security and Privacy*, 202–212. doi:10.1109/RISP.1994.296580

Forsati, R., & Shamsfard, M. (2015). Novel harmony search-based algorithms for part-of-speech tagging. *Knowledge and Information Systems*, *42*(3), 709–736. doi:10.1007/s10115-013-0719-6

Francis, R., & Chidambaram, I.A. (2015). Optimized PI+ load-frequency controller using BWNN approach for an interconnected reheat power system with RFB and hydrogen electrolyzer units. *Electric Power and Energy Systems, 67*, 381-392.

Frank, C., Garg, A., Sztandera, L., & Raheja, A. (2003). Forecasting womens apparel sales using mathematical modeling. *International Journal of Clothing Science and Technology*, *15*(2), 107–125. doi:10.1108/09556220310470097

Fred, G. (1996). Future Paths for Integer Programming and Links to Artificial Intelligence. *Computers & Operations Research*, *13*, 533–549.

Freitas, A. A., & Timmis, J. (2003). Revisiting the Foundations of Artificial Immune Systems: A Problem-Oriented Perspective. In J. Timmis et al. (Eds.), *ICARIS 2003, LNCS 2787* (pp. 229–241). doi:10.1007/978-3-540-45192-1_22

Fumi, Pepe, Scarabotti, & Schiraldi. (2011). Fourier analysis for demand forecasting in a fashion company. *International Journal of Engineering Business Management, 5*.

Gao, K. Z., Suganthan, P. N., Pan, Q. K., Chua, T. J., Cai, T. X., & Chong, C. S. (2014). Pareto-based grouping discrete harmony search algorithm for multi-objective flexible job shop scheduling. *Information Sciences*, *289*, 76–90. doi:10.1016/j.ins.2014.07.039

Compilation of References

Gao, K. Z., Suganthan, P. N., Pan, Q. K., Chua, T. J., Cai, T. X., & Chong, C. S. (2015). Discrete harmony search algorithm for flexible job shop scheduling problem with multiple objectives. *Journal of Intelligent Manufacturing*, *27*(2), 363–374. doi:10.1007/s10845-014-0869-8

Gao, X. Z., Wang, X., Jokinen, T., Ovaska, S. J., Arkkio, A., & Zenger, K. (2012). A hybrid PBIL-based harmony search method. *Neural Computing & Applications*, *21*(5), 1071–1083. doi:10.1007/s00521-011-0675-6

Garey, M. R., & Johnson, D. S. (1979). *Computers and intractability: a guide to the theory of np-completeness*. San Francisco, CA: Freeman.

Geem, Z. (2006). *Improved harmony search from ensemble of music players. In Knowledge-based intelligent information and engineering systems* (pp. 86–93). Heidelberg: Springer. doi:10.1007/11892960_11

Geem, Z. W. (2012). Effects of initial memory and identical harmony in global optimization using harmony search algorithm. *Applied Mathematics and Computation*, *218*(22), 11337–11343. doi:10.1016/j.amc.2012.04.070

Geem, Z. W., & Sim, K. B. (2010). Parameter-setting-free harmony search algorithm. *Applied Mathematics and Computation*, *217*(8), 3881–3889. doi:10.1016/j.amc.2010.09.049

Geem, Z. W., Tseng, C. L., & Park, Y. (2005). *Harmony search for generalized orienteering problem: best touring in China. In Advances in natural computation* (pp. 741–750). Berlin: Springer.

Gendreau, M., & Potvin, J.-Y. (Eds.). (2010). Handbook of Metaheuristics. Boston, MA: Springer US. doi:10.1007/978-1-4419-1665-5

Ghobbar, A. A., & Friend, C. H. (2003). Evaluation of forecasting methods for intermittent parts demand in the field of aviation: A predictive model. *Computers & Operations Research*, *30*(14), 2097–2114. doi:10.1016/S0305-0548(02)00125-9

Gil-López, S., Ser, J. D., Salcedo-Sanz, S., Pérez-Bellido, Á. M., Cabero, J. M., & Portilla-Figueras, J. A. (2012). A hybrid harmony search algorithm for the spread spectrum radar polyphase codes design problem. *Expert Systems with Applications*, *39*(12), 11089–11093. doi:10.1016/j.eswa.2012.03.063

Glover, F., & Laguna, M. (1997). *Tabu Search* (1st ed.). Boston, MA: Kluwer Academic Publishers. doi:10.1007/978-1-4615-6089-0

Goldengorin, B., Krushinsky, D., & Pardalos, P. M. (2013). The problem of cell formation: Ideas and their applications. In B. Goldengorin, D. Krushinsky, P. M. Pardalos, & M. Panos (Eds.), *Cell formation in industrial engineering* (pp. 1–23). New York, NY: Springer. doi:10.1007/978-1-4614-8002-0_1

Gomes, A., Antunes, C. H., & Martins, A. G. (2010). Improving the responsiveness of NSGA-II using an adaptive mutation operator: A case study. *Int. J. of Advanced Intelligence Paradigms*, *2*(1), 4–18. doi:10.1504/IJAIP.2010.029437

Gondim, P. R. L. (1996). Genetic Algorithms and The Location Area Partitioning Problem in Cellular Networks. *Proc. of IEEE 46th Vehicular Technology Conference*, 1835–1838. doi:10.1109/VETEC.1996.504075

Gonzalez, F. (2003). *A Study of Artificial Immune Systems Applied to Anomaly Detection*. (PhD Thesis). The University of Memphis.

Gonzalez, F., Galeano, J., & Veloza, A. (2005). A comparative analysis of artificial immune network models. *Proceedings of the 2005 Conference on Genetic and Evolutionary Computation*, 361–368.

Goss, S., Aron, S., Deneubourg, J. L., & Pasteels, J. M. (1989). Self-organized shortcuts in the Argentine ant. *Naturwissenschaften*, *76*(12), 579–581. doi:10.1007/BF00462870

Gottesman, D. (1996). *Stabilizer codes and quantum error correction, quant-ph/9705052* (PhD Thesis). Cal Tech.

Gozde, Taplamacioglu. (2011). Automatic generation control application with craziness based particle swarm optimization in a thermal power system. *Electrical Power and Energy Systems, 33*, 8-16.

Gozde, H., & Taplamacioglu, C. (2012). Comparative performance analysis of Artificial Bee Colony algorithm in automatic generation control for interconnected reheat thermal power system. *Electric Power and Energy Systems*, *42*(1), 167–178. doi:10.1016/j.ijepes.2012.03.039

Greensmith, J. (2007). *The Dendritic Cell Algorithm* (PhD Thesis). University of Nottingham.

Guney, K., & Onay, M. (2011). Optimal synthesis of linear antenna arrays using a harmony search algorithm. *Expert Systems with Applications*, *38*(12), 15455–15462. doi:10.1016/j.eswa.2011.06.015

Guo, Z. X., Yang, C., Wang, W., & Yang, J. (2015). Harmony search-based multi-objective optimization model for multi-site order planning with multiple uncertainties and learning effects. *Computers & Industrial Engineering*, *83*, 74–90. doi:10.1016/j.cie.2015.01.023

Hajipour, V., Rahmati, S. H. A., Pasandideh, S. H. R., & Niaki, S. T. A. (2014). A multi-objective harmony search algorithm to optimize multi-server location–allocation problem in congested systems. *Computers & Industrial Engineering*, *72*, 187–197. doi:10.1016/j.cie.2014.03.018

Hamaker, J. S., & Boggess, L. (2004). Non-euclidean distance measures in airs an artificial immune classification system. *Proceedings of the 2004 congress on evolutionary computation*, 1067–1073. doi:10.1109/CEC.2004.1330980

Ham, I., Hitomi, K., & Yoshida, T. (2012). *Group technology: applications to production management*. Hingham, MA: Kluwer.

Hamilton, A. J. S. (1998). The Evolving Universe. Kluwer Academic.

Compilation of References

Hardel, G. R., Yalapragada, N. T., Mandal, D., & Bhattacharjee, A. K. (2011). Introducing Dipper Nulls in Time modulated Linear symmetric Antenna Array Using Real Coded Genetic Algorithm. *IEEE Symposium on Computers and Informatics*, 249-254.

Harhalakis, G., Nagi, R., & Proth, J. (1990). An efficient heuristic in manufacturing cell formation for group technology applications. *International Journal of Production Research*, *28*(1), 185–198. doi:10.1080/00207549008942692

Harmer, P. K., Williams, P. D., Gunsch, G. H., & Lamont, G. B. (2002). An Artificial Immune System Architecture for Computer Security Applications. *IEEE Transactions on Evolutionary Computation*, *6*(3), 252–280. doi:10.1109/TEVC.2002.1011540

Hasan, B. H. F., Abu Doush, I., Al Maghayreh, E., Alkhateeb, F., & Hamdan, M. (2014). Hybridizing Harmony Search algorithm with different mutation operators for continuous problems. *Applied Mathematics and Computation*, *232*, 1166–1182. doi:10.1016/j.amc.2013.12.139

Hasancebi, O., Erdal, F., & Saka, M. P. (2009). An adaptive harmony search method for structural optimization. *Journal of Structural Engineering*, *137*, 419–431.

Hastings, W. K. (1970). Monte Carlo Sampling Methods Using Markov Chains and Their Applications. *Biometrika*, *57*(1), 197–109. doi:10.1093/biomet/57.1.97

Haupt, R. L. (1988). Adaptive nulling in monopulse antennas. *IEEE Transactions on Antennas and Propagation*, *36*(2), 202–208. doi:10.1109/8.1097

Haupt, R. L. (1997). Phase-only adaptive nulling with a genetic algorithm. *IEEE Transactions on Antennas and Propagation*, *45*(6), 1009–1015. doi:10.1109/8.585749

Hawking & Penrose. (1970). The Singularities of Gravitational Collapse and Cosmology. *Proc. of the Royal Society A: Mathematical, Physical and Engineering Sciences*, *314*(1519), 529 – 548.

Hawking, S. W. (1974). Black hole explosions? *Nature*, *248*(5443), 30–31. doi:10.1038/248030a0

Hehl, F., Kiefer, C., & Metzler, R. (1998). *Black Holes: A General Introduction*. Lecture Notes in Physics.

Hofmeyr, S. A., & Forrest, S. (1999). Architecture for an Artificial Immune System. *Evolutionary Computation*, *7*(1), 45–68. PMID:10199995

Holland, J. H. (1975). *Adaptation in Natural and Artificial Systems: An Introductory Analysis with Applications to Biology, Control, and Artificial Intelligence*. Ann Arbor, MI: University of Michigan Press.

Ho, S. L., Shiyou Yang, , Guangzheng Ni, , & Wong, H. C. (2001). An improved Tabu search for the global optimizations of electromagnetic devices. *IEEE Transactions on Magnetics*, *37*(5), 3570–3574. doi:10.1109/20.952664

Hosseini, S. D., Akbarpour Shirazi, M., & Karimi, B. (2014). Cross-docking and milk run logistics in a consolidation network: A hybrid of harmony search and simulated annealing approach. *Journal of Manufacturing Systems*, *33*(4), 567–577. doi:10.1016/j.jmsy.2014.05.004

Huang, Y.-F., Lin, S.-M., Wu, H.-Y., & Li, Y.-S. (2014). Music genre classification based on local feature selection using a self-adaptive harmony search algorithm. *Data & Knowledge Engineering*, *92*, 60–76. doi:10.1016/j.datak.2014.07.005

Hui, C. L., Lau, T. W., Ng, S. F., & Chan, C. C. (2005). Learning-based fuzzy colour prediction system for more effective apparel design. *International Journal of Clothing Science and Technology*, *17*(5), 335–348. doi:10.1108/09556220510616192

Hung, W. L., Yang, M. S., & Lee, E. S. (2011). Cell formation using fuzzy relational clustering algorithm. *Mathematical and Computer Modelling*, *53*(910), 1776–1787. doi:10.1016/j.mcm.2010.12.056

Hunt, J. E., & Cooke, D. E. (1996). Learning using an artificial immune system. *Journal of Network and Computer Applications*, *19*(2), 189–212. doi:10.1006/jnca.1996.0014

Inbarani, H. H., Bagyamathi, M., & Azar, A. T. (2015). A novel hybrid feature selection method based on rough set and improved harmony search. *Neural Computing & Applications*, *26*(8), 1859–1880. doi:10.1007/s00521-015-1840-0

J, A. P. S., & M, K. (2010). A Dynamic Location Management Scheme for Wirless Networks Using Cascaded Correlation Neural Network. *International Journal of Computer Theory and Engineering*, *2*(4), 581–585. doi:10.7763/IJCTE.2010.V2.205

Jagatheesan, Anand, Dey, & Ashour. (2016). Ant Colony Optimization algorithm based PID controller for LFC of single area power system with non-linearity and boiler dynamics. World Journal of Modeling and Simulation, 12(1), 3-14.

Jagatheesan, Anand, Dey, & Balas. (2016). *Load Frequency Control of Hydro-Hydro System with Fuzzy Logic Controller Considering Non-Linearity*. World Conference on Soft Computing, Berkeley, CA.

Jagatheesan, Anand, Santhi, Dey, Ashour, & Balas. (2016). Dynamic Performance Analysis of AGC of Multi-Area Power System Considering Proportional-Integral-Derivative Controller with Different Cost Functions. *Proceeding of IEEE International Conference on Electrical, Electronics, and Optimization Techniques*.

Jagatheesan, K., & Anand, B. (2014). Automatic Generation Control of Three Area Hydro-Thermal Power Systems considering Electric and Mechanical Governor with conventional and Ant Colony Optimization technique. *Advances in Natural and Applied Science, 8*(20), 25-33.

Jagatheesan, K., Anand, B., & Ebrahim, M.A. (2014). Stochastic Particle Swarm Optimization for tuning of PID Controller in Load Frequency Control of Single Area Reheat Thermal Power System. *International Journal of Electrical and Power Engineering, 8*(2), 33-40.

Compilation of References

Jagatheesan, K. (2015). Automatic generation control of Thermal-Thermal-Hydro power systems with PID controller using ant colony optimization. *International Journal of Service Science, Management, Engineering, and Technology, 6*(2), 18–34. doi:10.4018/ijssmet.2015040102

Jagatheesan, K. (2015). Performance analysis of double reheat turbine in multi -area AGC system using conventional and ant colony optimization technique. *Journal of Electronic and Electrical Engineering, 15*(1), 1849–1854.

Jagatheesan, K. (2016). Particle Swarm Optimization based Parameters Optimization of PID Controller for Load Frequency Control of Multi-area Reheat Thermal Power Systems. *International Journal of Artificial Paradigm*.

Jagatheesan, K., & Anand, B. (2016). Application of Flower Pollination Algorithm in Load Frequency Control of multi-area interconnected power system with non-linearity,". *Neural Computing & Applications*, 1–14.

Jagatheesan, K., Anand, B., Dey, N., & S, A. (2015). Artificial Intelligence in Performance Analysis of Load Frequency Control in Thermal-Wind-Hydro Power Systems. *International Journal of Advanced Computer Science and Applications, 6*(7), 203–212. doi:10.14569/IJACSA.2015.060727

Javadi, M. S., Esmaeel Nezhad, A., & Sabramooz, S. (2012). Economic heat and power dispatch in modern power system harmony search algorithm versus analytical solution. *Scientia Iranica, 19*(6), 1820–1828. doi:10.1016/j.scient.2012.10.033

Javaheri, H., & Goldoost-Soloot, R. (2012). Locating and Sizing of Series FACTS Devices Using Line Outage Sensitivity Factors and Harmony Search Algorithm. *Energy Procedia, 14*, 1445–1450. doi:10.1016/j.egypro.2011.12.1115

Jayasinghe, J. W., Anguera, J., & Uduwawala, D. N. (2013). Genetic algorithm optimization of a high-directivity microstrip patch antenna having a rectangular profile. *Radioengineering, 22*(3).

Jeddi, B., & Vahidinasab, V. (2014). A modified harmony search method for environmental/economic load dispatch of real-world power systems. *Energy Conversion and Management, 78*, 661–675. doi:10.1016/j.enconman.2013.11.027

Jerne, N. K. (1984). *Nobel Lecture: The Generative Grammar of the Immune System*. Karolinska Institutet, Stockholm. Retrieved from http://www.nobelprize. org/mediaplayer/index.php?id=1653

Jerne, N. K. (1974). Towards a Network Theory of the Immune System. *Annals of Immunology, 125C*(1-2), 373–389. PMID:4142565

Jin, H., Xia, J., Wang, Y.-q. (2015). Optimal sensor placement for space modal identification of crane structures based on an improved harmony search algorithm. *J Zhejiang Univ-Sci A (Appl Phys & Eng), 16*(6), 464-477.

Kanoh, H., & Tsukahara, S. (2010). Solving real-world vehicle routing problems with time windows using virus evolution strategy. *International Journal of Knowledge-Based and Intelligent Engineering Systems, 14*(3), 115–126. doi:10.3233/KES-2010-0194

Kao, Y., & Chen, C. C. (2014). Automatic clustering for generalised cell formation using a hybrid particle swarm optimisation. *International Journal of Production Research*, *52*(12), 3466–3484. doi:10.1080/00207543.2013.867085

Kao, Y., & Lin, C.-H. (2012). A pso-based approach to cell formation problems with alternative process routings. *International Journal of Production Research*, *50*(15), 4075–4089. doi:10.10 80/00207543.2011.590541

Karaboga, D., & Basturk, B. (2007). A powerful and efficient algorithm for numerical function optimization: Artificial bee colony (abc) algorithm. *Journal of Global Optimization*, *39*(3), 459–471. doi:10.1007/s10898-007-9149-x

Karaboga, D., & Basturk, B. (2009a). A comparative study of artificial bee colony algorithm. *Applied Mathematics and Computation*, *214*(1), 108–132. doi:10.1016/j.amc.2009.03.090

Karimi, Z., Abolhassani, H., & Beigy, H. (2012). A new method of mining data streams using harmony search. *Journal of Intelligent Information Systems*, *39*(2), 491–511. doi:10.1007/s10844-012-0199-2

Kashan, H. A., Karimi, B., & Noktehdan, A. (2014). A novel discrete particle swarm optimization algorithm for the manufacturing cell formation problem. *International Journal of Advanced Manufacturing Technology*, *73*(9), 1543–1556. doi:10.1007/s00170-014-5906-4

Kashyap & Sankeswari. (2014). A simulation model for LFC using fuzzy PID with interconnected hydro power systems. *International Journal of Current Engineering and Technology*, (3), 183-186.

Kaveh, A., & Ahangaran, M. (2012). Discrete cost optimization of composite floor system using social harmony search model. *Applied Soft Computing*, *12*(1), 372–381. doi:10.1016/j.asoc.2011.08.035

Kaveh, A., & Javadi, M. S. (2014). Shape and size optimization of trusses with multiple frequency constraints using harmony search and ray optimizer for enhancing the particle swarm optimization algorithm. *Acta Mechanica*, *225*(6), 1595–1605. doi:10.1007/s00707-013-1006-z

Kennedy, J., & Eberhart, R. C. (1995). Particle swarm optimization. *Proc. of IEEE International Conference on Neural Networks*, 1942 – 1948. doi:10.1109/ICNN.1995.488968

Khalili, M., Kharrat, R., Salahshoor, K., & Sefat, M. H. (2014). Global Dynamic Harmony Search algorithm: GDHS. *Applied Mathematics and Computation*, *228*, 195–219. doi:10.1016/j.amc.2013.11.058

Khator, S., & Irani, S. (1987). Cell formation in group technology: A new approach. *Computers & Industrial Engineering*, *12*(2), 131–142. doi:10.1016/0360-8352(87)90006-4

Khazali, A. H., & Kalantar, M. (2011). Optimal reactive power dispatch based on harmony search algorithm. *International Journal of Electrical Power & Energy Systems*, *33*(3), 684–692. doi:10.1016/j.ijepes.2010.11.018

Compilation of References

Kim, S.-S., & Kim, G., Byeon, J-H., & Taheri, J. (2012). Particle Swarm Optimization for Location Mobility Management. *International Journal of Innovative Computing, Information, & Control, 8*(12), 8387–8398.

Kirkpatrick, S., Gelatt, C. D., & Vecchi, M. P. (1983). Optimization by Simulated Annealing. *Science, 220*(4598), 671–679. doi:10.1126/science.220.4598.671 PMID:17813860

Knight, S. A., & Burn, J. (2005). Developing a Framework for Assessing Information Quality on the World Wide Web. *Informing Science Journal, 8*, 159–172.

Kong, X., Gao, L., Ouyang, H., & Li, S. (2015a). A simplified binary harmony search algorithm for large scale 0–1 knapsack problems. *Expert Systems with Applications, 42*(12), 5337–5355. doi:10.1016/j.eswa.2015.02.015

Kong, X., Gao, L., Ouyang, H., & Li, S. (2015b). Solving large-scale multidimensional knapsack problems with a new binary harmony search algorithm. *Computers & Operations Research, 63*, 7–22. doi:10.1016/j.cor.2015.04.018

Korepanov, V. O., & Novikov, D. A. (2013). The diffuse Bomb Problem. *Automation and Remote Control, 74*(5), 5, 863–874. doi:10.1134/S000511791305010X

Kothari, M. L., & Nanda, J. (1988). Application of optimal control strategy to automatic generation control of a hydrothermal system. *IEE Proceedings, 135*(4), 268-274. doi:10.1049/ip-d.1988.0037

Kougias, I. P., & Theodossiou, N. P. (2013). Multiobjective pump scheduling optimization using harmony search algorithm (HSA) and polyphonic HAS. *Water Resources Management, 27*(5), 1249–1261. doi:10.1007/s11269-012-0236-5

Koza, J. R. (1992). *Genetic Programming: on the Programming of Computers by Means of Natural Selection*. MIT Press.

Krushinsky, D., & Goldengorin, B. (2012). An exact model for cell formation in group technology. *Computational Management Science, 9*(3), 323–338. doi:10.1007/s10287-012-0146-2

Kułakowski, P., Vales-Alonso, J., Egea-López, E., Ludwin, W., & García-Haro, J. (2010). Angle-of-arrival localization based on antenna arrays for wireless sensor networks. *Computers & Electrical Engineering, 36*(6), 1181–1186. doi:10.1016/j.compeleceng.2010.03.007

Kulluk, S., Ozbakir, L., & Baykasoglu, A. (2012). Training neural networks with harmony search algorithms for classification problems. *Engineering Applications of Artificial Intelligence, 25*(1), 11–19. doi:10.1016/j.engappai.2011.07.006

Kumar, V., Chhabra, J. K., & Kumar, D. (2014). Parameter adaptive harmony search algorithm for unimodal and multimodal optimization problems. *Journal of Computational Science, 5*(2), 144–155. doi:10.1016/j.jocs.2013.12.001

Kusiak, A. (1987). The generalized group technology concept. *International Journal of Production Research, 25*(4), 561–569. doi:10.1080/00207548708919861

Kusiak, A., & Chow, W. S. (1987). Efficient solving of the group technology problem. *Journal of Manufacturing Systems*, 6(2), 117–124. doi:10.1016/0278-6125(87)90035-5

Langman, R. E., & Cohn, M. (1986). The complete idiotype network is an absurd immune system. *Immunology Today*, 7(4), 100–101. doi:10.1016/0167-5699(86)90147-7 PMID:25289798

Layeb, A. (2013). A hybrid quantum inspired harmony search algorithm for 0–1 optimization problems. *Journal of Computational and Applied Mathematics*, 253, 14–25. doi:10.1016/j.cam.2013.04.004

Lee, C. H., & Chang, F. K. (2010). Fractional-order PID controller optimization via improved electromagnetism-like algorithm. *Expert Systems with Applications*, 37(12), 8871–8878. doi:10.1016/j.eswa.2010.06.009

Lee, C. H., & Lee, Y. C. (2012). Nonlinear systems design by a novel fuzzy neural system via hybridization of electromagnetism-like mechanism and particle swarm optimisation algorithms. *Information Sciences*, 186(1), 59–72. doi:10.1016/j.ins.2011.09.036

Lee, S., & Mun, S. (2014). Improving a model for the dynamic modulus of asphalt using the modified harmony search algorithm. *Expert Systems with Applications*, 41(8), 3856–3860. doi:10.1016/j.eswa.2013.12.021

Levenshtein, Vladimir, I. (1966). Binary codes capable of correcting deletions, insertions, and reversals. *Soviet Physics, Doklady*, 10(8), 707–710.

Li, J., & Duan, H. (2014). Novel biological visual attention mechanism via Gaussian harmony search. *International Journal for Light and Electron Optics*, 125(10), 2313–2319. doi:10.1016/j.ijleo.2013.10.075

Lindemann-von Trzebiatowski, G., & Münch, I. (n.d.). *The Role Concept for Agents in Multi Agent Systems*. Retrieved from http://www.informatik.uni-hamburg.de/TGI/forschung/projekte/sozionik/journal/3/masho-3.pdf

Li, Y., Li, X., & Gupta, J. N. D. (2015). Solving the multi-objective flowline manufacturing cell scheduling problem by hybrid harmony search. *Expert Systems with Applications*, 42(3), 1409–1417. doi:10.1016/j.eswa.2014.09.007

Lotze, M. T., & Thomson, A. W. (2010). *Natural Killer Cells. Basic Science and Clinical Application*. Elsevier.

Luo, Q., Wu, J., Sun, X., Yang, Y., & Wu, J. (2012). Optimal design of groundwater remediation systems using a multi-objective fast harmony search algorithm. *Hydrogeology Journal*, 20(8), 1497–1510. doi:10.1007/s10040-012-0900-0

Luo, Q., Wu, J., Yang, Y., Qian, J., & Wu, J. (2014). Optimal design of groundwater remediation system using a probabilistic multi-objective fast harmony search algorithm under uncertainty. *Journal of Hydrology (Amsterdam)*, 519, 3305–3315. doi:10.1016/j.jhydrol.2014.10.023

Compilation of References

Madic, M. (2012). Performance comparison of meta-heuristic algorithms for training artificial neural networks in modeling laser cutting. *Int. J. of Advanced Intelligence Paradigms, 2*(4), 316–335.

Mahapatra, G. S. (2009). *Reliability Optimization in Fuzzy and Intuitionistic Fuzzy Environment.* Bengal Engineering and Science University.

Mahdavi, M., & Abolhassani, H. (2009). Harmony K-means algorithm for document clustering. *Data Mining and Knowledge Discovery, 18*(3), 370–391. doi:10.1007/s10618-008-0123-0

Mahdavi, M., Fesanghary, M., & Damangir, E. (2007). An improved harmony search algorithm for solving optimization problems. *Applied Mathematics and Computation, 188*(2), 1567–1579. doi:10.1016/j.amc.2006.11.033

Maheri, M. R., & Narimani, M. M. (2014). An enhanced harmony search algorithm for optimum design of side sway steel frames. *Computers & Structures, 136*, 78–89. doi:10.1016/j.compstruc.2014.02.001

Manahiloh, K. N., Nejad, M. M., & Momeni, M. S. (in press). Optimization of design parameters and cost of geosynthetic-reinforced earth walls using harmony search algorithm. *Int. J. of Geosynth. and Ground Eng.*

Mandal, D., Bhattacharjee, A. K., & Ghoshal, S. P. (2009, December). A novel particle swarm optimization based optimal design of three-ring concentric circular antenna array. In *Advances in Computing, Control, & Telecommunication Technologies, 2009. ACT'09. International Conference on* (pp. 385-389). IEEE. doi:10.1109/ACT.2009.101

Mandal, D., Ghoshal, S. P., & Bhattacharjee, A. K. (2009). Determination of the optimal design of three-ring concentric circular antenna array using evolutionary optimization techniques. *International Journal of Recent Trends in Engineering, 2*(5), 110–115.

Manjarres, D., Del Ser, J., Gil-Lopez, S., Vecchio, M., Landa-Torres, I., Salcedo-Sanz, S., & Lopez-Valcarce, R. (2013). On the design of a novel two-objective harmony search approach for distance- and connectivity-based localization in wireless sensor networks. *Engineering Applications of Artificial Intelligence, 26*(2), 669–676. doi:10.1016/j.engappai.2012.06.002

Martins, I. C., Pinheiro, R. G., Protti, F., & Ochi, L. S. (2015). A hybrid iterated local search and variable neighborhood descent heuristic applied to the cell formation problem. *Expert Systems with Applications, 42*(22), 8947–8955. doi:10.1016/j.eswa.2015.07.050

Marufuzzaman, M., Ahsan, K. B., & Xing, K. (2009). Supplier selection and evaluation method using Analytical Hierarchy Process (AHP): A case study on an apparel manufacturing organisation. *International Journal of Value Chain Management, 3*(2), 224–240. doi:10.1504/IJVCM.2009.026958

Matsumoto, M., & Nishimura, T. (1998). Mersenne twister: A 623-dimensionally equidistributed uniform pseudo-random number generator. *ACM Transactions on Modeling and Computer Simulation, 8*(1), 3–30. doi:10.1145/272991.272995

Matzinger, P. (2002). The danger model: A renewed sense of self. *Science*, *296*(5566), 301–305. doi:10.1126/science.1071059 PMID:11951032

McEwan, Ch., & Hart, E. (2011). On clonal selection. *Theoretical Computer Science*, *412*(6), 502–516. doi:10.1016/j.tcs.2010.11.017

Merzougui, A., Hasseine, A., & Laiadi, D. (2012). Application of the harmony search algorithm to calculate the interaction parameters in liquid–liquid phase equilibrium modeling. *Fluid Phase Equilibria*, *324*, 94–101. doi:10.1016/j.fluid.2012.03.029

Metropolis, N., Rosenbluth, A. W., Rosenbluth, M. N., Teller, A. H., & Teller, E. (1953). Equations of State Calculations by Fast Computing Machines. *The Journal of Chemical Physics*, *21*(6), 1087–1092. doi:10.1063/1.1699114

Michell, J., & Laplace, P. S. (1998). Black Holes: A General Introduction. Lecture Notes in Physics, 514, 3 – 34.

Miguel, L. F. F., Miguel, L. F. F., Kaminski, J. Jr, & Riera, J. D. (2012). Damage detection under ambient vibration by harmony search algorithm. *Expert Systems with Applications*, *39*(10), 9704–9714. doi:10.1016/j.eswa.2012.02.147

Miltenburg, J., & Zhang, W. (1991). A comparative evaluation of nine well-known algorithms for solving the cell formation problem in group technology. *Journal of Operations Management*, *10*(1), 44–72. doi:10.1016/0272-6963(91)90035-V

Morsali, R., Jafari, T., Ghods, A., & Karimi, M. (2014). Solving unit commitment problem using a novel version of harmony search algorithm. Front. *Energy*, *8*(3), 297–304.

Mostard, J., Teunter, R., & De Koster, R. (2011). Forecasting demand for single-period products: A case study in the apparel industry. *European Journal of Operational Research*, *211*(1), 139–147. doi:10.1016/j.ejor.2010.11.001

Muhsen, D. H., Ghazali, A. B., Khatib, T., & Abed, I. A. (2015). Extraction of photovoltaic module models parameters using an improved hybrid differential evolution/electromagnetism-like algorithm. *Solar Energy*, *119*, 286–297. doi:10.1016/j.solener.2015.07.008

Mukherjee, A., & De, D. (2016). ScienceDirect Location management in mobile network. *Survey (London, England)*, *19*, 1–14.

Mukhopadhyay, A., Roy, A., Das, S., & Abraham, A. (2008). Population-variance and explorative power of harmony search: An analysis.*Second National Conference on Mathematical Techniques Emerging Paradigms for Electronics and IT Industries (MATEIT 2008)*. doi:10.1109/ICDIM.2008.4746793

Mun, S., & Cho, Y.-H. (2012). Modified harmony search optimization for constrained design problems. *Expert Systems with Applications*, *39*(1), 419–423. doi:10.1016/j.eswa.2011.07.031

Murren, P., & Khandelwal, K. (2014). Design-driven harmony search (DDHS) in steel frame optimization. *Engineering Structures*, *59*, 798–808. doi:10.1016/j.engstruct.2013.12.003

Compilation of References

Naderi, B., Tavakkoli-Moghaddam, R., & Khalili, M. (2010). Electromagnetism-like mechanism and simulated annealing algorithms for flowshop scheduling problems minimizing the total weighted tardiness and makespan. *Knowledge-Based Systems*, *23*(2), 77–85. doi:10.1016/j.knosys.2009.06.002

Nanda, J., Kothari, M. L., & Satsangi, P. S. (1983). Automatic generation control of an interconnected hydrothermal system in continuous and discrete modes considering generation rate constraints. *IEE Proc., 130*(1), 17-27. doi:10.1049/ip-d.1983.0004

Nanda, J., & Kaul, B. L. (1978). Automatic generation control of an interconnected power system. *Proc. IEE*, 125(5), 385-390. doi:10.1049/piee.1978.0094

Nanda, P., Patnaik, S., & Patnaik, S. (in press). Modeling of Multi Agent Coordination using Crocodile Predatory Strategy. *International Journal of Reasoning-Based Intelligent Systems*.

Nasaroui, O., Gonzalez, F., & Dasgupta, D. (2002). The Fuzzy Artificial Immune System: Motivations, Basic Concepts, and Application to Clustering and Web Profiling.*IEEE International Conference on Fuzzy systems*, 711-716. doi:10.1109/FUZZ.2002.1005080

Nekkaa, M., & Boughaci, D. (2016). Hybrid harmony search combined with stochastic local search for feature selection.*Neural Processing Letters*,*44*(1), 199–220. doi:10.1007/s11063-015-9450-5

Nelder, J. A., & Mead, R. (1965). A Simplex Method for Function Minimization. *J. Computing.*, *7*(4), 308–313. doi:10.1093/comjnl/7.4.308

Newman. (2008). Indirect utility function. New York: The New Palgrave Dictionary of Economics.

Niu, Q., Zhang, H., Wang, X., Li, K., & Irwin, G. W. (2014). A hybrid harmony search with arithmetic crossover operation for economic dispatch. *International Journal of Electrical Power & Energy Systems*, *62*, 237–257. doi:10.1016/j.ijepes.2014.04.031

Nocedal, J., & Wright, S. J. (1999). *Numerical Optimization, Springer Series in Operations Research and financial engineering*. Springer.

Noktehdan, A., Seyedhosseini, S., & Saidi-Mehrabad, M. (2016). A metaheuristic algorithm for the manufacturing cell formation problem based on grouping efficacy. *International Journal of Advanced Manufacturing Technology*, *82*(1), 25–37. doi:10.1007/s00170-015-7052-z

Odell, J., Parunak, V. D., & Fleischer, M. (2003). The Role of Roles. *Journal of Object Technology*, *2*(1), 39–51. doi:10.5381/jot.2003.2.1.c5

Ohlmann, J. W., & Thomas, B. W. (2007). A Compressed-Annealing Heuristic for the Traveling Salesman Problem with Time Windows. *INFORMS Journal on Computing*, *19*(1), 80–90. doi:10.1287/ijoc.1050.0145

Oliva-Lopez, E., & Purcheck, G. (1979). Load balancing for group technology planning and control. *International Journal of Machine Tool Design and Research*, *19*(4), 259–274. doi:10.1016/0020-7357(79)90015-5

Omar, M., Solimn, M., Abdel Ghany, A.M., & Bendary, F. (2013). Optimal tuning of PID controllers for hydrothermal load frequency control using ant colony optimization. International Journal on Electrical Engineering and Informatics, 5(3), 348-356.

Omran, M. G. H., & Mahdavi, M. (2008). Global-best harmony search. *Applied Mathematics and Computation, 198*(2), 643–656. doi:10.1016/j.amc.2007.09.004

Onol, C., & Ergül, O. (2014). Optimizations of patch antenna arrays using genetic algorithms supported by the multilevel fast multipole algorithm. *Radioengineering, 23*(4), 1005–1014.

Osman & Laporte. (1996). Metaheuristics: A bibliography. *Ann. Oper. Res., 63*(5), 511 – 623.

Padhan, Sahu, & Panda. (2014). Application of Firefly Algorithm for Load Frequency Control of Multi-area interconnected power system. *Electric Power Components and Systems, 42*(13), 1419-1430.

Pan, C. T., & Liaw, C. M. (1989). An adaptive controller for power system load-frequency control,'. *IEEE Transactions on Power Systems, 4*(1), 122–128. doi:10.1109/59.32469

Pandi, V. R., & Panigrahi, B. K. (2011). Dynamic economic load dispatch using hybrid swarm intelligence based harmony search algorithm. *Expert Systems with Applications, 38*(7), 8509–8514. doi:10.1016/j.eswa.2011.01.050

Papaioannou, G., & Wilson, J. M. (2010). The evolution of cell formation problem methodologies based on recent studies (1997–2008): Review and directions for future research. *European Journal of Operational Research, 206*(3), 509–521. doi:10.1016/j.ejor.2009.10.020

Papa, J. P., Scheirer, W., & Cox, D. D. (2016). Fine-tuning Deep Belief Networks using Harmony Search. *Applied Soft Computing, 46*, 875–885. doi:10.1016/j.asoc.2015.08.043

Paqaleh, M. A., Rashidinejad, M., & Kasmaei, M. P. (2010). An implementation of harmony search algorithm to unit commitment problem. *Electrical Engineering, 92*(6), 215–225. doi:10.1007/s00202-010-0177-z

Parija, S. R., Addanki, P., Sahu, P. K., & Singh, S. S. (2013). *Cost Reduction in Reporting Cell Planning Configuration Using Soft Computing Algorithm.* Academic Press.

Patnaik, S. (2007). Robot Cognition and Navigation: An Experiment with Mobile Robots. Springer Science & Business Media.

Paydar, M. M., & Saidi-Mehrabad, M. (2013). A hybrid genetic-variable neighborhood search algorithm for the cell formation problem based on grouping efficacy. *Computers & Operations Research, 40*(4), 980–990. doi:10.1016/j.cor.2012.10.016

Percus, J. K., Percus, O. E., & Perelson, A. S. (1993). Predicting the size of the T-cell receptor and antibody combining region from consideration of efficient self-nonself discrimination. *Proceedings of the National Academy of Sciences of the United States of America, 90*(5), 1691–1695. doi:10.1073/pnas.90.5.1691 PMID:7680474

Compilation of References

Pergol, M., Mazur, W., Zieniutycz, W., & Sorokosz, L. (2011). Mutual Coupling Between IFF/SSR Microstrip Antennas with Reduced Transversal Size-Experimental Study. *Radioengineering, 20*(1).

Piegat, A. (2001). *Fuzzy Modelling and Control*. Berlin: Physica-Verlag Heidelberg. doi:10.1007/978-3-7908-1824-6

Pires, R. G., Pereira, D. R., Pereira, L. A. M., Mansano, A. F., & Papa, J. P. (2016). Projections onto convex sets parameter estimation through harmony search and its application for image restoration. *Natural Computing, 15*(3), 493–502. doi:10.1007/s11047-015-9507-4

Popentiu-Vladicescu, F., & Albeanu, G. (2016). Nature-inspired approaches in software faults identification and debugging. *Procedia Computer Science*. doi:10.1016/j.procs.2016.07.315

Prajod & Mabel. (2014). Design of PI controller using MPRS method for Automatic Generation Control of hydro power system. *International Journal of Theoretical and Applied Research in Mechanical Engineering, 2*(1), 1–7.

Prins, C. (2004). A simple and effective evolutionary algorithm for the vehicle routing problem. *Computers & Operations Research, 31*(12), 1985–2002. doi:10.1016/S0305-0548(03)00158-8

Purcheck, G. F. (1975). A linear–programming method for the combinatorial grouping of an incomplete power set. *Journal of Cybernetics, 5*(4), 51–58.

Purnomo, H. D., & Wee, H.-M. (2014). Maximizing production rate and workload balancing in a two-sided assembly line using Harmony Search. *Computers & Industrial Engineering, 76*, 222–230. doi:10.1016/j.cie.2014.07.010

Rajaguru, V., Sathya, R., & Shanmugam, V. (2015). Load Frequency Control in an Interconnected Hydro–Hydro Power System with Superconducting Magnetic Energy Storage Units. *International Journal of Current Engineering and Technology, 5*(2), 1243–1248.

Ramanand Kashyap, S. S. (2013). Load Frequency Control Using Fuzzy PI Controller Generation of Interconnected Hydro Power System. *International Journal of Emerging Technology and Advanced Engineering, 3*(9), 655–659.

Ram, G., Mandal, D., Kar, R., & Ghoshal, S. P. (2013). Optimized hyper beamforming of linear antenna arrays using collective animal behaviour. *The Scientific World Journal*. PMID:23970843

Rashedi, E., Nezamabadi-Pour, H., & Saryazdi, S. (2009). GSA: A gravitational search algorithm. *Inform. Science., 179*(13), 2232–2248. doi:10.1016/j.ins.2009.03.004

Rastgou, A., & Moshtagh, J. (2014). Improved harmony search algorithm for transmission expansion planning with adequacy–security considerations in the deregulated power system. *International Journal of Electrical Power & Energy Systems, 60*, 153–164. doi:10.1016/j.ijepes.2014.02.036

Rayman, D., Burns, D. J., & Nelson, C. N. (2011). Apparel product quality: Its nature and measurement. *Journal of Global Academy of Marketing, 21*(1), 66–75. doi:10.1080/12297119 .2011.9711012

Razfar, M. R., Zinati, R. F., & Haghshenas, M. (2011). Optimum surface roughness prediction in face milling by using neural network and harmony search algorithm. *International Journal of Advanced Manufacturing Technology*, *52*(5-8), 487–495. doi:10.1007/s00170-010-2757-5

Rechenberg. (1965). *Cybernetic Solution Path of an Experimental Problem*. Ministry of Aviation, Royal Aircraft Establishment.

Reynolds, C. W. (1987). Flocks, herbs, and schools: A distributed behavioral model. *Comput. Graph.*, *21*(4), 25–34. doi:10.1145/37402.37406

Roshanaei, V., Balagh, A. K. G., Esfahani, M. M. S., & Vahdani, B. (2009). A mixed-integer linear programming model along with an electromagnetism-like algorithm for scheduling job shop production system with sequence-dependent set-up times. *International Journal of Advanced Manufacturing Technology*, *47*(5), 783–793.

Ruby Meenaand, S. (2014). Load Frequency Stabilization of four area hydro thermal system using Superconducting Magnetic Energy Storage System. *IACSIT International Journal of Engineering and Technology*, *6*(3), 1564–1572.

Rzevski, G., & Skobelev, P. (2014). Managing Complexity. WIT Press.

Sahu, Panda, & Padhan. (2015). A hybrid firefly algorithm and pattern search technique for automatic generation control of multi area power systems. *Electric Power and Energy Systems, 64*, 9-23.

Sahu, B. K., Pati, S., Mohanty, P. K., & Panda, S. (2015). Teaching-learning based optimization algorithm based fuzzy-PID controller for automatic generation control of multi-area power system. *Applied Soft Computing*, *27*, 240–249. doi:10.1016/j.asoc.2014.11.027

Saikia, L. C., Sinha, N., & Nanda, J. (2013). Maiden application of bacterial foraging based fuzzy IDD controller in AGC of a multi-area hydrothermal system. *Electric Power and Energy Systems*, *45*(1), 98–106. doi:10.1016/j.ijepes.2012.08.052

Sakthivel, V., Elias, E. (2015). Design of low complexity sharp MDFT filter banks with perfect reconstruction using hybrid harmony-gravitational search algorithm. *Engineering Science and Technology, an International Journal*, *18*(4), 648-657..

Salcedo-Sanz, S., Manjarrés, D., Pastor-Sánchez, Á., Del Ser, J., Portilla-Figueras, J. A., & Gil-López, S. (2013). One-way urban traffic reconfiguration using a multi-objective harmony search approach. *Expert Systems with Applications*, *40*(9), 3341–3350. doi:10.1016/j.eswa.2012.12.043

Samanta, S., Acharjee, S., Mukherjee, A., Das, D., & Dey, N. (2013). Ant Weight Lifting Algorithm for Image Segmentation. *2013 IEEE International Conference on Computational Intelligence and Computing Research*,1-5. doi:10.1109/ICCIC.2013.6724160

Samiee, M., Amjady, N., & Sharifzadeh, H. (2013). Security constrained unit commitment of power systems by a new combinatorial solution strategy composed of enhanced harmony search algorithm and numerical optimization. *International Journal of Electrical Power & Energy Systems*, *44*(1), 471–481. doi:10.1016/j.ijepes.2012.07.069

Compilation of References

Sankaran, S., & Rodin, E. Y. (1990). Multiple objective decision making approach to cell formation: A goal programming model. *Mathematical and Computer Modelling*, *13*(9), 71–81. doi:10.1016/0895-7177(90)90079-3

Schrank, H. E. (1983). Low sidelobe phased array antennas IEEE Antennas Propagat. *Soc. Newslett.*, *25*(2), 4–9.

Schrijver. (1998). Theory of Linear and Integer Programming. John Wiley & Sons.

Sébastien, T., Michel, H., & Jean-Marie, C. (2003). Mean-term textile sales forecasting using families and items classification. *Studies in Informatics and Control*, *12*(1), 41–52.

Segura, T. G., Yepes, V., Alcalá, J., & Pérez-López, E. (2015). Hybrid harmony search for sustainable design of post-tensioned concrete box-girder pedestrian bridges. *Engineering Structures*, *92*, 112–122. doi:10.1016/j.engstruct.2015.03.015

Sekozawa, T., Mitsuhashi, H., & Ozawa, Y. (2011). One-to-one recommendation system in apparel online shopping. *Electronics and Communications in Japan*, *94*(1), 51–60. doi:10.1002/ecj.10261

Selçuk, Y. M., & Erdoğan, N. (2005). A Role Model for Description of Agent Behavior and Coordination. *Proceedings of the 6th international conference on Engineering Societies in the Agents World (ESAW'05)*.

Selim, H. M., Askin, R. G., & Vakharia, A. J. (1998). Cell formation in group technology: Review, evaluation and directions for future research. *Computers & Industrial Engineering*, *34*(1), 3–20. doi:10.1016/S0360-8352(97)00147-2

Setiawan. (2014). Fuzzy Decision Support System for Coronary Artery Disease Diagnosis Based on Rough Set Theory. *International Journal of Rough Sets and Data Analysis*, *1*(1), 65-80.

Shabani, Vahidi, & Ebrahimpour. (2015). A robust PID controller based on Imperialist competitive algorithm for load frequency control of power systems. *ISA Transactions*, *52*, 88–95.

Shafer, S. M., & Rogers, D. F. (1991). A goal programming approach to the cell formation problem. *Journal of Operations Management*, *10*(1), 28–43. doi:10.1016/0272-6963(91)90034-U

Shivaie, M., Ameli, M. T., Sepasian, M. S., Weinsier, P. D., & Vahidinasab, V. (2015). A multistage framework for reliability-based distribution expansion planning considering distributed generations by a self-adaptive global-based harmony search algorithm. *Reliability Engineering & System Safety*, *139*, 68–81. doi:10.1016/j.ress.2015.03.001

Sidhu, B., & Singh, H. (2007). Location Management in Cellular Networks. *Proceedings of World Academy of Science, Engineering and Technology*, *21*, 314–319.

Singh, J. A. P., & Karnan, M. (2010). Intelligent Location Management Using Soft Computing Technique.*2010 Second International Conference on Communication Software and Networks*, 343–346. doi:10.1109/ICCSN.2010.60

Sinsuphan, N., Leeton, U., & Kulworawanichpong, T. (2013). Optimal power flow solution using improved harmony search method. *Applied Soft Computing*, *13*(5), 2364–2374. doi:10.1016/j.asoc.2013.01.024

Sirjani, R., & Bade, M. G. (2015). A global harmony search algorithm for finding optimal capacitor location and size in distribution networks. *J. Cent. South Univ*, *22*(5), 1748–1761. doi:10.1007/s11771-015-2693-5

Sivakumar, N., & Vivekanandan, K. (2012). Agent Oriented Software Testing – Role Oriented Approach, International. *Journal of Advanced Computer Science and Applications*, *3*(12), 156–163.

Sivasubramani, S., & Swarup, K. S. (2011). Multi-objective harmony search algorithm for optimal power flow problem. *International Journal of Electrical Power & Energy Systems*, *33*(3), 745–752. doi:10.1016/j.ijepes.2010.12.031

Soto, R., Kjellerstrand, H., Duran, O., Crawford, B., Monfroy, E., & Paredes, F. (2012). Cell formation in group technology using constraint programming and Boolean satisfiability. *Expert Systems with Applications*, *39*(13), 11423–11427. doi:10.1016/j.eswa.2012.04.020

Spits, H., Bernink, J., Peters, Ch., & Mjosberg, J. (2012). Role of human innate lymphoid cells in IMID. *Journal of Translational Medicine*, *10*(Suppl 3), I16. doi:10.1186/1479-5876-10-S3-I16

Steudel, H. J., & Ballakur, A. (1987). A dynamic programming based heuristic for machine grouping in manufacturing cell formation. *Computers & Industrial Engineering*, *12*(3), 215–222. doi:10.1016/0360-8352(87)90015-5

Steyskal, H., Shore, R. A., & Haupt, R. (1986). Methods for null control and their effects on the radiation pattern. *IEEE Transactions on Antennas and Propagation*, *34*(3), 404–409. doi:10.1109/TAP.1986.1143816

Storn, R., & Price, K. (1996). Minimizing the real functions of the ICEC'96 contest by Differential Evolution. *IEEE Conference on Evolutionary Computation*, 842 – 844. doi:10.1109/ICEC.1996.542711

Stutzman, W. L., & Thiele, G. A. (2012). *Antenna theory and design*. John Wiley & Sons.

Subrata, R., Zomaya, A. Y., & Member, S. (2003). A Comparison of Three Artificial Life Techniques for Reporting Cell Planning in Mobile Computing. *IEEE Transactions on Parallel and Distributed Systems*, *14*(2), 142–153. doi:10.1109/TPDS.2003.1178878

Sun, Z. L., Choi, T. M., Au, K. F., & Yu, Y. (2008). Sales forecasting using extreme learning machine with applications in fashion retailing. *Decision Support Systems*, *46*(1), 411–419. doi:10.1016/j.dss.2008.07.009

Suryadi, D., & Kandi, Y. (2012). A Viral Systems Algorithm for the Traveling Salesman Problem. *Proceedings of the 2012 International Conference on Industrial Engineering and Operations Management*, 1989–1994.

Compilation of References

Suzuki, Y., & Cortes, J. D. (2016). A Tabu Search with Gradual Evolution Process. *Computers & Industrial Engineering, 100*, 25–57. doi:10.1016/j.cie.2016.08.004

Sycara, K. P. (1998). Multiagent systems. *AI Magazine, 19*(2), 79.

Sztandera, L. M., Frank, C., & Vemulapali, B. (2004). Predicting women's apparel sales by soft computing. *Proceedings of the 7th International Conference on Artificial Intelligence and Soft Computing,* 1193–1198. doi:10.1007/978-3-540-24844-6_187

Taheri, J., & Zomaya, A. Y. (2008). A modified hopfield network for mobility management. *Wireless Communications and Mobile Computing, 8*, 355–367.

Taleizadeh, A. A., Niaki, S. T. A., & Seyedjavadi, S. M. H. (2012). Multi-product multi-chance-constraint stochastic inventory control problem with dynamic demand and partial back-ordering: A harmony search algorithm. *Journal of Manufacturing Systems, 31*(2), 204–213. doi:10.1016/j.jmsy.2011.05.006

Tarakanov, A. O., Skormin, V. A., & Sokolova, S. P. (2003). *Immunocomputing: Principles and Applications.* New York: Springer-Verlag. doi:10.1007/978-1-4757-3807-0

Taylor, M. E. (2011). *Two decades of multi-agent teamwork research: past, present, and future.* Collaborative Agents-Research and Development. Springer Berlin Heidelberg.

Thanh, L. T., Ferland, J. A., Elbenani, B., & Thuc, N. D. et al.. (2016). A computational study of hybrid approaches of metaheuristic algorithms for the cell formation problem. *The Journal of the Operational Research Society, 67*(1), 20–36. doi:10.1057/jors.2015.46

Timmis, J., Hone, A., Stibor, T., & Clark, E. (2008). Theoretical advances in artificial immune systems. *Theoretical Computer Science, 403*(1), 11–32. doi:10.1016/j.tcs.2008.02.011

Timmis, J., & Neal, M. (2001). A resource limited artificial immune system for data analysis. *Knowledge-Based Systems, 14*(3-4), 121–130. doi:10.1016/S0950-7051(01)00088-0

Timmis, J., Neal, M., & Hunt, J. (2000). An Artificial Immune System for Data Analysis. *Bio Systems, 55*(1), 143–150. doi:10.1016/S0303-2647(99)00092-1 PMID:10745118

Toth, P., & Vigo, D. (2002). *The Vehicle Routing Problem.* SIAM. doi:10.1137/1.9780898718515

Toth, P., & Vigo, D. (2003). The Granular Tabu Search and Its Application to the Vehicle-Routing Problem. *INFORMS Journal on Computing, 15*(4), 333–346. doi:10.1287/ijoc.15.4.333.24890

Tripathy, S. C., Hope, G. S., & Malik, O. P. (1982). Optimization of load-frequency control parameters for power systems with reheat steam turbines and governor dead band nonlinearity. *IEE Proc., 129*(1), 10-16.

Tuo, S., Zhang, J., Yong, L., Yuan, X., Liu, B., Xu, X., & Deng, F. A. (2015). A harmony search algorithm for high-dimensional multimodal optimization problems. *Digital Signal Processing, 46*, 151–163. doi:10.1016/j.dsp.2015.08.008

Twycross, J., & Aickelin, U. (2007). Biological Inspiration for Artificial Immune Systems. *LNCS, 4628*, 300-311. doi:10.2139/ssrn.2831297

Tyagi, S., & Bharadwaj, K. K. (2014). A Particle Swarm Optimization Approach to Fuzzy Case-based Reasoning in the Framework of Collaborative Filtering. *International Journal of Rough Sets and Data Analysis, 1*(1), 48–64. doi:10.4018/ijrsda.2014010104

Valian, E., Tavakoli, S., & Mohanna, S. (2014). An intelligent global harmony search approach to continuous optimization problems. *Applied Mathematics and Computation, 232*, 670–684. doi:10.1016/j.amc.2014.01.086

Vega-rodr, M. A., & Juan, M. S. (2014). *Non-dominated Sorting and a Novel Formulation in the Reporting Cells Planning*. Academic Press.

Waghodekar, P., & Sahu, S. (1984). Machine-component cell formation in group technology: Mace. *International Journal of Production Research, 22*(6), 937–948. doi:10.1080/00207548408942513

Wang, C. M., & Huang, Y. F. (2010). Self-adaptive harmony search algorithm for optimization. *Expert Systems with Applications, 37*(4), 2826–2837. doi:10.1016/j.eswa.2009.09.008

Wang, G.-G., Gandomi, A. H., Zhao, X., & Chu, H. C. E. (2015a). Hybridizing harmony search algorithm with cuckoo search for global numerical optimization. *Soft Computing, 20*(1), 273–285. doi:10.1007/s00500-014-1502-7

Wang, L., & Li, L. P. (2013). An effective differential harmony search algorithm for the solving non-convex economic load dispatch problems. *International Journal of Electrical Power & Energy Systems, 44*(1), 832–843. doi:10.1016/j.ijepes.2012.08.021

Wang, Y., Liu, Y., Feng, L., & Zhu, X. (2015b). Novel feature selection method based on harmony search for email classification. *Knowledge-Based Systems, 73*, 311–323. doi:10.1016/j.knosys.2014.10.013

Watkins, A., Timmis, J., & Boggess, L. (2004). *Artificial Immune Recognition System (AIRS): An Immune-Inspired Supervised Learning Algorithm*. Kluwer. doi:10.1023/B:GENP.0000030197.83685.94

Weiss, G. (Ed.). (2013). *Multiagent Systems*. MIT Press.

Wheeler, J. A. (2000). *Exploring Black Holes: Introduction to General Relativity*. Addison Wesley.

Wilson, E. O. (1975). *Sociobiology: The new synthesis*. Belknap Press.

Xiao, Y., Zhao, Q., Kaku, I., & Xu, Y. (2012). Development of a fuel consumption optimization model for the capacitated vehicle routing problem. *Computers & Operations Research, 39*(7), 1419–1431. doi:10.1016/j.cor.2011.08.013

Xu, H., Zhang, X., & Patel, R. J. (2007). Developing Role-Based Open Multi-Agent Software Systems. *International Journal of Computational Intelligence Theory and Practice, 2*(1), 39–56.

Compilation of References

Yalcinalp, L. U. (1991). *Meta-programming for knowledge based systems in PROLOG* (PhD Thesis). Case Western Reserve University.

Yang & Deb. (2010). Engineering optimisation by Cuckoo search. *Int. J. Math. Modell. Numerical Optimization, 1*, 330 – 343.

Yang, S., Beng Gan, Y., & Qing, A. (2003). Moving phase center antenna arrays with optimized static excitations. *Microwave and Optical Technology Letters, 38*(1), 83–85. doi:10.1002/mop.10977

Yang, S., Gan, Y. B., & Qing, A. (2002). Sideband suppression in time-modulated linear arrays by the differential evolution algorithm. *IEEE Antennas and Wireless Propagation Letters, 1*(1), 173–175. doi:10.1109/LAWP.2002.807789

Yang, S., Gan, Y. B., Qing, A., & Tan, P. K. (2005). Design of a uniform amplitude time modulated linear array with optimized time sequences. *IEEE Transactions on Antennas and Propagation, 53*(7), 2337–2339. doi:10.1109/TAP.2005.850765

Yang, S., Gan, Y. B., & Tan, P. K. (2003). A new technique for power-pattern synthesis in time-modulated linear arrays. *IEEE Antennas and Wireless Propagation Letters, 2*(1), 285–287. doi:10.1109/LAWP.2003.821556

Yang, S., Gan, Y. B., & Tan, P. K. (2004). Comparative study of low sidelobe time modulated linear arrays with different time schemes. *Journal of Electromagnetic Waves and Applications, 18*(11), 1443–1458. doi:10.1163/1569393042954910

Yang, S., Gan, Y. B., & Tan, P. K. (2005). Linear antenna arrays with bidirectional phase center motion. *IEEE Transactions on Antennas and Propagation, 53*(5), 1829–1835. doi:10.1109/TAP.2005.846754

Yang, X. S. (2008). *Nature-Inspired Metaheuristic Algorithms*. Luniver Press.

Yan, H. S., Wan, X. Q., & Xiong, F. L. (2014). A hybrid electromagnetism-like algorithm for two-stage assembly flow shop scheduling problem. *International Journal of Production Research, 52*(19), 5626–5639. doi:10.1080/00207543.2014.894257

Yesil, E. (2014). Interval type-2 fuzzy PID load frequency controller using big bang-big crunch optimization. *Applied Soft Computing, 15*, 100–112. doi:10.1016/j.asoc.2013.10.031

Yurtkuran, A., & Emel, E. (2010). A new hybrid electromagnetism-like algorithm for capacitated vehicle routing problems. *Expert Systems with Applications, 37*(4), 3427–3433. doi:10.1016/j.eswa.2009.10.005

Zadeh, L. A. (1965). Fuzzy sets. *Information and Control, 8*(3), 338–353. doi:10.1016/S0019-9958(65)90241-X

Zeb, A., Khan, M., Khan, N., Tariq, A., Ali, L., Azam, F., & Jaffery, S. H. I. (2016). Hybridization of simulated annealing with genetic algorithm for cell formation problem. *International Journal of Advanced Manufacturing Technology, 86*(5), 1–12.

Zeng, Y., Zhang, Z., Kusiak, A., Tang, F., & Wei, X. (2016). Optimizing wastewater pumping system with data-driven models and a greedy electromagnetism-like algorithm. *Stochastic Environmental Research and Risk Assessment*, *30*(4), 1263–127. doi:10.1007/s00477-015-1115-4

Zheng, L., Diao, R., & Shen, Q. (2015a). Self-adjusting harmony search-based feature selection. *Soft Computing*, *19*(6), 1567–1579. doi:10.1007/s00500-014-1307-8

Zheng, Y.-J., Zhang, M.-X., & Zhang, B. (2015b). Biogeographic harmony search for emergency air transportation. *Soft Computing*, *20*(3), 967–977. doi:10.1007/s00500-014-1556-6

Zhu, H. ,., & Zhou, M. C. (2008). Role-Based Multi-Agent Systems. In *Personalized Information Retrieval and Access: Concepts, Methods, and Practices* (pp. 254–286). IGI Global. doi:10.4018/978-1-59904-510-8.ch012

Zimmermann, K. A. (2014). *Immune System: Diseases, Disorders & Function*. Retrieved from http://www.livescience.com/26579-immune-system.html

Zinati, R. F., & Razfar, M. R. (2012). Constrained optimum surface roughness prediction in turning of X20Cr13 by coupling novel modified harmony search-based neural network and modified harmony search algorithm. *International Journal of Advanced Manufacturing Technology*, *58*(1-4), 93–107. doi:10.1007/s00170-011-3393-4

About the Contributors

Srikanta Patnaik is currently working as a Professor in the Department of Computer Science and Engineering, Faculty of Engineering and Technology, SOA University, Bhubaneswar, India. He is an author of two text books and edited 17 books and few invited book chapters, published by leading international publisher like Springer-Verlag, Kluwer Academic, etc. He is the Editor-in-Chief of International Journal of Information and Communication Technology and International Journal of Computational Vision and Robotics published from the Inderscience Publishing House, England and also Editor-in-Chief of Book Series on Modelling and Optimisation in Science and Technology published from Springer, Germany. He is also Editor-in-Chief of the book series of Advances in Computer and Electrical Engineering (ACEE) and Advances in Medical Technologies and Clinical Practice (AMTCP) published by IGI-Global, USA and Series Editor of book Series in Automation, Control and Robotics published by River Publishing House.

* * *

Viacheslav Abrosimov received his MS from the USSR Military Academy, PhD and Doctors of Technical Science degree from the Research Institute of USSR Ministry of Defense in 1974, 1984 and 1994, respectively, all in Cybernetics. He is currently a Professor in Aerospace Department of Moscow Aviation Institute (National Research University) and Deputy Chief Designer of the "Smart Solutions" Company, Russia. His research field include artificial intellect, expert and neural systems, motion of aircrafts and vehicles, multi-agent technologies, and network-centric systems.

G. Albeanu received his B.S. in computer science (1984) and his Ph.D. in Mathematics (1996) from University of Bucharest, Romania with a thesis on nonlinear models (computational statistics approaches). From 1984 to 1989 he worked as software developer for ICAS and CCSIT-ITC in Bucharest (data analysis, computer aided design, information systems, real time operating systems, computer graphics).

Starting with 1991, till 2002 he has been assistant, lecturer, and associate professor of computer science at Bucharest University. He was appointed professor of computer science at University of Oradea in 2002. During the interval 2004 - 2007 he was the head (Chairholder) of the UNESCO IT Department at University of Oradea. Since 2007, he is professor of computer science at Spiru Haret University in Bucharest. His current research interests include different aspects of scientific computing, modelling and simulation, systems reliability, virtual reality techniques, soft computing and E-Learning. Grigore Albeanu has authored or co-authored more than 80 papers and 10 educational textbooks in applied mathematics and computer science. He is member of different scientific boards in Romania and abroad, being active as referee, reviewer, chairman, and invited professor.

Amira S. Ashour is currently an Associate Professor in the Electronics and Electrical Communications Engineering, Faculty of Engineering., Tanta University, Egypt. Amira Ashour was the Vice Chair of Computers Engineering Department, Computers and Information Technology College, Taif University, KSA or one year. She was the vice chair of Computer Science department, CIT college, Taif University, KSA, for 5 years. She is a Lecturer of Electronics and Electrical Communications Engineering, Faculty of Engg., Tanta University, Egypt. She received her PhD in Smart Antenna (2005) in the Electronics and Electrical Communications Engineering, Tanta University, Egypt. She had her Masters in Enhancement of Electromagnetic Non-Destructive Evaluation Performance using Advanced Signal Processing Techniques in Faculty of Engineering, Egypt, 2000. Her research interests include: image processing, medical imaging, smart antenna and adaptive antenna arrays.

Alireza Askarzadeh received the B.S. degree in electrical engineering from Shahid Bahounar University, Kerman, Iran, in 2007 and the M.S. and Ph.d. degrees in electrical engineering from Shahid Beheshti University, Tehran, Iran, in 2009 and 2012, respectively. He is currently with the Department of Energy Management and Optimization, Institute of Science and High Technology and Environmental Sciences, Graduate University of Advanced Technology, Kerman, Iran. His research interests are renewable energies, power system optimization and swarm intelligent computation.

R. Balamurugan has completed his Ph.D. in Information and Communication Engineering from Anna University Chennai and currently he is working as an Assistant Professor in Department of Computer Science and Engineering in Bannari Amman Institute of Technology, Sathyamangalam. He has published more than 13 papers in various international journals and conferences. His areas of interest include data mining and meta Heuristic optimization techniques.

Valentina E. Balas is currently Full Professor in the Department of Automatics and Applied Software at the Faculty of Engineering, "Aurel Vlaicu" University of Arad, Romania. She holds a Ph.D. in Applied Electronics and Telecommunications from Polytechnic University of Timisoara. Dr. Balas is author of more than 200 research papers in refereed journals and International Conferences. Her research interests are in Intelligent Systems, Fuzzy Control, Soft Computing, Smart Sensors, Information Fusion, Modeling and Simulation. She is the Editor-in Chief to International Journal of Advanced Intelligence Paradigms (IJAIP) and to International Journal of Computational Systems Engineering (IJCSysE), member in Editorial Board member of several national and international journals and is evaluator expert for national and international projects. She served as General Chair of the International Workshop Soft Computing and Applications in seven editions 2005-2016 held in Romania and Hungary. Dr. Balas participated in many international conferences as Organizer, Session Chair and member in International Program Committee. Now she is working in a national project with EU funding support: BioCell-NanoART = Novel Bio-inspired Cellular Nano-Architectures - For Digital Integrated Circuits, 2M Euro from National Authority for Scientific Research and Innovation. She is a member of EUSFLAT, ACM and a Senior Member IEEE, member in TC – Fuzzy Systems (IEEE CIS), member in TC - Emergent Technologies (IEEE CIS), member in TC – Soft Computing (IEEE SMCS). Dr. Balas was Vice-president (Awards) of IFSA International Fuzzy Systems Association Council (2013-2015) and is a Joint Secretary of the Governing Council of Forum for Interdisciplinary Mathematics (FIM), - A Multidisciplinary Academic Body, India.

Anand Baskaran received the B.E degree Electrical Engineering in 2001 from Government College of Engineering, Tirunelveli, Tamil Nadu, India, and the M.E degree in Power Systems Engineering in 2002 from Annamalai University, India and the Ph.D. degree in electrical Engineering in 2011 from Anna University Chennai, Chennai, India. Presently, he is with the Department of Electrical and Electronics Engineering, Hindusthan College of Engineering and Technology, Coimbatore, India. His research interest includes the development of hybrid intelligent system algorithms and application to the power system control problems.

David Cortes is a PhD Candidate in the Supply Chain and Information Systems Department at Iowa State Univerity. He is passionate about Supply Chain Management. In addition to his corporate experience attained in multiple Fortune 500 firms, he is also a published author in journals such as Transportation Research Part E and Computers and Industrial Engineering. David's research interests reside with issues of Supply Chain Design primarily focusing on Logistics (Transportation and Vehicle Routing). His teaching interests revolve around: Logistics and Operations Management.

Broderick Crawford received the Ph.D. degree from Universidad Técnica Federico Santa María, Chile, in 2011. He is currently profesor of computer science at the Pontificia Universidad Católica de Valparaíso, Chile. He has published about 200 scientific papers in different peer-reviewed international conferences and journals. His current research interest involves combinatorial optimization, constraint programming, and metaheuristics.

Nilanjan Dey, PhD., is an Asst. Professor in the Department of Information Technology in Techno India College of Technology, Rajarhat, Kolkata, India. He holds an honorary position of Visiting Scientist at Global Biomedical Technologies Inc., CA, USA and Research Scientist of Laboratory of Applied Mathematical Modeling in Human Physiology, Territorial Organization Of- Sgientifig And Engineering Unions, BULGARIA, Associate Researcher of Laboratoire RIADI, University of Manouba, TUNISIA. He is the Editor-in-Chief of International Journal of Ambient Computing and Intelligence (IGI Global), US, International Journal of Rough Sets and Data Analysis (IGI Global), US, Series Editor of Advances in Geospatial Technologies (AGT) Book Series, (IGI Global), US, Executive Editor of International Journal of Image Mining (IJIM), Inderscience, Regional Editor-Asia of International Journal of Intelligent Engineering Informatics (IJIEI), Inderscience and Associated Editor of International Journal of Service Science, Management, Engineering, and Technology, IGI Global. His research interests include: Medical Imaging, Soft computing, Data mining, Machine learning, Rough set, Mathematical Modeling and Computer Simulation, Modeling of Biomedical Systems, Robotics and Systems, Information Hiding, Security, Computer Aided Diagnosis, Atherosclerosis. He has 8 books and 160 international conferences and journal papers. He is a life member of IE, UACEE, ISOC, etc.

Juan A. Gomez-Pulido received the PhD degree in physics, electronics specialty, from the Complutense University, Madrid, Spain, in 1993. He is currently a professor in the Department of Computers and Communications Technologies, University of Extremadura. He has authored or co-authored 60 ISI journals, and almost 100 book chapters, and 300 peer-reviewed conference proceedings. He has participated in 19 funded research projects, leading some of them. His research lines fall within hot topics on reconfigurable and embedded computing based on FPGAs, multiobjective optimization and soft computing, wireless sensor networks and big-data analytics.

K. Jagatheesan received his B.E degree in electrical engineering in 2009 from Hindusthan College of Engineering and Technology, Coimbatore, Tamil Nadu, India and M.E. degree in Applied Electronics in 2012 from Paavai College of Engineering, Namakkal, Tamil Nadu, INDIA. He is currently working towards the Ph.D. degree with the faculty of Information & Communication Engineering, Anna University Chennai, Chennai, India. His area of interest includes Advanced Control System, Electrical Machines and Power system modeling and control and he published more than 35 papers in National/International journals and conferences. He is an Associate Member of UACEE, Member of SCIEI, IACSIT, IAENG, ISRD and Graduate Student Member of IEEE.

Premalatha Kandhasamy is currently working as a Professor in the Department of Computer Science and Engineering at Bannari Amman Institute of Technology, Erode, Tamil Nadu, India. She completed her Ph. D. in Computer Science and Engineering (CSE) at Anna University, Chennai, India. She did her Master of Engineering in CSE and Bachelor of Engineering in CSE at Bharathiar University, Coimbatore, Tamil Nadu, India. She has 20 years of teaching experience in academic field. She published 60 papers in national and international journals and presented more than 20 papers in international and national conferences. She completed three funded projects sponsored by Government of India. She organized conferences/workshops/seminars sponsored by DRDO, DBT, CSIR and ICMR. Her research interests include data mining, image processing, information retrieval and soft computing.

Jose M. Lanza-Gutierrez received the Ph.D. degree in computer science from the University of Extremadura, Caceres, Spain, in 2015. He is currently a postdoc researcher at Centre of Industrial Electronics, Universidad Politecnica de Madrid, Madrid, Spain. He has authored or co-authored more than 30 publications, including ISI journals, book chapters, and peer-reviewed conference proceedings. His current research interests fall on machine learning, big data, metaheuristics, and parallel and distributed computing.

Pragyan Nanda is currently pursuing her PhD in the Department of Computer Science and Engineering, Faculty of Engineering Technology Siksha 'O' Anusandhan University, Bhubaneswar, India. She received her Master degree from N.I.T, Rourkela. Her research interests include nature-inspired computing, business optimization, neral networks etc.

Nhu Gia Nguyen received the MSc and Ph.D. degrees in computer science from Dannang University and Ha Noi University of Science, Vietnam, respectively. Currently, Dr. Nguyen serves as vice dean of the Graduate School at Duy Tan University. His experience includes over 16 years of teaching, and he has more than 30 publications. His research interests include algorithm theory, network optimization, and wireless security. He is an associate editor of IJSES.

Smita Parija is continuing her ph.d at NIT,Rourkela.She received her Master degree from N.I.T Rourkela. Her specialization is in Communication System. Several publications in International journals and reputed international conference. She has supervised more than five PG Thesis and handling B tech projects also. Her research interests are wireless communication, neural network and Fuzzy logic.

Sritam Patnaik is currently pursuing his bachelor's degree in Computer Engineering at the National University of Singapore (NUS). He has also spent a year in Silicon Valley interning as a Software Engineer and studying technopreneurship at the NUS Overseas College - Silicon Valley.

Gopi Ram passed B. E. Degree in "Electronics and Telecommunication Engineering", from Government Engineering College, Jagdalpur, Chhattisgarh, India in the year 2007. He received the M. Tech degree in "Telecommunication Engineering" from National Institute of Technology, Durgapur, West Bengal, India in the year 2011. He joined as a full time institute research scholar in the year of 2012 at National Institute of Technology, Durgapur, West Bengal, India. His research interest includes Analysis and synthesis of antenna Array synthesis via Evolutionary Computing Techniques, Antenna Array optimization of various radiation characteristics. He received the scholarship from the Ministry of Human Resource and Development (MHRD), Government of India for the period 2009-2011 (M. Tech) and 2012-2016 (Ph.D). Currently is working as Senior Assistant Professor in the department of ECE at Madanpalle Institue of Technology & Science (MITS) (UGC Autonomous). His research interests are antenna array pattern optimization, Applications of soft computing techniques in electromagnetic. He has published more than 40 research papers in International Journals and Conferences.

Kannimuthu S is currently working as Associate Professor in Karpagam College of Engineering, Coimbatore, Tamil Nadu, India. He is also an In-Charge for the Center of Excellence in Algorithms. He did PhD in Computer Science and Engineering at Anna University, Chennai. He did his M.E (CSE) and B.Tech (IT) at Anna University, Chennai. He has more than 10 years of teaching and industrial experience. He is the recognized supervisor of Anna University, Chennai. He is guiding 6 PhD Research Scholars. He has published 19 research articles in various International Journals. He has presented a number of papers in various National and International conferences. He has visited more than 40 Engineering colleges and delivered more than 50 Guest Lectures on various topics. He is the reviewer for 4 Reputed Journals and 3 Books. He has successfully completed the consultancy project through Industry-Institute Interaction for ZF Wind Power Antwerpen Ltd., Belgium. He has received fund two times from DRDO to conduct two workshops.

He has guided a number of research-oriented as well as application oriented projects organized by well known companies like IBM. His area of research interest includes data mining, optimization and distributed computing.

Sudhansu Sekhar Singh is working as Professor in School of Electronics Engineering, KIIT University, Bhubaneswar, Odisha. He has 21 years of working experience out of which more than 14 years in teaching in reputed engineering colleges and universities. He has done his Ph.D from Jadavpur University, Kolkata, and M.E Electronics system and communication from REC, Rourkela. More than fifty publications in International journals and reputed international conference proceedings are to his credit. He has supervised more than twenty PG Thesis and examined several doctoral dissertations. His broad research area is in wireless and mobile communication, Specifically multicarrier CDMA, MIMO- OFDM and Wireless Sensor Networks.

Ricardo Soto was born in Viña del Mar, Chile, in 1979. He received the PhD degree in Computer Science from the University of Nantes, France, in 2009 under the supervision of Pr. Laurent Granvilliers. He is currently Associate Professor of Computer Science at the Pontifical Catholic University of Valparaíso, Chile. His interest research interests include Constraint Programming, Metaheuristics, Global Optimization, and Autonomous Search. In this context, he has published about 180 scientific papers in different international conferences and journals, some of them top ranked in Computer Science, Operational Research, Artificial Intelligence and Programming Languages.

Yoshinori Suzuki is Dean's Professor of Supply Chain Management and Associate Department Chair at the College of Business, Iowa State University. He holds a Bachelor of Science degree in Business and Economics from Sophia University (Tokyo Japan), a Master of Business Administration degree in Marketing from New York University Stern School of Business, and a Doctor of Philosophy degree in Business Logistics from The Pennsylvania State University Smeal College of Business. He has participated in many publicly and privately funded research projects, and has published over 40 research papers. He is currently serving as the co-editor of Transportation Journal, and associate editor of Decision Sciences and Journal of Business Logistics.

Swati Swayamsiddha is working as Assistant Professor in School of Electronics Engineering, KIIT University, Bhubaneswar since 2009 and doing her research at IIT, Kharagpur. She has supervised many PG and UG thesis. Her research interests spans the area of mobile communications, adaptive signal processing, cognitive radio networks, nonlinear optimization, Nature-inspired meta-heuristics, soft and evolutionary computing. She is a member of ISC and IET.

Florin Popenţiu Vlădicescu graduated in Electronics and Telecommunications from University POLITEHNICA of Bucharest in 1974 and holds a PhD in Reliability in 1981. He has been appointed Director of the "UNESCO Chair" in Information Technologies Department at University of Oradea. Professor Florin Popenţiu Vlădicescu has published over 100 papers in international journals and conference proceedings. Also he author of one book co-author of 4 books. He has worked for many years on problems associated with software reliability and has been Co-Director of two NATO Research Projects. Also he is on the advisory board of several international journals and currently Associated Editor to IJICT – Inderscience Publishers. He is an independent expert for the Seventh Framework Programme - H2020 for Net Services – Software and Services, Cloud. Professor Popenţiu Vlădicescu is currently Visiting Professor at "ParisTech". He also lectures at the Technical University of Denmark. He was elected Fellow of the Academy of Romanian Scientists in 2008.

Index

A

agent 192-193, 198-202, 204, 206, 208-209, 211-216, 218-219, 222-224
Ant Colony Optimization 26, 61, 153-154, 158, 167-169, 187
antenna arrays 16, 30, 115-116, 122, 129, 131-132
apparel industry 190-193, 195-197, 204
Approximate solving-technique 60-61
Artificial Bee Colony Optimization 62
Artificial Immune Systems (AIS) 92, 105
Automatic generation control 153, 166-170

B

binarization 37, 39, 50

C

cell formation 37, 41, 55-60
choice 103, 109, 117, 195, 206, 213
clonal selection 92-93, 96, 100, 107, 111, 113
collective animal behavior (CAB) 115, 129
continuous optimization 36, 38, 40, 55, 60
control object 206-207, 209, 212
Cuckoo search 25, 36, 62, 66, 90, 166-167

D

demand forecasting 190, 192-194, 196-203
directivity 126-129
discrete optimization 60, 174
discrete problem 37, 40, 60

E

engineering optimization problems 1-2, 15, 25, 66
evolution 14, 28, 58-59, 61, 64-65, 69-71, 84, 88, 90, 95, 97, 99, 132-136, 141-142, 148-150, 179, 187-188
Exact Solving-Technique 60

F

function 2-7, 9, 12-14, 16-24, 41, 43, 50, 63, 65, 75, 83, 85, 87-90, 95, 99, 102-105, 107, 110-111, 114, 117-118, 121, 142, 145, 153, 156-160, 162, 164-165, 176, 179, 187, 193, 206, 211-217, 219-220, 222-223
fuzzy numbers 103-104, 206, 211, 213, 215, 217-218, 222

G

global optimization 1, 29, 55, 89, 174
global optimum 2, 62-64, 79
group 17, 37-38, 41, 50-55, 57-60, 111, 149, 191-192, 194, 197-198, 206-211, 214, 217-218, 222-223
group technology 37-38, 55, 57-60

H

heuristic 15, 17, 19, 26, 39-40, 45, 55-59, 61, 63, 111, 149-150, 159
hydro-hydro power system 156-157, 160, 165

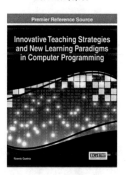

Stay Current on the Latest Emerging Research Developments

Become an IGI Global Reviewer for Authored Book Projects

Premier Reference Source
Solutions for High-Touch Communications in a High-Tech World

Premier Reference Source
Advanced Research on Biologically Inspired Cognitive Architectures

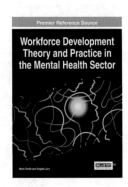
Premier Reference Source
Workforce Development Theory and Practice in the Mental Health Sector

Premier Reference Source
Resource Management and Efficiency in Cloud Computing Environments

The overall success of an authored book project is dependent on quality and timely reviews.

In this competitive age of scholarly publishing, constructive and timely feedback significantly decreases the turnaround time of manuscripts from submission to acceptance, allowing the publication and discovery of progressive research at a much more expeditious rate. Several IGI Global authored book projects are currently seeking highly qualified experts in the field to fill vacancies on their respective editorial review boards:

Applications may be sent to:
development@igi-global.com

Applicants must have a doctorate (or an equivalent degree) as well as publishing and reviewing experience. Reviewers are asked to write reviews in a timely, collegial, and constructive manner. All reviewers will begin their role on an ad-hoc basis for a period of one year, and upon successful completion of this term can be considered for full editorial review board status, with the potential for a subsequent promotion to Associate Editor.

If you have a colleague that may be interested in this opportunity, we encourage you to share this information with them.

Become an IRMA Member

Members of the **Information Resources Management Association (IRMA)** understand the importance of community within their field of study. The Information Resources Management Association is an ideal venue through which professionals, students, and academicians can convene and share the latest industry innovations and scholarly research that is changing the field of information science and technology. Become a member today and enjoy the benefits of membership as well as the opportunity to collaborate and network with fellow experts in the field.

IRMA Membership Benefits:

- **One FREE Journal Subscription**

- **30% Off Additional Journal Subscriptions**

- **20% Off Book Purchases**

- Updates on the latest events and research on Information Resources Management through the IRMA-L listserv.

- Updates on new open access and downloadable content added to Research IRM.

- A copy of the Information Technology Management Newsletter twice a year.

- A certificate of membership.

IRMA Membership $195

Scan code or visit **irma-international.org** and begin by selecting your free journal subscription.

Membership is good for one full year.

Encyclopedia of Information Science and Technology, Third Edition (10 Vols.)

Mehdi Khosrow-Pour, D.B.A. (Information Resources Management Association, USA)
ISBN: 978-1-4666-5888-2; **EISBN:** 978-1-4666-5889-9; © 2015; 10,384 pages.

The **Encyclopedia of Information Science and Technology, Third Edition** is a 10-volume compilation of authoritative, previously unpublished research-based articles contributed by thousands of researchers and experts from all over the world. This discipline-defining encyclopedia will serve research needs in numerous fields that are affected by the rapid pace and substantial impact of technological change. With an emphasis on modern issues and the presentation of potential opportunities, prospective solutions, and future directions in the field, it is a relevant and essential addition to any academic library's reference collection.

Take An Extra

30% Off[1]

[1] 30% discount offer cannot be combined with any other discount and is only valid on purchases made directly through IGI Global's Online Bookstore (www.igi-global.com/books), not intended for use by distributors or wholesalers. Offer expires December 31, 2016.

Free Lifetime E-Access with Print Purchase

Take 30% Off Retail Price:

Hardcover with Free E-Access:[2] **$2,765**
List Price: $3,950

E-Access with Free Hardcover:[2] **$2,765**
List Price: $3,950

E-Subscription Price:

One (1) Year E-Subscription: $1,288
List Price: $1,840

Two (2) Year E-Subscription: $2,177
List Price: $3,110

Recommend this Title to Your Institution's Library: www.igi-global.com/books

[2] IGI Global now offers the exclusive opportunity to receive free lifetime e-access with the purchase of the publication in print, or purchase any e-access publication and receive a free print copy of the publication. You choose the format that best suits your needs. This offer is only valid on purchases made directly through IGI Global's Online Bookstore and not intended for use by book distributors or wholesalers. Shipping fees will be applied for hardcover purchases during checkout if this option is selected.

The lifetime of a publication refers to its status as the current edition. Should a new edition of any given publication become available, access will not be extended on the new edition and will only be available for the purchased publication. If a new edition becomes available, you will not lose access, but you would no longer receive new content for that publication (i.e. updates). Free Lifetime E-Access is only available to single institutions that purchase printed publications through IGI Global. Sharing the Free Lifetime E-Access is prohibited and will result in the termination of e-access.